# TRANSACTIONS

*of the*

American Philosophical Society

*Held at Philadelphia for Promoting Useful Knowledge*

VOLUME 78, Part 4

# The Artist at Work:
## Narrative Technique in Chrétien de Troyes

## EVELYN MULLALLY
Queen's University, Belfast, Northern Ireland

THE AMERICAN PHILOSOPHICAL SOCIETY

Independence Square, Philadelphia

1988

Library of Congress Catalog
Card Number 88-71547
International Standard Book Number 0–87169–784–X
US ISSN 0065–9746

# CONTENTS

# The Artist at Work:
## Narrative Technique in Chrétien de Troyes

### Evelyn Mullally

# Introduction

The rediscovery of Chrétien de Troyes in the nineteenth century has given rise, over the last hundred years or so, to a vast quantity of critical work devoted to him.[1] He is now firmly established as the most important vernacular writer of the twelfth–century renaissance. As a Frenchman, he was at a decided advantage, for the twelfth century in France was like no period before or since. With the single exception of law, in which the Italians took the lead, this was a renaissance dominated by the French, who influenced the whole course of European culture by their revival of art, architecture, philosophy, theology, music and literature.[2]

Chrétien, a native of Troyes in Champagne, was patronized by two powerful nobles, the Countess of Champagne and the Count of Flanders; he was thus well placed to compose the courtly literature that characterized his time. His five romances are important in the history of European literature: *Erec et Enide* is the earliest known Arthurian romance; *Cligès* provides the earliest, most sustained and most hostile commentary on the legend of Tristan and Iseut; the *Chevalier de la Charrette* is the earliest known version of the story of Lancelot and Guinevere; the *Chevalier au Lion* is Chrétien's most original work, widely exploited by later romancers, and his *Conte del Graal* is the earliest known romance about the Grail.

As well as being the most original of twelfth–century romancers,

---

[1]Chrétien scholarship is so extensive that it is impossible to do justice to it in the confines of a study such as this. A comprehensive list of critical works appears in Kelly, *Chrétien de Troyes: An Analytic Bibliography*. The most useful general introduction to Chrétien is still Frappier's study, *Chrétien de Troyes*. The vicissitudes of his reputation between the twelfth century and the eighteenth are traced by Pickford, "The Good Name of Chrétien de Troyes." See Bibliography for complete references.

[2]On the twelfth-century renaissance, see Haskins, *Renaissance of the Twelfth Century*. Developments in education are treated by Paré, Brunet and Tremblay in *Renaissance du XIIe siècle*. The origins of this European renaissance in the late tenth and eleventh centuries are explored by Southern, *Making of the Middle Ages*. Marc Bloch placed the beginning of what he called the second feudal age in the middle of the eleventh century; see his *Société féodale*, 97-99 and 157-64. For recent scholarship on the subject see *Renaissance and Renewal in the Twelfth Century*, ed. Benson and Constable. For the law, Bologna, where Gratian's *Decretum* was written c. 1140, remained the greatest centre of legal studies throughout the Middle Ages, though Gratian himself may have studied in Paris; see Brooke, *Twelfth Century Renaissance*, 75. Twelfth-century French sculpture is analysed by Mâle in *L'Art religieux du XIIe siècle en France*. Philosophy and theology are treated in all these general studies and also by Gilson, *Philosophie au Moyen Age*. For music, see Seay, *Music in the Medieval World*. The courtly literature of Chrétien's period is surveyed in the third part of Bezzola's study: *Origines et formation de la littérature courtoise*. The evolution of Arthurian literature is traced in *Arthurian Literature*, ed. Loomis.

1

Chrétien is also the most accessible. *Erec et Enide*, for example, is so close to modern literary preoccupations that it has been claimed as the first European novel.[3] Nevertheless, the very attractiveness of Chrétien's work is its most treacherous aspect when we come to examine his romances critically. We know nothing of his life, nothing of the circumstances in which he wrote, apart from the few meagre scraps of information we can glean from the texts themselves. We cannot hope to read his romances with exactly the same literary sensibilities as his first audiences heard them eight hundred years ago, but we can take a few reasonable precautions against anachronism in our response.

First of all, it is essential to replace Chrétien in his context as a writer. Great innovator though he was, he did not create the matter of his fictions *ex nihilo*. Nor was he writing alone in a literary void. True, when we turn from the earlier narratives of the twelfth century to Chrétien's romances, his originality makes a powerful impact. Here, everyone must feel, is a truly creative artist, a master of his material who handles his subjects with complete confidence. Yet much of the material he worked on already existed in oral or written form.

Chrétien's debt to orally-transmitted literature cannot be assessed with any precision. At an unknown number of removes, he may well have drawn on the literatures of countries as far apart as Ireland and Iran.[4] Unfortunately, the exploration of these possible links is hampered both by the obscurity of the surviving texts and by problems of transmission, and the results of over a century of investigations, though they have shed fascinating light on comparative mythology and folklore, tend to lead us away from Chrétien's texts rather than elucidating his literary techniques.

We are on surer ground with the surviving texts of Chrétien's own country and century, and with the classical and post-classical texts with which every educated person in the twelfth century was familiar. Chrétien is very much a man of his time in this respect: in his prologue to *Cligès*, he shows himself to be conscious of France's pre-eminence in chivalry and culture and proud to place himself in a tradition that he, like his contemporaries, traced back to Greece and Rome. In the same prologue he alludes to his debt to Ovid, for he mentions his translations of the *Ars Amatoria* and of some of the *Metamorphoses*.

Chrétien is also aware of the native French tradition of the *chanson de geste* which had come to maturity in the earlier part of his century. In *Erec* he alludes to a character in the William of Orange cycle. In *Cligès* and *Yvain* he alludes to the legend of Roland.[5] His own narratives, however, are far removed from the epic tradition of the chanson de

---

[3]Gallais, "De la naissance du roman."

[4]See Loomis, *Arthurian Tradition*, and *The Grail*. For a critical appraisal of Loomis, see Luttrell, "The Arthurian Traditionalist's Approach." For the Tristan story, see Schoepperele, *Tristan and Isolt*. The possible Iranian sources are dealt with by Gallais in *Perceval et l'initiation* and "Tristan et Iseut" et son modèle persan.

[5]See Owen, "Chrétien and the *Roland*."

geste. The transition from the epic, which first flourished in the early part of the twelfth century, to the romance which dominated the later part, is an intriguing and complex literary phenomenon. It may be characterized as a move in predominant interest from the heroic to the romantic, that is, from celebrating the exploits of a leader and his men to narrating the adventures of an individual knight, from depicting a male-dominated environment to showing a newer one in which women have an important role, and a change from the native and historic or would-be historic to the remote and exotic. On a formal level, it is a move away from the ponderous accumulations of assonating 'laisses' to the light and fluent rhythms of the octosyllabic rhyming couplet.[6]

Half-way between epic and romance are the narrative poems written in the middle years of the century, the so-called romances of antiquity: the *Roman de Thèbes* and the *Roman d'Eneas*, both anonymous, and the *Roman de Troie* by Benoît de Sainte-Maure. All these poems are based on epics, but on the epics of remote countries in the distant past which could be treated with romantic exoticism. All are largely concerned with the epic theme of heroic warfare, but they are also all written in the octosyllabic rhyming couplets that will become characteristic of romance; they all give at least an episodic importance to their female characters, and they all betray their debt to Ovid in their analyses of women's feelings.[7] A couple of anonymous short tales from the *Metamorphoses* also survive: *Narcisse* and *Piramus et Tisbé* both concentrate on the analysis of tragic love. The short romance of *Floire et Blancheflor* is both more exotic and more optimistic. Chrétien had some acquaintance with all of these works and was undoubtedly keenly interested in the productions of his contemporaries and rivals, Gautier d'Arras and Thomas.

He was also aware of the new style of love-lyric being written by the troubadours of southern France. Two lyrics survive which are generally believed to be his, and in one he reproduces the sentiments of the greatest of the Occitan love poets, Bernard de Ventadour.[8] Chrétien is a narrative rather than a lyric writer, however, and his most characteristic use of lyric themes will be to transpose them on to the plane of romance, as he does in *Lancelot*.

Chrétien assuredly had some knowledge of the great source-book of

---

[6]The transition from epic to romance is treated on a very general level by Ker, *Epic and Romance*. The contrast between indigenous epic and exotic romance is pointed out by Griffin, "The Definition of Romance." The formal aspects of the two genres are dealt with by Auerbach in chapters 5 and 6 of *Mimesis* and by Vinaver, *Rise of Romance*, chapters 1 to 3. Epic and romance are treated as successive parts of a larger generic cycle by Frye, *Anatomy of Criticism*. On a more abstract level, the problems of definition are treated by Jauss, "Littérature médiévale et théorie des genres."

[7]See Wilmotte, *Evolution du roman*; also *Eneas*, ed. Salverda de Grave, xxxv–xxxvi; *Troie*, ed. Constans, 6:354; *Narcisse*, ed. Thiry-Stassin and Tyssens, 50–53. *Eneas* has received the most attention because of the great influence of the monologues of Lavinia. See Faral, *Sources latines*; Laurie, "*Eneas* and the *Lancelot* of Chrétien de Troyes," and Jones, *Theme of Love*.

[8]See Zai, ed., *Chansons courtoises de Chrétien de Troyes*, 95.

Arthurian legend, Geoffrey of Monmouth's *Historia Regum Britanniae*, though it may have been through the medium of Wace's translation, the *Roman de Brut*.[9] It is also possible that he knew a later work by Wace, the *Roman de Rou*. The Arthur of Geoffrey and Wace is still a heroic figure: his vast conquests are reminiscent of Charlemagne's. When we meet him again in Chrétien's first romance, his character and function have both been radically transformed.

Another legend Chrétien was very familiar with and made conscious efforts to transform was the story of Tristan and Iseut. He alludes to it explicitly in *Erec* and tells us in the *Cligès* prologue that he himself had written something (now lost) about King Mark and Iseut la Blonde. It is the most pervasive, one could say the most obsessive, of Chrétien's literary influences and, perhaps even more than Ovid, helps to shape his concept of love.[10] Tristan is undoubtedly a heroic figure but it is in his story that love becomes the dominant theme, perhaps for the first time in twelfth–century narrative literature. It is here that the critical encounter of the heroic and romantic occurs. Indeed, as Joseph Bédier put it: "Entre la *Chanson de Roland* et le roman d'*Erec*, si *Tristan* n'existait pas, il faudrait l'inventer".[11]

It is in *Erec*, his earliest work, that Chrétien shows, naturally enough, the clearest traces of a good twelfth–century education: he mentions Macrobius, he shows some acquaintance with Boethius and perhaps also with Chalcidius, and displays his competence in the art of rhetoric.[12] It has been suggested that he also came under the influence of his contemporaries who wrote in Latin: Bernard Silvester, John of Salisbury, Alain de Lille.[13] His fellow romancer Thomas alludes to the work of Petrus Alfonsi and it is possible that Chrétien knew it too. He is certainly familiar with a number of literary attitudes expressed by Giraldus Cambrensis and Walter Map and it is even possible that he had some echo of the letters of Abelard and Heloise.

The literature that he might have been aware of is very considerable indeed. We cannot, of course, always be sure that he in fact knew all that he could have known. Marie de France, for instance, who must

---

[9]See Pelan, *L'Influence du "Brut" de Wace*, 17–70.

[10]There is a brief but useful survey in Gallais, *"Tristan et Iseut" et son modèle persan*, chap. 7. Most studies concentrate on the influence of the Tristan story on *Cligès*. See Paris, "*Cligès*"; Van Hamel, "*Cligès* et *Tristan*"; Micha, "Tristan et Cligès"; Bertolucci, "Di nuovo su 'Cligès' e 'Tristan' "; and Lonigan, "The *Cligès* and the Tristan Legend." Two articles on *Lancelot* consider the prose romance as well as Chrétien's: Lot-Borodine, "Tristan et Lancelot," and Payen, "Lancelot contre Tristan."

[11]. Bédier, ed., *Le Roman de Tristan par Thomas*, 1:153.

[12]For Macrobius, see *Erec*, ll. 6738 and 6741; for indirect reference to Boethius, see ll. 2784–86; there is a possible allusion to Chalcidius at ll. 1515–16 according to Hunt, "Redating Chrestien de Troyes," 218. Chrétien's use of rhetoric is most evident in his descriptive passages. See Faral, *Arts poétiques*, 75–85, and Colby, *Portrait in Twelfth-Century French Literature*.

[13]See Wetherbee, *Platonism and Poetry*; Luttrell, *Creation of the First Arthurian Romance*; and Hunt, "Redating Chrestien de Troyes."

have been roughly contemporary with him and who shows the same acquaintance with Ovid, Boethius and Wace, shows no awareness of Chrétien, nor he of her. Nevertheless, even when no source relationship can be established, it is still instructive to compare the way Chrétien solves his narrative problems with the way his contemporaries solved theirs.

Our first task, of course, is to determine what his problems were. It is in this area, more than anywhere else, that the traps of anachronistic sensibility lie in wait for us. For a start, to be original was considered shameful rather than praiseworthy.[14] Chrétien can boast of making his *Erec et Enide* into a masterpiece while making it plain that an Erec story is already familiar to his audience. Marie de Champagne, if no-one else, knew what was going to happen in *Lancelot*, the romance she had personally commissioned; as for *Cligès* and *Perceval*, Chrétien claims that he got the material for them out of existing books and, even though he tells us nothing further about his authorities, the last thing he wants is for us to think that he invented the plots.

It is also unlikely that one of Chrétien's concerns as a narrator was the modern preoccupation with suspense. If the plot is not new, what true suspense can there be? We find, for example, that Benoît de Sainte-Maure, as if to pre-empt all suspenseful interest in his immense *Roman de Troie*, prefaces it with nearly seven hundred lines of summary so that no part of his narrative can take us by surprise.

More radically still, we have to face the possibility that Chrétien's romances contain nothing of what we mean when we talk about psychology.[15] There is no trace in his works of any kind of Romantic perception of the individual valued simply as an individual rather than for his intrinsic worth. Those critics who are most concerned with the psychological dimension of fiction tend to favour *Erec* and *Yvain*, the romances in which there is the highest level of what is now called "human interest."

Perhaps the most delicate problem is the one of tone. The prevailing tone of our own culture is ironic. But can we be sure that an author as remote as Chrétien is in harmony with our ideas of the absurd, or that when he chooses to distance himself from his narrative, he is doing it for the same reasons as a writer might in the twentieth century?

The rational solution would be to read Chrétien's works in the light of the expectations proper to their genre, the romance.[16] The problem here

---

[14]See Lewis, *Discarded Image*, 210–15, and Hunt, "Rhetorical Background to Arthurian Prologue," 4–5.

[15]Vinaver rejected as anachronistic the attempts of French scholars to interpret medieval texts in the light of seventeenth–century concepts of art and twentieth–century concepts of psychology; see *A la recherche d'une poétique médiévale*, 35. Similar observations are made by Payen, "Une approche classiciste du roman médiéval."

[16]The essence of romance for most modern readers is a quality of idealized fantasy. See Ker, *Epic and Romance*, 4 and 326; Beer, *The Romance*, 9; Stevens, *Medieval Romance*, 21 and 28. Jackson, in "The Nature of Romance," argues that fully-fledged examples of romance

is a historical one: Western European romance cannot be traced back
any farther than Chrétien himself. The authors of the romances of
antiquity laid the foundations, but the first fully-fledged romance, the
first full-length narrative to cut all ties with the classical or Carolingian
past, is *Erec et Enide*. To define rules for Chrétien on the basis of what he
appears to have invented is simply to beg the question.

Reading Chrétien's texts, therefore, requires a negative approach in
the first instance. We need to read him in a passive state of receptivity,
with minds emptied as far as possible of any narrative expectation. The
most important romance in this respect is *Erec*, for it is in his first
romance that Chrétien lets us know, both explicitly and implicitly, what
he considers to be the norms of his narrative. If, then, in this ideal state
of suspended expectation, we listen to the way Chrétien goes about
telling a story, it becomes apparent that the method of narration he
chooses is linked with the particular bias he is giving his theme, and that
the preoccupation he betrays in each narrative causes him to adapt his
material in a particular way or alter his presentation of character or
action.

Chrétien as a narrator is primarily concerned with bringing together
the formal and thematic elements at his disposal in such a way as to
enhance the overall sense of his narrative. As we shall see, his methods
vary considerably from one romance to the next, but within each tale the
narrative technique is a unifying principle, or at least a principle of
continuity. The widespread concern with deciding how many sections
Chrétien's narratives should be divided up into has begun to seem
excessive.[17] For a writer so explicitly concerned with *conjointure*, it is of
more interest to see how he links his episodes together.

Leaving aside Chrétien's last work, the unfinished *Conte del Graal*,
which raises so many special problems that it would require a study all
to itself, Chrétien's first four romances offer a substantial field of
investigation into the development of his techniques as a narrator.
Certain sections of the romances are of obvious importance in any
analysis of technique. Chrétien's prologues, which have deservedly attracted a good deal of attention, are a continual source of enlightenment.
Likewise the opening scene of each romance merits special attention, for
it is here that the author establishes the norms of his narrative though
they sometimes contradict what the prologue has led us to expect. The
way in which the central characters are introduced is a matter of considerable importance, for it is on them that our narrative expectations will
be focussed. Then the author's interventions and comments are of undeniable importance, though they are often absent when we might welcome them and disconcerting when they are included. It goes

---

must have existed before *Erec*, but if so, none survive. For a concise recent assessment of
the nature of romance in Chrétien's period, see Hunt, *Chrestien de Troyes: Yvain*, chap. 1.
  [17]See Maddox, "Trois sur deux."

without saying that the explicit preoccupations of the author must be given particular analysis in determining how he adapted his material for his purpose, though an author's stated intentions are far from exhausting the possible significance of his work.

A study of this kind requires a reliable text to work on, and unfortunately no adequate modern edition of Chrétien yet exists. The attractive modern presentation of the romances in the Classiques Français du Moyen Age series does not, regrettably, make up for the unsatisfactory method of editing. All citations are therefore taken from the older critical editions of Wendelin Foerster.[18]

In investigating the evolution of Chrétien's art we are confronted with the difficult problem of his chronology. It is generally agreed that his romances were written some time between c. 1170 and c. 1190, and that *Erec* is his first romance and *Cligès* his second. The relative chronology of *Lancelot* and *Yvain* has, however, been a cause of dispute. It has been suggested that *Yvain*, or at least parts of *Yvain*, must have been written before *Lancelot*, but as no actual proof has yet been put forward, there is good reason to return to the conviction of earlier scholars, who contended that *Lancelot* must come first, for the simple reason that it contains no allusions to *Yvain*, whereas *Yvain* contains three allusions to *Lancelot*.[19]

The problem of dates, and consequently of influences, is an acute one in the history of twelfth-century literature. The single vernacular text which can be indisputably dated is Wace's *Brut*, for the author tells us it was written in 1155. For all other literary texts in French, we are forced to rely on the uncertain guide-lines afforded by the state of development of the language, on external allusions, whether to patrons or to historical events, or on references to other, less uncertainly dated texts.

It is illuminating to compare Chrétien's narrative technique with that of writers we know preceded him. When he repeatedly adapts the same situation borrowed from one of the tales in the *Metamorphoses*, when he exploits from a new angle one of the numerous episodes of the Tristan story available to him, when he gives a new slant to well-worn anti-feminist material, then indeed we can be sure of seeing him assert his personality as a writer. Even though the relative chronology is uncertain, when we find another writer of the period solving a narrative problem one way and Chrétien solving it differently, we still learn something about his art, for it is where he is most unlike others that he

---

[18]On the unsatisfactory nature of the CFMA series, see Reid, "Chrétien de Troyes and the Scribe Guiot"; Frappier, "Remarques sur le texte du *Chevalier de la Charrette*"; Vinaver, *"Les deux pas de Lancelot"*; and Hunt, "*Chrestien de Troyes: The Textual Problem.*" New editions of *Erec*, *Cligès* and *Perceval* are currently in preparation. For details of existing editions, see Kelly's bibliography.

[19]See Mullally, "Order of Composition of *Lancelot* and *Yvain*." Throughout the present study, the *Chevalier de la Charrette* is referred to either by its full title or, more commonly, by the shortened forms *Charrette* and *Lancelot*. Similarly, the *Chevalier au Lion* is referred to as the *Yvain*, in accordance with common convention.

is most himself. He may simply be preferring one style to another, or he may have some aesthetic or moral objection to the available material. His preference may be a purely formal one and, having set out with a specific narrative purpose in mind, he subordinates all incidental material to his overall plan. We cannot assume that what is characteristic of Chrétien in one romance will be characteristic of him throughout his career. Even a superficial reading of his romances reveals the range of their matter, so it is not unreasonable to expect change and variety in their manner. All these considerations should help us to do justice to Chrétien as a craftsman. They should also protect us against anachronistic judgments, which present us with a particularly difficult problem when we turn to his first romance, *Erec et Enide*.

# EREC ET ENIDE

# I. The Norms of the Narrative

Throughout his first romance, Chrétien never presents himself as anything but orthodox in his opinions. His approach could be defined as that of an optimistic rationalist for, from one end of the romance to the other, right and reason not only prevail, but are shown to prevail. Moreover, the author's attitudes influence both the themes of his narrative and his technique of narration, as can be inferred from the prologue.[1]

The prologue of *Erec* is not, however, without its surprises. Though designed to give pleasure, the romance opens on an unequivocally didactic note. How often, Chrétien remarks, do people fail to value things that are worth more than they imagine. It is noteworthy that he does not make this remark in his own name. It is neither a merely personal opinion nor a *sententia* requiring reference to an authority. It is, he says, a peasant's proverb, a saying so widely diffused that it is part of common human experience, a generally recognized reality.[2] Everyone, he continues, has a duty to develop the talents God has given him.[3] This recommendation is none the less serious for being directed here not, as one might expect, towards moral perfection, but towards an aesthetic ideal. Everyone ought to strive to express himself well and to teach well. The art of *bien dire*, though primarily the means of transmitting knowledge, acquires an all but autonomous value from the aesthetic excellence his skill can confer on it.

The subject matter of his romance is not original. There is nothing unusual about this. Mere novelty, as C. S. Lewis pointed out,[4] had no appeal in the Middle Ages. On the contrary, in a world that was confidently rational, that rejected the absurd as absurd, it would have been ridiculous to incorporate the new, which must be false, into the rational scheme of things as they already existed in a fully created world. But though novelty might be equated with falsehood, it does not equally

---

[1] Citations are from Foerster's 1934 edition; see Bibliography. For a recent study of the romance, which includes an analysis of the prologue, see Burgess, *Chrétien de Troyes: Erec et Enide*, chap. 1.

[2] The popularity of proverbs among the literate classes is attested by the number of surviving collections. For this proverb, see Morawski, *Proverbes français*, 2313. Geoffroi de Vinsauf recommends poets to begin their work with a proverb or an example. See Faral, *Arts poétiques*, 58.

[3] The sense of moral obligation attached to the transmission of knowledge is widespread in the twelfth century, even among writers of romance. In the *Roman de Thèbes*, ll. 1–20 and the *Roman de Troie*, ll. 1–34, we find the same idea even more strongly expressed. See also Curtius, *European Literature*, 87–89.

[4] *Discarded Image*, 208–15.

follow that a narrative that already exists must be true in any very obvious sense. The story of Erec, son of Lac, is already well known at royal and noble courts, but Chrétien does not claim that the story he is about to retell is true, as, for example, Marie de France claims that some of her *lais* are true.[5] Erec is neither a historic nor a legendary figure. He has nothing of the epic hero about him. His tale will not be a recital of some characteristic exploit, like Count William's ingenious entry into Nîmes or his capture of Orange. The subject is the man himself, "Erec le fil Lac" (1. 19).

Chrétien's claim to fame is made on aesthetic rather than on factual grounds. He is not offering us a version of the story that corresponds to a historical reality, nor one that is supported by a literary authority, but rather his own carefully coherent and therefore rational and true version. Out of this popular adventure story, disjointed and distorted by ignorant jongleurs, Chrétien, the educated clerk, boasts that he will extract a very beautiful and coherently organized work.[6] The beauty of his conjointure may entail a concept of moral coherence, but the aesthetic principle is the one that is most clearly communicated. The assemblage of the fragments of narrative is to be Chrétien's prime concern. We can foresee that it will be in the matter of linking episodes that he will deploy his greatest efforts of skill. The coherence of the structure will justify the closing boast of the prologue. Chrétien's work will have the coherence of beauty for as long as the coherence of orthodoxy prevails: the romance will endure "tant con durra crestiantez" (1. 25).

Nevertheless, the opening of the story proper contains none of the explanatory matter which a modern reader would expect. "On an Easter day, in spring, in his castle at Cardigan, King Arthur held court" (ll. 27–29). The casual abruptness with which Arthur is introduced presupposes a good deal of familiarity on the part of the audience, though even without it a fair amount of information can be registered. A display of secular power which expressly coincides with the most important feast of the Church is to be understood in a clearly Christian context. The spring setting strikes a literary rather than a naturalistic note for it was already familiar to the point of banality in twelfth-century lyric verse. Cardigan, too, is no doubt envisaged as a literary rather than a factual location, for Chrétien's geography remains vague in this romance and Erec will pass from one "Bretagne" to the other without apparently crossing the sea. For Chrétien, no doubt, as for other

[5]*Lais* (ed. Rychner): *Guigemar*, 1. 19; *Bisclavret*, 1. 316; *Chievrefoil*, 1. 3 and *Eliduc*, ll. 1–4.
[6]For a summary of critical interpretations of the first lines of *Erec*, see Vinaver, *A la recherche d'une poétique médiévale*, chap. 5. Kelly, "Source of Meaning," 200, defines conjointure as "specifically the result of the interlacing of different elements derived from the source or sources." Ollier, "Author in the Text," 30, prefers the more extended definition: "textual organization in its entirety." It is impossible to define Chrétien's use of the term with absolute precision, but even the most restrictive interpretation indicates that he is preoccupied with the formal arrangement of his narrative.

continental writers, Arthur's castles are all situated in the equal remoteness of romance.

The King Arthur mentioned here undoubtedly owes his existence to the Arthur of Wace's *Roman de Brut*, which in turn derives from Geoffrey of Monmouth's *Historia Regum Britanniae*, but the absence of any introductory matter indicates clearly enough that Chrétien's Arthur has broken the last tenuous links with history.[7] Arthur's immediately recognizable and acceptable function here is as a holder of courts without any need of personal or political justification. The great plenary court at Caerleon-on-Usk, so plausibly imagined by Geoffrey and so aptly embellished by Wace, has here been cut loose from the chronicle. Here, as in countless later romances, King Arthur is an arbitrary holder of courts, and he has become a figure in the world of literary imagination.

The Arthurian court that Chrétien goes on to describe, though situated in a temporal vacuum, is nevertheless firmly rooted in what the author presents as the reality proper to literature, the abstract reality of ideal social excellence. Arthur's court derives more directly from Wace than from Geoffrey: whereas Geoffrey emphasized Arthur's military and political supremacy, Wace added a note of moral excellence. No-one, he says, could be counted as courtly who had not sojourned at the court of Arthur; men came from far and wide to appreciate for themselves not only Arthur's incomparable prowess but also his unequalled courtesy and liberality (*Brut*, ll. 9761–92). Chrétien's Arthur continues this theme: his courtly gathering is of an unprecedented splendour, reminiscent of the superlatives of folktale: "Ains si riche ne fu veüe" (l. 30). All the courtiers are paragons of appropriate excellence; the knights are all brave, the ladies all beautiful and high-born. We know at once the norms of existence and behaviour that will be required of the characters in the romance.

Yet Arthur's court provides something more than a convenient point of departure and, in due course, an aesthetically satisfying point of return. Divorced though it is from historical reality, and from the vestigial reality which underlies such native legends as the epics of the William cycle, the Arthurian court is still all that Chrétien allows us in the way of referential reality. This court, though remote from the world Chrétien and his continental audience knew, is nevertheless presented as the sole determining milieu for the characters of his romance. Erec's social identification is as the son of King Lac, but his personal identification is as a highly regarded member of Arthur's Round Table. It is at Arthur's court that all values, social, moral and even aesthetic, are tested and validated. Erec, though the hero of the story, is the son of a king who is necessarily lower in status than Arthur. He is placed

---

[7] For possible verbal echoes of the *Brut* in *Erec*, see Pelan, *L'Influence du "Brut" de Wace*, 21–40. The mention of the Round Table in *Erec*, l. 83, is enough to show that Chrétien is not dependent on Geoffrey for his information, for Wace is the first writer to mention the "Roünde Table" (*Brut*, l. 9751).

second in rank to Arthur's nephew Gawain to witness the ritual kiss given to Enide. Gawain is the one who remains, right to the end of Chrétien's work, the criterion of chivalry. There is implied criticism of him in the later romances, but it is irrelevant to his narrative function. Arthur himself is less idealized in *Erec* than in his earlier, more heroic manifestations, but his static qualities, besides offering a striking contrast to the dynamic character of the hero, provide a solid and stable background for the action of the romance.

Arthur is an exemplary Christian king, but Christianity as such remains in the background in *Erec*. The centre of the stage is taken up with secular concerns. Chrétien deals with human qualities and failures, and the conflicts and triumphs he describes are all physical or emotional. The story is remarkably secular in tone. For a romance which frankly acknowledges the influence of the Tristan legend, it is noteworthy that *Erec* does not even contain an Ogrin figure, the type of holy hermit in the woods who offers moral advice, encouragement or consolation to the hero and who quickly becomes one of the stock figures of Arthurian romance.[8] Lancelot, Yvain and Perceval will all encounter a holy man in the course of their adventures: Erec takes advice from no-one. He and Enide struggle to re-establish a proper equilibrium in their marriage, drawing only on their individual qualities.

The Tristan story offers another point of comparison, this time with the central episode of Enide's unlucky 'parole' through which Erec learns of his lost reputation. Tristan, in the Beroul fragment, has essentially the same experience as Erec: it is abruptly brought home to him that he has neglected his chivalrous duties for love. But for Tristan the realization prompts an outpouring of repentance as for a sin (Beroul, ll. 2160–76).[9] It is remarkable that though both Tristan and Iseut feel no sense of guilt at their adultery, they both feel remorse for its social effects. They have abandoned their duties to society by abandoning the court, and they appeal to the hermit Ogrin to help repair the damage done to society by a love too egotistically indulged.

With Erec it is different. No-one can doubt that he feels his disgrace keenly,[10] all the more as he did not have Tristan's moral alibi of a love potion. But whereas it was necessary for Tristan to explain the change that came over him when the effects of the potion wore off, there was no need for Erec to express a change of heart, for his heart had not changed. He had maintained a proper appreciation of chivalry

---

[8]Kennedy, "Portrayal of the Hermit Saint," shows that the hermit, in spite of his holy calling, was often portrayed in ways that accentuated the secular, aristocratic spirit of French Arthurian literature.

[9]Citations are from Ewert's edition; see Bibliography.

[10]The episode of the 'parole' and Erec's reactions to it have been very variously interpreted. See Payen, *Motif du repentir*, 366–76; Press, "Comportement d'Erec envers Enide"; Zaddy, *Chrétien Studies*, 1–23; and Ménage, "Erec et Enide."

throughout his honeymoon, continuing to support it among his men. He has no acceptable excuse to make for his behaviour, so he makes none. He expresses his regret not by words, but by instant action. His vocabulary of course contains the conventional Christian formulas of politeness. When, for example, he rides off in haste after Yder, he says to the queen: "Je m'an vois. A Deu vos comant" (l. 271). This is only the well-bred twelfth-century equivalent of "I must go. Goodbye." Even the vain Count Galoain, after proposing adultery and murder to Enide, thinks nothing of bidding her a pious goodnight: "Si la comande a Deu çant foiz" (l. 3423).

The absence of any very personal religious feeling in the hero should not be taken to indicate that Chrétien's humanism is tinged with scepticism. On the contrary, the rational framework of things is more taken for granted in *Erec* than in any of the later romances. All, he might have said at the end of *Erec*, is for the best in the best of all chivalrous worlds. All, even at the darkest moments of the romance, makes sense.

Chrétien's use of aphorisms is illustrative of his general attitude, for he never employs them with witty intent. There is nothing of the La Rochefoucauld about him. The maxims and proverbs he employs are never designed to shock or amuse or sting his public into self-awareness. They simply elucidate some aspect of his story by referring to the universal truths of human experience, accessible even to the peasant of the opening proverb. So, if Enide's parents weep when they give her in marriage, it is because they are following a human impulse that needs no explanation: such is nature (l. 1463). If Erec does not rush into combat unarmed, it is because everyone knows that folly is not bravery (l. 231).

True, Chrétien is aware that in life appearance and reality do not always coincide, but this too is part of inherited wisdom. Everyone knows that people talk big and act small and that expectations are not always justified by events. Chrétien's concern is not to invent brilliant maxims, but to show how his hero can implement acknowledged general truths. So he makes Erec's experience move from the particular to the general. In his first combat, with Yder, Erec thinks of nothing but the specific motivations that spur him on, the vengeance due to the queen and himself and the honour due to Enide. Later, when he sets out on the less specific mission of personal rehabilitation, his first encounters are with groups of robber knights who have no individualized personalities and who constitute only a generalized enemy of the honour he is seeking to regain. They are a depersonalized embodiment of unchivalrous vices, as Chrétien makes clear by the generality of his condemnation: "Covetousness is an evil thing; fools overreach themselves" (ll. 2939–44).

Individualist though he is, Erec's experiences become more generalized as he nears his goal of public glory regained. By the time he has reached the stage of disinterested combat on behalf of Cadoc, he is capable of generalizing the scorn he feels for his opponents: big boasts may herald little actions (l. 4435). He is the moral victor before he even begins to fight. When at last he approaches his final adventure in the orchard of King Evrain, he is challenged by a mysterious tall knight who calls on him to fight on the pretext that Erec was not worthy to approach the knight's damsel. Erec generalizes his response to this challenge in a whole series of maxims which ally his cause with the moral experience of Chrétien's public and may be roughly rendered: it is as easy to talk folly as sense; there is nothing to be gained by threats; many a slip twixt cup and lip; boasting goes before defeat (ll. 5919–28).

The actions of the heroine are similarly absorbed into the aphorisms of common experience, but adapted to her character. Enide's outstanding virtue is her wisdom, but it is essentially a passive quality. So too in the matter of maxims. Enide does not apply them to others: she is the object of them herself. Sometimes they are the superficial maxims of men capable only of understanding a baser kind of woman. Count Galoain rationalizes his rejection by reflecting that flattery makes women proud and that they respond better to rougher treatment (ll. 3350–53). This, of course, is truth at a very low level. No-one, indeed, challenges its validity and it is possible that it might have had its application to women such as the selfish 'amie' of the knight in the orchard. But Enide is set on a higher plane, equally inaccessible to the brutal maxim of the other count, the Count of Limors: "Lamentations never brought anyone back to life"(l. 4797). Enide reproaches herself for her 'parole', reminding herself that "silence never hurt anyone" (l. 4630). Discretion may be the prudent way to self-preservation, but Chrétien never allows us to think that Enide's 'parole' has detracted from her essential 'sagesse'. On the contrary, he allows no-one to comment unfavourably on her. When she deceives Count Galoain, her speech is so plausible and courteous that Chrétien feels the need to reassure us that it is not true: she thinks one thing and says another (l. 3384). Taken in isolation, such a remark might be seen as a cynical comment on female duplicity, but Chrétien evidently takes the same line as Beroul's hermit Ogrin who contends in effect that the end justifies the means and that in a difficult moral situation a lie is justifiable (Beroul, ll. 2353–54). Internal reality is of greater importance than external appearance. Enide hides her grief as Erec approaches Evrain's perilous orchard, for grief felt in the heart means more than grief expressed by the mouth (ll. 5831–32). For Chrétien, there is a body of opinion accepted as true which he shares with his public. Not once does he claim to be contradicting common experience or setting up his individual judgment against accepted wisdom. On the contrary, his interventions are designed to reassure us that he acknowledges the value of common experience and that if his characters deviate from observed truth it is only, as in the case of Enide, to rise above it to a more ideal plane.

Chrétien's personal interventions are few. He makes no direct comment on the central episode of Enide's 'parole'. He does, however, give us an indirect comment on the effects of the crisis, in the lamentation of Enide. From the obscurity she had lived in at the beginning of the romance she has been abruptly raised to heights of glory and happiness, and is now even more abruptly faced with the prospect of misery and misfortune. With orthodox piety, Enide attributes her great joy to God and makes her present ills the work of Fortune who had taken her up and then dropped her (ll. 2782–86). The role of Fortune in human affairs had been exploited by innumerable writers since Boethius described the operations of her treacherous wheel,[11] and nowhere in romance are the implications more clearly marked than here. God is the source of all true joy; the impermanent goods of this world are given and snatched away again by the pseudo-goddess; true wisdom can alone survive the losses inflicted by Fortune. Even thus grossly oversimplified, the value of the Boethian approach is obvious for any writer dealing with the problem of undeserved misfortune. The goodness of God is not compromised. The injustices of common experience are given a philosophic perspective and coherence, and the anguish of the absurd is avoided. Enide does not indeed follow the implications to their logical conclusion, where even human relations are seen as falling under the jurisdiction of Fortune and therefore to be viewed with detachment: for the heroine of a romance such scorn of the bonds of society would be inappropriate. She makes her point: she is prepared to meet any of the blows of Fortune except the hatred of her lord (ll. 2787–90). There can be no doubt that Enide's ability to credit God with her joy and rise above the caprices of Fortune in all material matters is a characteristic and essential part of her 'sagesse'.

Thus far, however, God remains so to speak in the wings. Not, indeed, because He is a *Dieu caché*, but because He is sufficiently manifest, for a secular romance, in the manifestly rational order of things. Most of the time God need only play a brief part in the story and then only at those critical moments when divine support is required to uphold what is right. Erec may be lacking in effusive piety, but Chrétien never allows him to uphold any but a just cause. He is instantly perceived as the instrument of divine protection by Cadoc when he comes to rescue him from the evil giants (ll. 4475–77).

Erec stands in need of divine intervention more than once. When Galoain plots to seduce Enide and murder Erec, Chrétien, in his capacity as omniscient author, announces that divine help is on the way to the still unsuspecting hero (ll. 3426–29). In this instance, the necessary help comes primarily through Enide's prudence, here very much a divine part of her 'sagesse'. A more directly divine intervention is imagined at the beginning of the last adventure, the *Joie de la Cort*. The townspeople of Brandigan voice their apprehensions in chorus: Erec will certainly die

---

[11]*Philosophiae Consolatio*, ed. Bieler, book 2.

unless God protects him (ll. 5524–25). There is a corresponding choral thanksgiving when he is victorious: God is called on to bless the man He has protected (ll. 6377–78).

Enide needs direct divine help when she is overcome by grief at Erec's apparent death. She is about to kill herself, Thisbe fashion, on Erec's sword but, characteristic of Chrétien's optimism, not only is the Pyramus figure not really dead at all, but the heroine, once she has given this supreme proof of her love — which is the only function of the episode in the economy of the plot — is also saved in the nick of time. She looks at the sword, but "God, who is full of mercy, made her delay a little" (ll. 4670–73), just long enough in fact for a rescuer to ride up and show Enide and us that "God did not wish to forget her" (l. 4680). The rescuer, Count Oringle of Limors, almost immediately assumes a more hostile function, but Chrétien has now prepared us to expect that God will not forget Enide in whatever emergency.

Enide's rescue may seem almost too pat, but the same cannot be said for her first adventure, which involves the award of the hawk and which sets out the principles of divine support in their most complete and most bewildering form. The Custom of the Hawk is the key adventure that establishes the status of both hero and heroine. In this episode, Erec, who had been lashed by the dwarf of the knight Yder, will fight Yder for the prize of the hawk, to be bestowed upon Enide. The queen prays that God will protect Erec from evil (ll. 271–72), and Erec's heroism derives from his ability to fight evil and uphold right with success. The transition from the negative role of wiping out his shame to the positive one of championing right is what marks his accession as a hero. When he hears that Yder will challenge all comers to deny that the qualities of his 'amie' merit the award of the hawk, Erec sees the opportunity of rightfully upholding the vastly superior claims of Enide (ll. 641–46). The general public are in agreement that Enide's beauty is such that she fully deserves the hawk (ll. 759–60). It is their remark about Erec that is puzzling:

> "Mout doit estre hardiz et fiers
> Qui la bele pucele an mainne."          (ll. 754–55)

If Enide's claim is so overwhelmingly right, why must it be assumed that she has an exceptionally able knight to defend it? On the other hand, if Erec is exceptionally able to begin with, he need not necessarily be defending a rightful cause to gain a victory. But for Chrétien the point of a romance of chivalry is to show that true right and might are inseparable, and perhaps nothing better illustrates the optimism of *Erec* than the way that the just, such as Enide's father and the courteous Cadoc, are introduced to us not as men oppressed without hope but, on the contrary, at the very moment when they are to be rescued from undeserved misfortune by the chivalrous action of the hero. If right must ultimately prevail, as orthodox Christianity contends, then this is the essential truth of any conflict, and the ideal world of romance is appropriately used to illustrate it.[12]

The rightness of Erec's motivation is an essential point and Chrétien gives it the maximum emphasis by telling us that Erec does not win because he is a better fighter than Yder. In skill there is nothing to choose between them (ll. 961–62); Erec's only superiority is in his motivation. Yder has causelessly insulted the queen and wrongfully put forward the claim of his lady to the hawk. Erec, on the other hand, is bound in honour to avenge himself and the queen, and is bound by love, gratitude and reason to uphold Enide's better claim to the prize. So, though Yder may fight as hard as Erec and even though his lady may weep and pray as hard as Enide (ll. 890–94), they can be given no prospect of victory in a wrongful cause. Erec takes fresh strength from a renewed consciousness of his double motivation—the sight of Enide and the memory of his wrongs (ll. 911–20)—and, as the battle is resumed, even a powerful blow from Yder which cuts through his armour from helmet to hauberk fails to injure him, for God protects him (l. 948). Right is the extra help given to Erec and withheld from Yder who, deprived of divine protection, finally succumbs, exhausted.

Erec's defence of Enide has a significant corollary: if he acts for what is right, then she *is* right. Her beauty is a manifestation of the ultimate good. Chrétien takes pains to point out its divine origin and her status as an unmatchable exemplar. In his enthusiasm, he allows Nature, God's vicar, to give way to God Himself in the making of Enide (ll. 411–36). Her beauty is a mirror for others to see themselves in (ll. 437–41).[13] He tells us nothing of what Erec sees in it when Enide tells him of his lost reputation, other than that he instantly acknowledges the truth of its reflections. Beauty is so closely allied with truth as to be indistinguishable from it.[14]

Erec, too, manifests this divine attribute. Chrétien insists on his personal beauty (ll. 87–88) and his perfect equality with Enide in this respect (ll. 1504–16). His beauty inspires a quasi–religious awe among the female subjects of King Evrain, who bless themselves at the sight of it (ll. 5506–07). Most telling of all is the way that his beauty is closely allied with his prowess. A young squire tells Count Galoain that he was given a horse by a very courteous knight, the most handsome he had ever seen. It is as if courtesy and beauty were facets of the one excellence (ll. 3226–27). This is certainly how Galoain understands it, for he replies,

---

[12]On the legal procedure of direct appeal to divine judgment, and its decline in the twelfth century, see Southern, *Medieval Humanism*, 51–52.

[13]The mirror motif is discussed by Colby; *Portrait in Twelfth–Century French Literature*, 143–44.

[14]There is a Platonic ring to the portrayal of human beauty as a manifestation of the divine. Gilson remarked of medieval thought: "Platon lui-meme n'est nulle part, mais le platonisme est partout," in *Philosophie au Moyen Age*, 268. The influence of Platonic cosmography on twelfth–century Latin and vernacular poets is studied by Wetherbee in *Platonism and Poetry*.

with a promptness that would be absurd if only externals were involved, that he is sure that the unknown knight is not handsomer than himself. The squire insists that he is, and that if there is any temporary eclipse in his beauty, it must be due to the recent exercise of extraordinary prowess. Both the squire and the count evidently expect that the finer man will manifest his superiority in his person as well as in his actions.

The converse of the principle equally applies. When the queen sends her attendant to Yder in the forest, the girl has her way blocked by Yder's dwarf who, Chrétien states baldly, was full of "felenie" (l. 164). His dwarfish deformity corresponds with the evil he promptly manifests by striking the girl. It is evidently no part of his code of behaviour to believe that "granz vitance est de ferir fame" (l. 1018), the reproach Erec addresses to the vanquished Yder. It is noteworthy that Yder, who is described as "bel et adroit" (l. 150), did not commit this outrage himself—unlike the later and blacker villain, Oringle of Limors, who is blamed by his barons for striking Enide (ll. 4826–36). Chrétien preserves as much of Yder's chivalrous character as possible, as he will later be needed to relay Erec's triumph worthily to Arthur's court. He therefore allows all the evil in the knight to be transferred to the wholly evil, almost symbolic figure of the hideous dwarf.

At the other extreme of physical disproportion are the evil and cruel giants who attack Cadoc (l. 4345). Like the dwarf, they have no concept of behaviour ruled by a code of chivalry. Erec asks for Cadoc's release in the name of courtesy (ll. 4413–18), but courtesy is as far from their villainous actions as beauty is from their grotesque bodies.

Chrétien's identification of good with beautiful and bad with ugly receives a certain refinement in his treatment of two more important secondary figures. The brave and loyal Guivret is a small man. It may well be that in the original tale he too was a dwarf. But he has nothing of dwarfish deformity in the romance. Chrétien takes care to impress on us that he is not, as we evidently might expect, small in character as well as in stature, but a man of great heart (ll. 3678–80). The other figure, Mabonagrain, is treated more ambiguously. Chrétien deploys much art in preparing us for a formidable adversary to meet Erec in Evrain's orchard, but as he intends to integrate Mabonagrain into courtly society, he does not make another uncouth giant of him, but instead a knight of Erec's class; the only blemish on his otherwise considerable beauty is his rather excessive height (ll. 5901–05). The blemish of excess manifests itself both in his person and his personality, for he has indulged to excess an attitude that would have been honourable in the right circumstances, namely obedience to his mistress.

Both Guivret and Mabonagrain, being essentially sympathetic characters, need to be absolved from the contamination of evil that ugliness evidently represents. The evil envisaged, however, is limited to its social effects. Given that the narrative deals exclusively with secular social relations, it is understandable that the concepts of good and evil are not so much internal and spiritual as external and social. What evil characters are reproached for is their 'viltance', that is, conduct unbecoming to free men.

In our egalitarian age, it is not easy to accept Chrétien's assumption that high rank presupposes a higher and more refined code of behaviour and even higher intrinsic human worth. At Erec's coronation, when he is finally established as being of the greatest possible social consequence, Chrétien emphasizes the glory and honour of the occasion by telling us that only the higher grades of society were allowed to be present and that the lower orders were excluded (ll. 6907-13). This concept of relative value explains the attitude of Enide's father. He is fully conscious of his daughter's qualities and it is her intrinsic value that has made him refuse any son-in-law whose social worth does not match her moral worth and who is not as noble in class as she is noble in heart. Poor though he is, he has a deeper sense of what is fitting than to give Enide to a mere baron, however rich or powerful. He is waiting, confidently, it would seem, for God to grant her a higher honour, for "avanture" to bring them a king or a count for her (ll. 526-32). His faith in the rightful ordering of the world is no sooner expressed than it is vindicated. 'Avanture' brings Enide the royal husband she deserves, and in such a context cannot be thought of as the random operation of chance, but something closer to providence, directed by the same God who will not forget Enide in her later peril.[15]

It is true that two noblemen, Count Galoain and Count Oringle, blot their escutcheons fairly badly, but Galoain repents and Oringle is severely reprimanded by his men, so that the high standards of nobility are maintained at least in theory. Chrétien does not, however, pretend that we are in anything but an ideal world. He does not allude to any contemporary kings or counts to prove his point. On the contrary, given that his ethical standards in the romance are dependent on a king principally derived from foreign fictions, we are not surprised to find that all the allusions in the story derive not from contemporary experience but from the more conveniently universal examples of literature and antiquity.

There had been no greater literary success in Chrétien's lifetime (though it seems to have been a *succès de scandale*) than the story of Tristan and Iseut. Knowing that this is the criterion by which his story will be judged, he protests that his heroine is even more beautiful than Iseut (ll. 424-26; 4845-46), his hero even more of a liberator than Tristan (ll. 1247-49) and better yet, that no Brangien has interfered with the natural course of events on their wedding night (ll. 2075-77).

Classical comparisons are used to establish Erec's nobility. When he leaves Arthur's court with Enide, everyone joins in praise of him. Again

---

[15]Burgess, *Contribution à l'étude du vocabulaire pré-courtois*, 44-55, shows how the word 'aventure' evolves towards this providential sense.

there is no reference to experience, but to the great models of biblical and classical history: he resembled Absalom in his face, Solomon in his speech and Alexander in his liberality (ll. 2266–70). At Erec's coronation, Arthur's liberality is similarly established by comparison with rulers from ancient history, Alexander and Caesar (ll. 673–82). As for Erec's coronation robe, Chrétien calls on Macrobius to help him interpret the significance of the quadrivium depicted on it (ll. 6736–90). The four ways of higher learning, like the eloquence of Solomon and the generosity of Alexander, evoke the exemplary attributes of ideal rather than real sovereigns.

It is not that Chrétien is unconcerned with real life, but he is dealing only with a rational reality, arranging the elements of his romance into a pattern in which reason always triumphs. Hence the extremely rational behaviour of his characters, which risks appearing incomprehensible in an age no longer so confident of human reason. The ethos of his romance, which determines the behaviour of the characters, can be summed up in two precepts: first, given that honour and glory are good, it is right to pursue them; second, true love can only be inspired by merit and experienced by noble natures. Erec and Enide act throughout on the basis of these two principles.

The desirability of obtaining chivalrous honour is displayed in its plainest form in the final adventure, the Joie de la Cort. Guivret's warnings of possible shame (l. 5446) are outweighed by Erec's eager anticipation of possible honour (l. 5454). Yet the undertaking lacks the motivation we have come to expect of Erec. The service the adventure will render is not made clear until after the event. Evrain will tell him nothing about the horn in the orchard except that the man who will sound it will increase his fame and honour before everyone in the country (ll. 5817–19). That is enough for Erec. Evrain could not have expressed himself thus if the challenger's role had been shameful or unworthy. The adventure is designed in this mysterious way in order to throw into relief the disinterestedness of Erec's pursuit of honour. His services have not been asked for, as they were for the rescue of Cadoc, and he has nothing left to prove to Enide, as their reconciliation has already taken place. The public nature of the acclaim promised to the victor is the added incentive.

Purely spiritual virtues can be developed in private, but the only way that the chivalrous virtue of prowess can be proved is in public. Hence the importance of reputation throughout the romance. The first thing Chrétien tells us about Erec is that he already has a great reputation at Arthur's court (ll. 83–92). The only narrative justification for the tournament at Tenebroc is to emphasize the height of glory Erec had reached just before his fall. He is concerned to fight well "por ce que sa proesce apeire" (l. 2218). Even Enide, who never doubts him, is gratified at being given ocular proof of his prowess when he defeats the robber knights (ll. 3113–14). But no reputation is gained once and for all. Arthur himself cannot afford to neglect appearances. His regal generosity is displayed at Erec's coronation "por ce que sa corz miaudre apeire" (l. 6666). So, when Erec ceased to prove himself publicly, his value dropped, his "pris an est abeissiez" (l. 2548). His value as a knight, and consequently as a person, has been diminished, for 'pris' is reserved exclusively for the worthy. It is plainly Erec's duty, both to himself and to the unquestioned values of chivalry, to re-establish his reputation.

Given these principles, Erec's position, when he is jolted out of his honeymoon torpor, is clear enough. The remarkable part is the rational corollary. Erec, like every other character in the story, reacts with perfect reasonableness. He makes no attempt at excuse or self-justification. His critics are right. His inaction has been wrong. Remedial action is put into effect right away (ll. 2576–83). There is no need to imagine that Erec is suffering from injured pride, for it is extraordinary the way every character in the romance accepts what we would regard as humiliating situations with a lack of false shame which sometimes sounds like superhuman humility and which certainly jars on our accepted notions of normal psychology.[16] Enide's father takes no offence when Erec asks him why his daughter is dressed so badly, but explains the situation with perfect simplicity (ll. 503–07). The arrogant Yder acknowledges Erec's superiority readily and obediently goes and recounts his humiliating defeat to the queen (ll. 1047–54; 1183–97). The queen is delighted to let her husband salute Enide as the most beautiful lady of the court and to offer her his respectful love (ll. 1763–1840). Count Galoain, deceived by Enide and unhorsed by Erec, has nothing but remorse for his treachery and admiration for Enide's discretion (ll. 3632–56). The boorish Kay is not ashamed to tell Arthur the truth about his discomfiture at the hands of Erec (ll. 4075–77). Cadoc and his 'amie' are humbly and unreservedly grateful for being rescued from a situation they were unable to cope with by themselves (ll. 4475–569). Mabonagrain is content to accept defeat when he discovers that he has been vanquished by a man he considers better than himself, even though his defeat takes place before the eyes of his lady (ll. 6010–47).

Most astonishing of all is Enide, who accepts the humiliating reality of her situation with unimaginable sweetness. She and Erec may be equal in beauty and courtesy, but neither of them ever forgets that he is the giver and she the receiver of benefits. Her very last speech is a declaration of admiration and gratitude in which she reminds her cousin that Erec is a king's son who married her when she was "povre et nue" (ll. 6310–11). Indeed, Erec had insisted on presenting her to Arthur and Guinevere in the rags he found her in, so the reality of the social gulf between them could not go unnoticed. Rank being an unquestioned

---

[16]Vinaver, *A la recherche d'une poétique médiévale*, 77, makes a remark about the *Tristan* of Beroul that can well be applied to *Erec*: "Lorsqu'un écrivain du XIIe siècle ne dit pas tout ce qu'il devrait dire pour combler notre attente, il se peut qu'il nous cache quelque chose; mais il se peut aussi qu'il ne nous cache rien." There is no indication that Chrétien is hiding anything from us in *Erec*.

good, Enide has made an unquestionably good match. Though she is given away by her father without any reference to her own opinions or feelings, she is treated less high-handedly than we might perhaps imagine, for she thinks exactly like her parents and is happy to be given to Erec because he is brave and courteous and she knows that he will be king some day and she will be queen (ll. 687–90). She is given to him like a piece of property. Erec actually refers to her as a rich gift (l. 1274). So it is logical of her to fear that she may be disposed of by him like property. It is thus wholly reasonable that on the one hand Erec should accept the truth of her 'parole' and be impatient to efface his shame, and on the other hand that Enide, conscious of her inferior status, should face the possibility of suffering for what might be seen as ungrateful impertinence.

It is undeniable, of course, that Chrétien wishes us to be convinced of the reality of the love the couple have for one another, especially after their reconciliation (ll. 4917–38; 5238–58; 5827–59). For Chrétien, how-ever, love conforms strictly to the principle of an *amour d'estime*. Nowhere in his work does he admit that the right kind of love may have an irrational source. Even in *Erec*, where the physical side of love is made more explicit than in the later romances (ll. 1479–1516; 2069–108), love depends for its continued existence on respect, and respect is grounded in merit. Love here most closely approximates to the ideal love between friends, as laid down by Cicero: such love can only be inspired by true merit and only experienced by the meritorious; the true friend will be loyal, but he will give and receive justified criticism in a rational spirit.[17] This ideal is realized in Chrétien's romance, but given a specifically twelfth-century colouring. Chrétien elaborates the hint given by Geoffrey of Monmouth, who tells us that in the exemplary court of King Arthur no lady thought any man worthy of her love who had not proved himself three times in battle.[18] There is no room for gratuitous sentiment in this rational scheme of things: worthy love is the reward of chivalrous merit.

The only work of literature which seriously challenges this view in the twelfth century is the Tristan story, in which the love of the hero and heroine is caused not by the merits of the lovers, considerable though these are, but by the irrational power of a magic potion accidentally swallowed. To Chrétien, love brought about by such means was unworthy of the dignity of human reason and human will. He sums up his position categorically in his lyric *D'amor qui m'a tolu a moi*:[19]

---

[17]*De Amicitia* v, viii and xiii.

[18]Despite the epic tone of Geoffrey's *Historia*, the concept of love as the reward of chivalrous merit already exists: "Facetae etiam mulieres [. . .] nullius amorem habere dignabantur, nisi tertio in militia probatus esset. Efficiebantur ergo castae quaeque mulieres, et milites pro amore illarum nobiliores." (ed. Faral, 246). This corresponds to Wace, *Brut*, ll. 10511–21.

[19]Raynaud, 1664. See Brakelmann, 46–48.

Onques del bevrage ne bui
Dont Tristans fu enpoisonez;
Mais plus me fait amer que lui
Fins cuers et bone volentez.                    (ll. 28–31)

A noble heart and the right exercise of the will are what make the experience of true love possible, so it is an experience available only to the élite. Appropriate merit in another calls love into being. So, from the beginning of his romance, Chrétien insists on the merits of his hero: Erec is of high rank, high reputation and exceptional beauty and his first action in the story is to prove himself in battle against the capable Yder. Enide's parents can take it for granted that he will inspire love in their daughter, for her dispositions are as meritorious as his. If she is of lower rank than Erec, she is still, as he points out to the queen (ll. 1563–64), the niece of a count. The equality of the pair in physical and moral attributes is emphasized by Chrétien as they set off to be married (ll. 1504–16). Just as Chrétien reaffirms Erec's prowess at Tenebroc before he falls into 'recreantise', so Chrétien shows us how Enide's beauty, nobility, courtesy, generosity and wisdom are acknowledged by all before the episode of the 'parole'. We cannot doubt that the merit which is the essential basis of love still exists in both parties, though Erec's neglect of arms is culpable and Enide has reason to reproach herself with being the innocent cause of his fault.

The critical part is that it is impossible, in Chrétien's mind, for a woman to love a man she cannot respect. This is why the efforts of Oringle of Limors are doomed to failure. He is rational enough up to a point: her grief is useless; God will comfort her in time; she should be consoled by the prospect of marrying him and becoming a countess (ll. 4693–705). His heartless reasoning is not what makes a villain of him, for it is exactly the same reasoning that Charlemagne in the *Chanson de Roland* applies to Aude: a woman who has lost one man in battle is offered a socially acceptable replacement. The fact that for Enide as for Aude no replacement could be adequate in value serves to highlight the excellence of the hero, not the insensitivity of the offer. The love Oringle offers Enide may be honourable in the sense that it is legal and socially suitable, but it has no value for Chrétien because it is offered by someone so morally inadequate. Love can only be inspired by proven worth. Indeed, it is only when Erec and Enide have proved themselves to one another that Erec can declare that they are now sure of one another's love (ll. 4923–25).

It may seem a poor compliment to Chrétien to say that all his characters are rational creatures in a wholly rational world. Chrétien, however, is far from conventional as a romancer. It is precisely his struggle to maintain rational human values in the face of irrational narrative tradition that constitutes his greatest originality in *Erec*, as we shall see in his rejection of the "marvellous."

## II. The Rejection of the "Marvellous"

The apparent gratuitousness of l. 710 of *Erec et Enide* contrasts disconcertingly with the rapidity and economy of the narrative up to that point. Erec, about to fight on behalf of Enide, is armed for the combat by the heroine herself:

> La pucele meïsme l'arme,
> N'i ot fet charaie ne charme. (ll. 709–10)

Chrétien's denial is vigorous and surely unnecessary. We have no reason to suppose that Enide had the ability or the inclination to cast spells or charms on the armour. On the contrary, the poverty of the hospitable vavassour and the ragged clothes of his beautiful daughter have been heavily emphasized (ll. 407–517). Chrétien's description of a noble family who have lost everything as the result of long-drawn-out wars has the realistic impact of a *tranche de vie* when incorporated into a *conte d'aventure*: it is an unlikely environment for an enchantress to live in.

Chrétien's emphatic negative makes his literary intention quite clear: he is wrenching the narrative sequence away from the magical and the "marvellous," which the story line had evidently led his public to expect, and he is anxious to substitute something else. The "marvellous" sequence he is rejecting is easy to discern below the surface of the text: Enide arming the hero vividly recalls some enchantress who provides her lover with magic arms in order to facilitate his victory. Chrétien's reasons for rejecting this kind of plot line were probably twofold. On the one hand, the advantage in purely human terms that the hero gains from the absence of any magic props is immediately evident: Erec has no outside help and gains his victory through his own prowess and the strength and rightness of his motivations. On the other hand, back in the prologue Chrétien had specifically despised his predecessors for their inept handling of the story and claimed a greater mastery over his material. A "marvellous" tale could have offered him little scope. The superficial variety of the fairy tale and the compelling sameness of its structure have been thoroughly analysed by Vladimir Propp.[1] If Chrétien was to impose his own order on the narrative data, he had to break away from the magical. As we saw in the prologue, he will be telling of Erec, son of Lac: he has chosen to emphasize the man rather than the marvels.

---

[1] *Morphologie du conte.*

26

Enide, too, stands to lose on the human level by being identified with an enchantress. But which enchantress did Chrétien have in mind? It has been suggested that Chrétien wishes to distinguish her from "the traditional Celtic fairy mistress"[2] but the parallel is remote. On the other hand, a surviving French text, written in Chrétien's lifetime, offers an enlightening comparison: the story of Medea and Jason as told by Benoît de Sainte-Maure at the beginning of his *Roman de Troie*.

As Benoît tells the story, Medea is sympathetic as well as beautiful. She loves Jason sincerely, and it is in order to ensure that he is victorious in his quest for the Golden Fleece that she equips him with a whole trousseau of magic aids, a "figure," an ointment, a ring, an "escrit" and some "gluz" (*Troie*, ll. 1663–763). All Jason has to do is to remember to carry out her instructions for using each of these items. The conquest of the Golden Fleece is reduced to an unheroic mechanical exercise.

There is evidence to show that Chrétien knew the *Roman de Troie* when he was writing *Erec*.[3] He also alludes to Medea and her enchantments by name in *Cligès*[4] and makes direct use of her ring in *Yvain*.[5] Despite her magic powers, she is unable to hold Jason, who deceives and abandons her. If Medea is indeed the enchantress Chrétien had in mind when writing l. 710 of *Erec*, it is not difficult to see why he would want to reject any comparison of his heroine with her.

Magic armour, in any case, was already familiar from the other two *romans d'antiquité*. In *Eneas* Venus gives the hero magic arms forged by Vulcan (*Eneas*, ll. 4297–549), and in the *Roman de Thèbes* Eteocles makes himself invincible with a "marvellous" hauberk and an unerringly deadly sword (*Thèbes*, ll. 6203–28). Whatever the kind of "marvellous" in Chrétien's basic material or in contemporary literature, the independence he shows in rejecting it marks him as an original writer, intent on extending the scope of literary expression.

Not that the marvels of his material are excluded at a stroke, once and for all. The "marvellous" always remains close to the surface of *Erec* as a possibility for the narrative, an option which Chrétien systematically rejects, but not before he has put it to use. The ambivalent status of the "marvellous" in this romance is conveyed at the very beginning when Arthur, the focal point of the chivalrous world, announces that he

---

[2]Topsfield, *Chrétien de Troyes*, 323.

[3]Wilmotte, *L'Evolution du roman français*, 18–20, argues that Chrétien may have known the *Roman de Troie* when he was writing *Erec* for three reasons: he mentions Helen of Troy at l. 6342; *Erec* ll. 2407–08 are very similar to *Troie*, ll. 1557–58; and the exotic creatures on Erec's coronation robe closely resemble those on the robe Briséida wears (*Troie*, ll. 13327–409).

[4]See Wilmotte, *Evolution du roman*, 20–21. Thessala knows more about magic and charms than Medea (*Cligès*, ll. 3021–24). She is the confidante of the heroine and "l'avoit norrie d'anfance, Si savoit mout de nigromance" (*Cligès*, ll. 3003–04), a couplet which recalls Medea herself: "Mais jo sai tant de nigromance, Que j'ai aprise dès m'enfance (*Troie*, ll. 1419–20). Cligès mentions the joy with which Helen was received at Troy, a theme Benoît had exploited at length (*Troie*, ll. 4853–80).

[5]See *Yvain*, ed. Reid, notes to ll. 1023, 2600 and 2952.

intends to renew the custom of hunting the White Deer (ll. 37–38). His wish is expressed with the arbitrary abruptness of a fairy-tale king, but it was enough to orient the expectations of his public. The nature of these expectations has been excellently summed up by Reto R. Bezzola. He notes that white deer and other mysterious white animals are common in folklore and that they appear fairly frequently in twelfth-century courtly literature. He refers to the lais of *Guigemar, Tyolet, Graelent* and *Guingamor* and to the romance of *Partenopeus de Blois* and concludes that the White Stag in *Erec* must have roused similar super-natural expectations:

L'animal blanc avait donc toujours pour mission de faire accéder un élu au suprême bonheur terrestre, s'exprimant dans l'amour d'une femme de beauté surnaturelle (à l'origine même un être surnaturel) qui enlevait le héros dans un monde où regnait ni mort ni vieillesse. [. . .] Dès le début de la lecture, l'attente du surnaturel plonge donc l'auditoire dans cette atmosphère mi-réelle, mi-féerique qui restera jusque dans les temps modernes un des charmes les plus attrayants du roman,—et cela sans que Chrétien ait vraiment recours au surnaturel.[6]

Surely, however, if the tradition is so well established, Chrétien's refusal to follow it deserves some investigation? There would be no point in departing from a tried and tested scenario except for some definite purpose. It is remarkable how Chrétien manages to keep the White Deer and all its associations on the one hand, and to avoid any "recourse to the supernatural" on the other.

Arthur's brusque announcement drops into the opening scene without explanation or justification. Gawain, however, is provoked into protest and we see Chrétien solving three narrative problems at a stroke. Gawain's objections furnish a pretext for exposing to the public the rules of the hunt, his indignation plunges the plot into dramatic conflict without loss of time, and the rationalistic nature of his arguments offers the first challenge to the "marvellous." If the victor is to kiss the most beautiful lady of the court, and if each of the five hundred ladies there has a lover ready to uphold her claim to that title, then seriously disruptive results must inevitably follow. Gawain here preserves the character of peace-loving *raisonneur* conferred on him by Wace (*Brut,* ll. 10765–74), the tone of common sense being heightened by the contrast with the fairy-tale opening lines. Chrétien wants to maintain the static and arbitrary world of the "marvellous" as a foil for any other new material he may wish to introduce.

No change or development is possible in the field of the "marvellous" itself. Arthur, while recognizing the justice of Gawain's remarks, refuses to change his plans, and crystallizes the fairy-tale atmosphere by his order:

---

[6]Bezzola, *Sens de l'aventure,* 94–95.

Demain matin a grant deduit
Irons chacier le blanc cerf tuit
An la forest avantureuse.
Ceste chace iert mout mervelleuse.                    (ll. 63–66)

Adventures and marvels, associated by the rhyme, undergo a contamination of meaning.[7] In a popular tale, the hero's adventures become more and more "marvellous" in order to hold our attention, and the framework of the tale is filled out with any number of adventures, each sparked off by a suitable marvel. Marvels and adventures were, no doubt, the sterile norms of the conte d'avanture. If Chrétien evokes them, it is both to stimulate the conventional expectations in his audience and to surprise them into renewed attention when he breaks with tradition.

The break is made as soon as the hero appears. Erec, though introduced in conventional terms as a member of the Round Table, is immediately placed in opposition to the "marvellous." Arthur's hunt literally passes him by. The White Deer, being of no interest to the hero, loses its prestige. Having fulfilled its function of getting the action under way, it is deprived of its magic epithet and hunted like any other beast (ll. 117–22). Moreover, it is deprived of its traditional role. Erec, instead of being enticed away into a land of marvels, stands fast in a clearing while his supernatural guide disappears into the depths of the forest (ll. 125–37). We never get a glimpse of the White Deer until it is being destroyed (ll. 277–83). Once the Deer has prepared the public to expect a guide to be sent to the hero, it is rapidly eliminated in favour of the real guide, another knight.

There is no "marvellous" aspect to Yder, his lady or his dwarf. Yder, as a knight, exists in the narrative on the same plane as the hero. His knightly excellence is boasted of by his accompanying dwarf (ll. 173–74), and his 'vilain' behaviour is only shocking by contrast with the chivalrous response his appearance would suggest. The insult offered by his dwarf is physically brutal. Chrétien could hardly make it clearer that it is not any supernatural charm that beckons on the hero, but the plain human impulse to be avenged. Erec is galvanized into action so speedily that no preparation is possible. The hero and the narrative are swept forward with the maximum urgency.

Yder carries through his role of guide by bringing the hero into contact with the heroine. If Enide's poverty was a surprise to literary expectations, so too is her appearance. She is no supernatural being. She is not even a "femme de beauté surnaturelle," to quote R. Bezzola. On the contrary, Chrétien insists that she is the work of Nature (ll. 411–13). All possibility of ambiguity ends, as we have seen, with the explicit rejection of the idea that Enide can or will cast spells (l. 710).

---

[7]Foerster prints "mervelleuse" relying on the Guiot ms. in his first edition of the text (Halle, 1890). In later editions he chooses "delitose" from ms. H, Paris B.N. 1450.

It could be argued that the rejection of the "marvellous" is structurally immaterial. The development of the plot line is not affected by the substitution of one agent for another. On a functional level, the White Deer and Yder are interchangeable. However, the structural identity of the former could not be extended beyond this single function, and in a complex narrative sequence the human agent has obvious advantages. Whereas a white animal is a spent force once it has accomplished its mission, Yder can and does assume different narrative functions and provides the story with greater continuity and coherence. By surrounding the hero with figures of comparable stature, the strands of the narrative can be woven together more tightly. Unlike a white animal, Yder can be sent back to Arthur's court to provide an active link between Erec's present, past and future.

The White Deer and the knight Yder both contribute to establishing the sense of Erec's first chivalrous adventure, the Custom of the Hawk. The Custom of the White Deer is a preliminary sketch for the second custom, upheld by Yder and challenged by Erec. In each case, a supremely beautiful woman is to have her claim to supremacy publicly acknowledged. However intrinsically improbable, the existence of such customs has been established from the beginning of the romance.[8] But whereas Arthur had renewed his custom without giving any reason and without having any ready solution to the problem of choosing the right lady, Erec has no such difficulty. The incomparable beauty of Enide offers him a thoroughly justified reason for upholding her claim in a contest that was thrust upon him. Besides, whereas the White Deer led a harmless if nebulous existence, the violence offered by Yder's dwarf presented Erec with a pressing motivation for vengeance. Given that the actions a chivalrous hero like Erec can perform are extremely limited in kind, it becomes essential to differentiate them in degree. The hero of a romance is almost invariably reduced to fighting in single combat with an enemy. In his encounter with Yder, Erec's distinguishing features are his double justification and his lack of all magical support.

Once the point has been made clear about the rejection of "marvellous" solutions for his hero, Chrétien relaxes and allows himself certain exceptions to his policy of exclusion. The victorious Erec is taking away Enide as his bride when her cousin offers her the gift of a palfrey, which is certainly wonderful, if not quite supernatural, for it goes faster than a bird flies and its rider travels more smoothly than in a boat (ll. 1392–402). The nuance here is very discreet, but towards the end of the romance, in a parallel situation, Chrétien admits a more explicit degree of the "marvellous," because he has by then firmly established the code of conduct enacted by his heroes. Enide, as she leaves the Castle of Penevric, is presented with another palfrey. A decidedly bizarre note is struck here, for the piebald face of the sorrel mount is marked by a stripe

---

[8]For a study of both feudal and fictional customs, see Köhler, "Le Rôle de la 'coutume'."

that is greener than a vine-leaf (l. 5328). Taken in isolation, this would certainly indicate that we have crossed the boundary of the rational, though multicoloured mounts are not unknown in the comparatively sober romans d'antiquité,[9] and it is clear from the way Chrétien describes it that he is unaware that he may be straining our credulity. As far as he is concerned, it is only insofar as it differs from Enide's previous palfrey that this new horse is considered worthy of description at all. Its value is declared to be not inferior to that of the previous horse, but nothing more (ll. 5320–21).

The odd flourish of greenery brings to a climax Chrétien's description of the horse as such and acts as a transition to the really "marvellous" part of the gift, the wonderfully splendid harness. The description of this runs to over twenty lines (ll. 5330–51), constituting a rhetorical *tour de force* of a kind already exemplified in the romance, notably in the descriptions of Enide's beauty and of the robes given her by the queen (ll. 411–41; 1587–625).[10] The story of Aeneas, carved in ivory on the palfrey's trappings, evokes a magnificent legendary past which only serves to make the present time of the narrative more immediate and vital by contrast. The last and most complete example of this kind of rhetorical description deals with Erec's coronation robe (ll. 6733–809). It is as if Chrétien allows himself to indulge in the exotic aspect of the "marvellous" in the static parts of his romance, where the action and motivation of the characters are not in question and where the story is not vulnerable to the mechanical contamination of the "marvellous."

At first it seems as if the "marvellous" triumphs at a critical part of the intrigue. The episode of the White Deer does after all come to a happy conclusion. Arthur can justify his insistence on renewing the custom, and he does so at length (ll. 1793–814). Nevertheless, the hunting of this "marvellous" beast had, as Gawain predicted, led the court to the brink of disaster and the expected clashes were only averted by Erec, the very man who had not taken part in the hunt.

Arthur's self-justification is not without interest. To Gawain's earlier objection, he had merely replied that he could not go back on his royal word, once pledged (ll. 59–62). When a crisis is imminent, he appeals to Gawain to save his honour, but no solution other than temporization can be found (ll. 285–341). Arthur's static and inflexible helplessness is underlined. When all turns out well, he justifies his rigidity, saying that it is his royal duty to preserve exactly those customs which his ancestors had established, without introducing any changes or modifications (ll. 1793–814). Thus the whole Arthurian ethos consists in maintaining a solid context of immovable tradition, composed of customs which had

---

[9]Capaneüs has a horse of four extraordinary colours (*Thèbes*, ll. 9019–26) and Camilla rides an amazing animal of eight different colours (*Eneas*, ll. 4049–68).

[10]On the possible classical sources of the exotic kind of "marvellous," see Faral, *Sources latines*, 307–88; for the rhetorical aspects of these descriptions, see Faral, *Arts poétiques*, 75–85.

become arbitrary in character from being long divorced from their original *raison d'être*. On the level of the narrative, the static quality of Arthur and his rule gives added relief to the dynamic quality of the hero and to the central action of the romance.

The splendour of the Arthurian décor assumes a new importance on the occasion of Erec's wedding, to such a degree, indeed, that it temporarily eclipses the hero. Erec, having performed the heroic deed that has won him Enide, retires for the moment to the background during the festive gathering. The "marvellous," the exotically static, is left free to fill our view. There is nothing inappropriate, of course, in evoking Arthurian splendour in order to gild the triumph of the man who has preserved the peace of the Arthurian court. Yet the guests who assemble at Arthur's bidding, while they bear witness to the extent of his domain, nevertheless introduce a note which comes close to the grotesque. The extreme youth of the men brought by Ban de Gomeret (ll. 1974–78) is balanced by the immense age of the men who accompany Kerrin, King of Riel (ll. 1985–91). If the dwarf King Bilis and his men (ll. 1993–2011) lack gigantic counterparts, it is no doubt because the presence of giants would threaten to eclipse Arthur's sovereignty in his own court. The dwarves come from the Antipodes: Maheloas comes from a country even more remote, for in it there are no toads or serpents or intemperate weather (ll. 1845–51). The overall purpose is clear enough: Arthur's power and influence extend even to the most distant and unexplored territories.[11]

Only one of the guests strikes a frankly fairy-tale note and that is Guigomar, lord of the isle of Avalon:

> De cestui avons oï dire
> Qu'il fu amis Morgain la fee,
> Et ce fu veritez provee.                    (ll. 1956–58)

Why does Chrétien bring in Morgan la Fay, after so firmly rejecting any association of his heroine with supernatural charms? His attitude to Morgan is uneasy: within the space of two lines a rumour is transformed into a proven truth. This is the first time in the course of the rapid, fluent, almost arrogantly presented narrative that there has been any question of proving anything. Nor is proof forthcoming: Chrétien does not even hint at an authority, but passes swiftly on. The brief allusion to Morgan adds to the decorative background of the wedding without threatening the development of the narrative. Once evoked in this

---

[11]Note in this connection that the tympanum of Vézelay (sculpted c. 1125–30), which represents Christ sending out the apostles to convert the world, shows Christ as a large and majestic figure in the centre, the apostles as smaller but still imposing figures, and the remoteness of the peoples that are to be brought under Christian rule is conveyed by representing them as small and sometimes highly grotesque figures around the outer edge of the tympanum and on the lintel. See Mâle, *L'Art religieux du XIIe siècle en France*, 326–32.

relatively relaxed context, she can be reintroduced later, when she is needed for more utilitarian ends.

The requirements of the plot demand that Erec should pass through a series of combats which naturally do not leave him unscathed. The requirements of Chrétien's style, always rapid and concise apart from the descriptive interludes, demand that no time be lost in getting the hero ready for the next encounter. So when Erec, with his crisis still unresolved, is courteously ambushed by Gawain and brought wounded to Arthur's court, a solution must be found to avoid a longueur in the narrative. In a similar situation, Benoît de Sainte-Maure had Hector's wounds rapidly healed between battles by a "marvellous" oriental physician who administers a potion that has an instantaneously beneficial effect (*Troie*, ll. 10245–51). Arthur, for his part, promptly brings out an ointment "Que Morgue, sa suer, avoit fet" (l. 4220). Its efficacy is such that a daily application can heal any wound within a week. Morgan is not described as a fairy here. In such close connection with the hero, it is only her medical knowledge and her relationship to the king that are mentioned. Later in the story, Guivret's sisters, who perform similar medical marvels, are even more carefully rationalized. There is also more leisure here, as the reconciliation with Enide has just taken place. Erec again needs treatment, and he is brought to these learned ladies, who strive hard to heal him (l. 5196). There is no question now of effortless magic, but of a serious, laborious, scientific procedure, and it is a full fortnight before the exertions of the sisters succeed in abating Erec's sufferings (ll. 5200–21).

If Chrétien is so reluctant to allow his hero to benefit from magic concoctions even in cases of medical necessity, it is scarcely surprising that he should make it clear that no love potion was needed on the wedding night. The legend of Tristan had already been twice alluded to in the romance (ll. 424–26; 1247–50). Chrétien implicitly acknowledges the prestige of the tragedy of fatal passion but, just as with his other allusions, whether to literary or oral tradition, he rejects any comparison that involves the use of the "marvellous." On his heroine's wedding night, there is no Brangien, no substitution (ll. 2075–77), just as there had been no previous deceit or enchantment in the relationship, nothing but what is natural. Like a hunted stag who thirsts for the stream, like a hungry hawk who responds eagerly to the call of the one who feeds him, so Erec and Enide hasten to satisfy their appetites (ll. 2081–88). It is appropriate that the two animals which have brought them together should be recalled at such a moment and noteworthy that each should be deprived of all possible supernatural ambience. On the contrary, it is their basic animal appetites which are evoked, a discreet indication that the relations of the hero and heroine are still on an instinctual level and that a fuller human development is still to come.

A change of viewpoint on the "marvellous" is briefly sketched soon after the wedding. At the Tenebroc tournament the hero amazes the spectators with his skill: "A mervoilles s'an esbaïrent" (l. 2212). Erec, whose victorious progress has been exposed to us with such rational plausibility that his feats at the tournament can scarcely surprise us, is suddenly metamorphosed into a marvel himself. A change of viewpoint gives a change of vision: marvels are now in the eye of the beholder.[12]

It is in the last of Erec's adventures that Chrétien makes the most complex use of the "marvellous," before, inevitably, rejecting it. The Joie de la Cort, once criticized as an *hors d'oeuvre*, is now universally accorded a vital place in the overall sense of the romance.[13] Nevertheless, on the level of the narrative, it presents the public with problems, particularly with regard to the use of the "marvellous." Chrétien shows us Erec and Enide, their personal relationship renewed, setting off for Arthur's court accompanied by Guivret. They come to a fine castle surrounded by a moat which is filled with deep and fast-flowing water, and Erec asks Guivret its name (ll. 5367-86). Guivret's reply is the first indication of strain: he promises Erec that he will tell him the truth about it (ll. 5387-88), a protest which immediately opens up the possibility of the false and the unreal. We are reminded of the protest over Morgan la Fay. Guivret is in fact reluctant to tell the whole truth, knowing that Erec will be tempted by the perilous adventure (ll. 5428-45). Chrétien himself, when it comes to describing the site of the adventure, betrays an even greater uneasiness. Concerning this orchard, he will, he protests, tell us something true (ll. 5735-38). Thus warned, we are prepared for a garden that will need a lot of explaining and indeed Chrétien has scarcely named its first feature, the wall of air, than he attributes it to "nigromance" (l. 5742). There is no sense that the author is taking pleasure in a romantic and mysterious atmosphere. On the contrary, it is as if Chrétien wishes to explain away the garden, and abdicate responsibility for it by assigning its existence to the operation of anonymous powers.

The owner of the castle, King Evrain, and his fortified town have nothing magical about them. Evrain expresses the same chivalrous prudence voiced by the Arthurian court when they begged Erec to give up his quest and stay with them. (ll. 4233-55; 4286-89). Evrain duly warns Erec against the adventure in the orchard, but his is the thankless role of the *raisonneur*, whose only function is to indicate what is reasonable so that the hero may surpass it:

> Erec antant et bien otroie
> Que li rois a droit le consoille;
> Mes con plus granz est la mervoille
> Et l'avanture plus grevainne,
> Plus la covoite et plus se painne.          (ll. 5642-46)

---

[12] As Kelly points out, "Matière and genera dicendi in Medieval Romance," 149: "émerveillement seems to derive from the singularity of the merveille rather than from its setting or supernatural quality alone, although it may include the latter."

[13] See Sturm-Maddox, "Hortus non conclusus: Critics and the Joie de la Cort".

The adventure is a marvel, but the joy the adventure produces lies in the destruction of the marvel. The mysterious attraction of the orchard is sinister. After the steady human progress of the hero's adventures, the presentation of this "marvellous" site jars by its static qualities (ll. 5746-64). There is no natural revolution of the seasons; no kind of change is permitted. The garden's beauty is fixed in a deadly immobility. Even its fruit cannot be taken outside and eaten. The link with the outside world is a narrow one (ll. 5765-67). Erec goes bravely down this narrow passage with, indeed, a presentiment of the Joie, but armed for combat; and a combat is inevitably what ensues.

The townspeople had marvelled, looking at the newcomer and bewailing his anticipated fate in chorus (ll. 5501-09). Now all attention is focussed on the marvel Erec will encounter. He thinks of the joy, *but* he sees a marvel (l. 5774). The marvel is in fact a horror fit to terrify the most intrepid epic hero, a row of heads spiked on stakes. The one headless stake bears a horn. It is a marvel, but it is not allowed to remain a mystery, for Evrain at once undercuts any possibility of marvelling by explanation: the empty stake is waiting for the head of the next victim; the horn will be blown by the man who succeeds in returning victorious (ll. 5792-826).

Erec goes forward alone into this gruesome garden, and discovers a maiden reposing under a tree on a rather incongruous silver bed. As he seats himself beside her, a knight appears with almost mechanical promptitude and issues a challenge. The stranger is "granz a mervoilles" (l. 5900), but he is no giant of myth or folklore. Nor is he to be compared with the two brutal giants Erec had fought earlier. The giants who attacked Cadoc enlarged Erec's horizon, both because the reason for fighting them was, for the first time in the hero's career, purely altruistic, and because the fight itself was the first in which the rules of chivalry did not apply.

The knight in the orchard is very different from these. He quickly shows that he belongs to Erec's world. Even his height, which might have been supernaturally grotesque, is only a relatively small blemish on an otherwise perfect beauty (ll. 5901-02). Chrétien's brief excursion into the "marvellous" is over. The knight's fierce challenge is accorded no special respect: Erec reasons with him coolly and refuses to be intimidated by his threats (ll. 5935-39). The fight is not distinguished in any way from other such combats described in the romance. Duly defeated, the adversary reveals himself to be Mabonagrain, nephew of Evrain and well known to Erec's father Lac (ll. 6037-41). When his 'amie' turns out to be Enide's cousin (ll. 6246-62), the last vestiges of the mysterious and the "marvellous" vanish in an atmosphere of family reunion.

The Joie de la Cort comes about precisely when Mabonagrain is released from the "marvellous" garden: joy and marvels are in direct opposition. As Mabonagrain explains to Erec, his 'amie' had taken

advantage of his submission to her and forced him to stay with her in
the garden, thinking that she could keep him to herself for the rest of his
life "an prison" (l. 6097). Since Mabonagrain was dubbed knight in this
very orchard "veant mainz prodomes" (l. 6071), then the excluding wall
of air must be due to the excluding 'amie', and after Erec's victory we
hear no more about it.

Mabonagrain, at the end of the story, like Arthur to a lesser extent at
the beginning, is a slightly mechanical figure, a puppet pulled by the
strings of arbitrary conventions. His situation provides the right foil of
fixity needed to estimate just how far Erec, in contrast, has progressed.
The contrast is even more striking, and is indeed made perfectly explicit,
between their two ladies (ll. 6192-323). We can see more clearly now
how fortunate Erec was to find an 'amie' who pressed on him neither
magic help nor magic hindrance, and who was prepared to suffer herself
rather than let her love harm him. Not that the damsel of the orchard is
described as an enchantress. Since she is a blood relation of Enide, it
would be most inappropriate that she should be a fairy mistress. The
'nigromance' that produced the wall of air would appear to be the
product of an impersonally evil power, for the lady was as much
trapped by it as her lover.

The enchanted orchard is a pseudo-paradise in which a pair of lovers
cut themselves off from the rest of the world. It is not without its charm,
for the perfectly static offers at least the illusion of perfect security. But
it constitutes a rejection of the claims of the individual and the claims
of society that Chrétien is not prepared to countenance. The liberation
of the couple causes joy to the court and eventually joy to themselves.
The selfish and anti-social constraints that imprisoned the couple in
the orchard are characteristically expressed by Chrétien in terms of
the artificial limitations placed on human freedom of action by the
"marvellous."

Throughout the romance, Chrétien is at pains to show us his hero and
heroine acting as free and responsible human agents. From the moment
they appear, Erec and Enide are in an almost continual state of spatial
and personal progression. The character of each is defined by opposition
to possible "marvellous" alternatives. Erec's dynamism is defined by
contrast with the rigid conservativism of Arthur and the frustrated
subjection of Mabonagrain, as well as by the absence of any of the
"marvellous" aids offered to the heroes of the romans d'antiquité. The
full measure of Enide's 'sagesse' is seen by contrast with the paralysing
effect her cousin's love has on Mabonagrain. Chrétien's strongest point
is made in favour of what is human and against everything artificial. It
is precisely because they have not stayed secluded in a magic garden but
have exposed themselves to the challenge of the world that Erec and
Enide achieve a stability powerful enough to enable them to liberate
others from the constraints expressed by the "marvellous."

## III. The Problem of Narrative Continuity

Everything we have seen so far about Chrétien's literary preoccupations poses a problem when we come to consider the "bele conjointure" (l. 14) of his narrative. If his characters are rational creatures in a rational world, then he cannot make use of explanation as a means of linking episodes and justifying action. In a perfectly coherent order of things, explanations are superfluous. It is only romancers like, for example, Balzac, writing in a confused post-Revolutionary world, who can profit from the general uncertainty in order to create self-contained literary worlds, and people them with characters whose actions are to be explained by reference to the author's own experience of reality, arranged or invented for the occasion. Had Chrétien been living in such a world, he might have written explanatory introductory phrases such as: "Like all rich young men, Erec . . ." or perhaps: "Enide was one of those rare persons who . . ." or other such highly artificial devices of the realistic novel.

As it is, Chrétien is deprived both of the necessity and the support of explanation, and he voluntarily deprives himself of any help to be had from the resources of the "marvellous." It is paradoxical that the effect produced by an author writing of a perfectly rational world is to present us with a story devoid of rational explanation.[1] Since rationalizing and justification are foreign to his purpose, he deploys several purely technical devices in order to produce a satisfactory narrative continuity.

First and simplest is pace. The sheer speed of *Erec* is a powerful means of forcing our acceptance of the narrative. Swept along by the pace of the action, we are simply not allowed the leisure to reflect on the relative probability or improbability of each new episode, as we shall be able to later in the more static and introspective romance of *Cligès*. When we first see Erec, he is spurring his horse after Arthur and "galopant vint tot le chemin" (l. 96). With the queen, he rides into the forest "a grant esploit" (l. 115) and scarcely relaxes his pace for the rest of the romance. Over and over again, he and the characters he comes into contact with are stated to be progressing 'isnelement', 'araument', 'sanz demorance', and 'maintenant sans nule demore'. It is revealing to examine this device further as it is exploited in three different but characteristic situations.

---

[1]The single exception occurs at ll. 2826–28, where he explains that it was the custom for knights to attack an enemy knight one by one. This is a concession to physical probability, for he tells us that otherwise the robbers would have killed Erec. Renaut de Beaujeu, who borrows this custom from *Erec*, is uneasy about it, for he adds that life has changed a great deal since this custom was in force. See *Renaut de Beaujeu: Le Bel Inconnu*, ll. 1016–84.

Each time Erec plunges into a new situation where explanation of the
circumstances would be warranted, the pace increases so that he is well
entrenched in the adventure before there is time to ask questions. Very
early in the romance, just after he has received Yder's challenging insult
(which, by the way, is never explained or justified at all), Erec sets out
in pursuit without even waiting to collect his armour. He tracks his
quarry to a fortified town and follows him to his lodgings. Nearby he
sees a white-haired vavassour sitting alone and pensive on some steps
and he thinks that he might give him shelter:

> Parmi la porte antre an la cort:
> Li vavassors contre li cort.
> Ainz qu'Erec li eüst dit mot,
> Li vavassors salué l'ot.
> "Biaus sire!", fet il, "bien veigniez!"          (ll. 383–87)

By what telepathy does the vavassour immediately divine Erec's needs?
Erec is an unarmed stranger and Chrétien has made a point of telling us
just a few lines previously that the crowd who welcomed Yder ignored
Erec because they did not know him (ll. 361–67). It is as if the dynamic
urgency of Erec's requirements galvanizes a passive character into
action. Once drawn into Erec's ambience, the exceptional courtesy of the
vavassour will bring easily in its wake the exceptional virtues of his
daughter. Erec's urgency is so great, and the hospitality of the vavassour
so pressing, that despite the poverty of the household, entertainment
is provided with astonishing speed (ll. 490–500). Erec—and the reader—
is already established in Enide's house before there is time to ask
questions.

Moreover, while speed at the start of the story may be necessary to
arouse the public's interest and prevent us from brooding over the
possible and the probable in the data of the plot, Chrétien feels it
necessary to maintain the initial impetus throughout the story, as the
main line of his narrative is expressed in violent action. It is therefore
natural enough that, at the crisis of the story produced by Enide's
'parole,' he should imagine a reaction for his hero that is active rather
than discursive. Enide has her palfrey saddled without delay (ll.
2616–22); Erec's valet runs to collect his master's arms (ll. 2624–32). Erec,
explaining nothing to his bewildered entourage, calls for his Gascon bay
and tells his valet to run and make Enide hurry as she is keeping him
waiting too long: she is to mount horse at once (ll. 2665–71). The valet
hastens to transmit the command to hasten (ll. 2671–79). Enide goes
down to the courtyard; King Lac runs after her (ll. 2685–87) and the
knights run "qui miauz miauz" (l. 2687) to offer their companionship.
Erec sweeps all objections aside, puts his affairs in order with the utmost
expedition and sets off with Enide, commanding her to ride ahead
"grant aleüre" (l. 2768).

This emphasis on Erec's speed is more than a convenient way of

getting us from one episode to the next without heavy-handed justification. It is also a means of illustrating the hero's characteristic knightly
excellence, the capacity to act fast and effectively. When Erec's capacity
to act becomes the centre of interest, as it does the moment he and Enide
set off, it causes another narrative problem. We take it in our stride
when Erec rapidly overcomes three robbers and then, with even greater
proportional speed, disposes of five more, but this kind of progression
could quickly become ridiculous. So Chrétien devises a situation which
absolutely necessitates speed. The couple, on the point of being betrayed by Count Galoain, are obliged to escape with all urgency. Enide
lets the exhausted Erec sleep as long as possible, then wakes him to
explain what is afoot and to urge him to get going quickly (ll. 3469-70). To
which he naturally replies that they had better saddle their horses
quickly and run to call their host (ll. 3488-90). He dresses hurriedly,
settles his account with his host, who is astounded by such haste, and
they make their escape just before the enemy arrives. The baffled
Galoain pursues them, swearing he will have Erec's head the moment
he catches him, and he urges his companions to ride even faster
(ll. 3530-38). Enide hears them coming and calls to Erec to ride faster still
to the cover of the forest (ll. 3556-57). At this point, Chrétien is careful
not to let the pace of the action become too facile and automatic. The
direction of the movement is abruptly reversed. Erec "se retorne
maintenant" (l. 3571), sees the count's seneschal approaching on a fast
horse, runs him through, and is ready for Galoain himself who rides up
at full speed. Erec unhorses him, turns again and gallops off into the
forest (ll. 3572-620). The repentant count sends his men off home
"isnelemant" (l. 3639) and Erec rides "toz esleissiez" (l. 3663) with his
wife until they come to a drawbridge. Then "isnelemant passent le pont"
(l. 3674) and we are straight into the episode of Guivret le Petit.
     The same technique, with variations, is used in the later episode of the
more brutal Count Oringle of Limors. After Erec rescues Cadoc and his
'amie' from the giants, he brushes aside their thanks and rides back as
fast as he possibly can to Enide (ll. 4575-89). But he falls as if dead at her
feet and Enide, in despair, is about to kill herself when God makes her
delay just long enough for a count to ride up, "grant aleüre," (l. 4676),
naturally, and prevent her. The Count of Limors has a bier made for
Erec "promptly and without delay" (l. 4726), but his speedy forcefulness
is perhaps better conveyed by his instant proposal of marriage to the
supposed widow and his refusal to take no for an answer. At the critical
moment, back at his castle, Erec revives, draws his sword quickly
(l. 4861), runs to where his wife is, dispatches the count, sends everyone
fleeing in terror, runs to get his shield, chases them all down to the
courtyard where his horse is being held ready saddled, hastens to
mount it, followed by Enide, whom he comforts as they ride off "grant
aleüre" (l. 4936). Here the effect of speed has been sustained over a
single long episode by distributing the pressure between hero and

villain; in turn Erec, Oringle and again Erec have initiated an action
which interlocks with the following one to provide the rapid links of a
satisfying sequence of movement.

The glaring exception to the general preoccupation with speed is
Chrétien's equal fondness for passages of description. He finds it hard
to resist the temptation to display his skill at this essentially rhetorical
exercise, though he is well aware that it conflicts with the interests of
narrative progression. When the appetites of both his hero and his
public have been whetted by the prospect of the adventure of the Joie de
la Cort, and Erec is on the point of requesting Evrain's permission to
attempt it, this is not the moment to hold the story up with a description
of the interior decoration of the castle. No indeed, for

> Le tans gasteroie an folie,
> Ne je ne le vuel pas gaster,
> Einçois me vuel un po haster;
> Car qui tost va la droite voie
> Passe celui qui se desvoie.          (ll. 5574–78)

In this respect Chrétien is like his hero. For the author as for the
protagonist there is a quasi-moral obligation to go straight to his goal
without wasting time in self-indulgent 'folie'. Over and over again
Chrétien protests that he is going ahead without wasting time on
unnecessary pauses (ll. 1084; 2070; 6174–75; 6386–87; 6444).

It is noteworthy that it is only splendours of the kind Evrain possesses
that tempt Chrétien to hold up his narrative.[2] In *Erec*, only the beautiful
and the magnificent warrant detailed report. When Enide's father
equips Erec with a very modest mount, Chrétien forbears without
difficulty from describing the trappings:

> Del hernois a parler ne fet;
> Car la granz povretez ne let.          (ll. 735–36)

Understandably, once his hero has reached his goal, Chrétien feels more
at liberty to indulge himself. The coronation of Erec, as befits the
apotheosis of a hero now past compare, is marked by splendours that
provide a positive *embarras de richesses* for the rhetorician. It is madness
to attempt to describe them, but Chrétien cannot resist the temptation:

> Donc vuel je grant folie anprandre,
> Qui au descrivre vuel antandre.          (ll. 6707–08)

He plunges in recklessly:

> Mes puis que feire le m'estuet,
> Or avaingne qu'avenir puet,
> Ne leisserai que je ne die
> Selonc mon san une partie.          (ll. 6709–12)

[2]See Faral, *Sources latines*, 320–28 and 335–48.

It is more remarkable that the narrative was halted near the beginning in order to accommodate a thirty-line description of the heroine's beauty (ll. 411–41). This is a true rhetorical portrait, as much encomium as description.[3] It is a static moment in the narrative, providing indirect justification for future action. Once Enide's exceptional merits, both moral and physical, have been established, the outcome of the customs of the Hawk and the Deer need no further justification, any more than Erec's condescension in marrying her.

When the subject of the description is inanimate and material, Chrétien integrates it as much as possible into the narrative flow by associating it with the prevailing speed. On the magnificent formal occasion when the queen, at Erec's request, bestows a ceremonial robe on Enide, no detail of the robe's splendour is omitted, but the giving of it is done in a flurry of activity which both underlines the queen's ready generosity to a newcomer, and confers a factitious air of movement to the description. To Erec's request,

> . . . la reïne maintenant
> Li respont: "Mout avez bien fet!
> Droiz est que de mes robes et.
> Et je li donrai buene et bele,
> Tot or androit, fresche et novele."
> La reïne erraumant l'an mainne
> An la soe chanbre demainne
> Et dist qu'an li aport isnel
> Le fres blïaut et le mantel.                    (ll. 1582–90)

The elaborate description of the robe ends with the queen calling for magnificent gold cords for the mantle:

> Ele les fist tot maintenant
> Metre el mantel isnelement.                     (ll. 1627–28)

In this way the static is framed as far as possible with the dynamic.

Speed is actually incorporated into the first gift Enide receives, the palfrey her cousin gives her, which can travel faster than a bird and carry its rider more smoothly than a ship (ll. 1387–402). The second palfrey she receives later, from Guivret, has a harness that gives Chrétien full scope for his descriptive powers (ll. 5316–56). Nevertheless, it is introduced on a note of urgency:

> Guivrez de monter les semont
> Maintenant sanz nule demore.
> Ja ne cuide veoir cele ore
> Enide, qu'il soient monté.                       (ll. 5312–15)

The long and apparently self-indulgent description of the strange mount and its exotic harness has an underlying tension which reasserts

---

[3]See Faral, *Arts poétiques*, 76.

itself at the end when Enide mounts the palfrey eagerly and the others follow suit "isnelemant" (l. 5360).

Chrétien's constant preoccupation with speed is a narrative device designed to keep a story of adventure on the move. On the level of character, it has another important effect. The movement of the plot and the movements of the hero are so closely fused that the unjustified nature of the narrative confers an unjustified character on Erec's actions. Devoid of explanation and justification, his will alone successfully sweeps aside all obstacles and propels him towards his goal. Speed is the primary manifestation of the will, imposing itself arbitrarily on the action.

The power of the will is first expressed through Arthur. The first action of the story is introduced by the arbitrary expression of his will when he announces that he wishes to hunt the White Deer.[4] The reasonable objections of Gawain are set aside; right or wrong, the royal will is not subject to justification (ll. 39–62). Arthur's will is unchallengeable and it sweeps all with him. Next morning he rises, rouses his knights, who are followed by the queen, who is followed by Erec. The king's will has produced a snowball effect on the action, and Erec is caught up in it without more ado. He is already an actor in the drama before he is formally introduced to us. Once in the forest, it is the queen's expression of will, again arbitrary, which provokes the adventure, for it is she who wishes to know who Yder is (ll. 149–52).

Erec, the son of a king and destined to be a king in his turn, plausibly assumes this regal ability to direct the action by the expression of will. The strength of his will is made clear early in his relations with Enide. He proposes to take her in her present rags to Arthur's court, stating that he wishes the queen to give her a robe (l. 1350). Enide's cousin, described by Chrétien as "mout preuz, mout sage, mout vaillanz" (l. 1354), and whose suggestions therefore appear to warrant a favourable reception, says that she wishes to present Enide with a suitable robe to go to court in. Without reference to anyone, Enide least of all, Erec refuses the offer, giving no other reason than that he does not wish it (ll. 1374–78). The count and his family give way at once to the superior force of Erec's will and he then declares that he wishes Enide to accept the alternative gift of the palfrey (ll. 1403–06).

The rejection of the robe and the consequent re-affirmation of Erec's will do not directly affect the action, but the incident establishes the imperious character of his will and accounts for the style of his future actions. When, for example, Erec wishes to leave Cardigan for Carnant,

[4]Köhler, "Le rôle de la coutume," 394, claims that the upholding of customary laws by Arthur "élimine tout arbitraire royal" and that in *Erec* Arthur justifies himself for maintaining the customs of his father (ll. 1803–14). Nevertheless, in Chrétien's narrative, the custom of the White Deer is presented first as an unmotivated expression of Arthur's will, then as a positive danger to the court, and only after the hero circumvents the danger can Arthur justify himself in retrospect.

King Arthur is obliged to bow to his wishes and reluctantly give him leave (ll. 2279–83). Later on Arthur's very reasonable wish that Erec should stay with him to be healed is even more firmly overruled (ll. 4231–60). His will is so strong that his own men do not dare question him (ll. 2653–56) but they, like his wife and his father, make haste to discover Erec's will and then obey. Erec sets out with Enide "ne set quel part, an avanture" (l. 2767), but it is no aimless wandering. Erec's will is strong enough to carve out a moral path, the "voie" he will refuse to abandon (l. 4257).

The encounters that make up his 'voie' invariably entail physical opposition and it is obviously necessary that his opponents should have their share of arbitrary and aggressive will. The first robber is determined to have Enide's palfrey (l. 2813). Kay insists on knowing Erec's identity (ll. 3990–91). Oringle of Limors is intent on marrying Enide whether she will or no (ll. 4721–22). His will is only held in check by her stronger will, rooted in her rational preference for a better man (ll. 4844–52). But there is no room for rational argument between Erec and Oringle, nor is the mere expression of will enough to decide the issue here. The deciding factor in a chivalrous context is the ability to express will in action. Chrétien ends, as always, by cutting the knot in the intrigue with the sword of the hero.

Actions provide another solution to the problem of continuity, in the most natural possible way. The characteristic action of romance is normally made up of two parts, as mutually dependent as the two sides of a coin. Once we have been shown one part, we expect the other, without any need of justification. Erec formulates the arrangement very early in the action by requesting Enide's father to grant him

> ". . . un don,
> Don je vos randrai guerredon."                    (ll. 631–32)

The 'don', a knightly gift or service or honour is the chivalrous act for which the correct and indeed the inevitable response is the 'guerredon', the guerdon or reward or formal recognition of the 'don'. In this case the 'don' is the honour of upholding Enide's claim to the Hawk and the 'guerredon' will be Erec's offer of marriage. As he says to the vavassour after his victory:

> "Mout m'avez grant enor portee;
> Mes bien vos iert guerredonee."                    (ll. 1323–24)

In the same way, when Galoain's squire offers Erec and Enide the timely service of refreshment after their night in the forest, Erec rewards him with the 'guerredon' of one of the horses he has won (ll. 3183–84).

This aspect of knightly behaviour is exploited by Chrétien to link together a variety of situations. The simplest extension is to make the 'guerredon' provoke a further response of its own. In the case just mentioned, the excellence of the horse given to the squire prompts him to boast to his master Count Galoain of the high qualities of the donor (ll. 3222–30). Galoain's vanity is provoked, and the motivation for the next episode provided.

The 'guerredon' may be extended by repetition. The honour bestowed by the vavassour on Erec in giving him Enide is twice rewarded later in the romance. As the couple leave for Arthur's court, Erec promises to make the vavassour lord of Roadan and Montrevel (ll. 1328–40). He grants this 'guerredon' in due course (ll. 1877–86) It is the only action whose completion spans the two sections or "vers" of the romance. But it is only at the end of the romance that he fully recompenses the vavassour, by presenting him to King Arthur and acknowledging publicly the extent of the honour done him (ll. 6601–03).

The honouring of the worthy by the worthy lends itself particularly well to the extending and delaying of reciprocal action. Guivret, for example, feels it an honour to be vanquished by someone like Erec and presses on his victor the service of help and healing (ll. 3890–904). Erec accepts only the minimum of what is offered, and the guerdon remains available for completion later in the narrative. Erec hopes that Guivret will not forget him should he hear that he is in some emergency (ll. 3905–12) and so, very naturally, as soon as Guivret hears of the sensational events at the castle of Limors, "erraumant d'Erec li sovint" (l. 4955). Guivret can at last complete his 'guerredon' by having Erec healed at his castle of Penevric (ll. 5187–239).

Given that such reciprocity is the norm of chivalrous behaviour, considerable effect can be derived from the suppression of the 'guerredon'. When Erec rescues Cadoc from the giants, he performs a service that it is beyond the power of those rescued to reward. Cadoc's 'amie' says to Erec that they should both be his to honour and serve him,

> "Mes qui porroit guerredoner
> Ceste desserte nes demie?"                    (ll. 4568–69)

Erec courteously replies:

> ". . . Ma douce amie!
> Nul guerredon ne vos demant.
> Anbedeus a Deu vos comant."                    (ll. 4570–72)

No reward can be adequate and none is asked. Erec, however, increases his reputation with the reader for his disinterestedness and increases his reputation at Arthur's court when the couple spontaneously go there to recount his exploit (ll. 4576–79), the only 'guerredon' in their power to give.

It is, of course, one thing to acknowledge one's inability to return a service and quite another to make no acknowledgement of the service at all. Mabonagrain's lady obtains an enormous concession from her lover, uses emotional blackmail to gain her ends and feels no sense of obligation. As the unfortunate knight explains to Erec:

> . . . "ele me demanda
> Un don, mes ne le noma mie.
> Qui veeroit rien a s'amie?"                      (ll. 6056–58)

But, though their love is supposed to be mutual (ll. 6052–53), she makes no returning concession to him in respect of his wishes or knightly duties, and the conspicuous absence of the expected guerdon underlines the inadequacy of their relationship.

When the pattern of the 'don' and 'guerredon' is reduced to an active stimulus provoking an appropriate response, it is easy to see that the formula can be filled negatively and that instead of the positive chivalrous service which provokes gratitude, the essential pattern will be the same if we are presented with a negative 'don', such as an insult, to which there will be the correspondingly inevitable response of vengeance. Erec knows that Yder's insult offers him only one possible course of counteraction, which has only two possible outcomes:

> ". . . itant prometre vos vuel
> Que, se je puis, je vangerai
> Ma honte ou je l'angreignerai."                 (ll. 244–46)

In the same way Erec faces the provocation posed by the shame of his own 'recreantise'.

The balance of action and counteraction appears most clearly, perhaps most mechanically, in the battle scenes. In his combat with Yder, Erec deals blow for blow and the action swings to and fro like a pendulum. Yder's sword cuts through Erec's helmet, and the action swings in his favour. Erec pays him back what he owes (l. 952) and strikes a correspondingly heavy counterblow, getting Yder on the shoulder. As Chrétien tells us, both fighters are fierce and equal combatants (ll. 961–62). Finally, Erec manages to stun his opponent (ll. 973–74). On the structural level, it is only this last stroke that counts, being the only one to advance the plot, but the balance of blows that preceded it builds up our picture of Erec as a competent fighter and our understanding that the world of chivalry is regulated by the call to action and counteraction. The final great duel in the orchard takes place over a longer span of time, "tant que l'ore de none passe" (l. 5999). It is described more briefly, as the rules of the game have been set out fully in the earlier episode, but here again the combatants strike great blows of perfectly equal effect for the greater part of the fight. Even after they are both half-blinded by blood and sweat neither can gain an advantage, until exhaustion weakens Mabonagrain's resistance to Erec's superior stamina (ll. 6000–07).

Both Yder and Mabonagrain are accorded mercy when they sue for it, a 'don' for which they return the 'guerredon' of gratitude. Yder agrees to spread Erec's glory by recounting his defeat to Arthur. Mabonagrain glorifies Erec even more instantly by the gratifying relief with which he hears that his conqueror is the son of Lac (ll. 6010–47). Such chivalry is probably not true to life, but it is so satisfactory on the moral and aesthetic level that it is justification enough in itself.

A more subtle and negative 'don' is exploited by Chrétien in the shape of a non-action which calls for a positive response as a vacuum calls for air. Chrétien creates narrative vacuums for the purpose of filling them, and makes us so impatient for him to fill them that he can then proceed to do so without any further justification. A striking example of this technique occurs early in the romance, in the scene of the hunt of the White Deer. Erec and the queen are following the movement of the hunt, riding in all haste into the forest. Ahead of them the huntsmen have started the Deer; they are raising a cry and sounding their horns; the hounds follow in full cry; the archers let fly; Arthur himself is at the head of the hunt (ll. 117-124). The queen, Erec and the queen's maid are in the wood, straining for sounds of the hunt. They pause in a clearing beside the path taken by the hunt which has by now vanished into the forest. The stage has thus been dramatically emptied of sound and action, yet impregnated with attention and expectation. Into this vacuum rides Yder, and the queen's attention transfers to him. We find it so appropriate to have this vacuum filled that there is no need to give a reason for the queen's curiosity and, more important, no need to give a reason for Yder's abrupt irruption into the narrative.

Anxiety, remorse, or any strong desire can create an emotional vacuum to be filled promptly without need of explanation. Three typical examples occur in the episode dealing with the Count of Limors. The first illustrates the acute emotional vacuum brought about by the distress and anxiety of absence. Erec, after restoring Cadoc to his 'amie', hastens back as fast as he can to Enide. He is terrified that someone may have abducted her, while she is terrified that he may have abandoned her (ll. 4580-89). Their fears are rationally grounded, yet it is emotion rather than reason that propels them towards one another with such urgency and we realize that reconciliation is imminent.

Before it occurs, however, Chrétien shows us the reaction to another negative 'don', remorse. When Erec collapses before her eyes, Enide assumes he is dead and blames herself. In her overwrought state, she declares that his death demands that vengeance be wrought on her, and that Erec's own sword is the right weapon to redress the balance of justice (ll. 4660-67). The chivalrous theme of a wrong calling for revenge is here transferred to the emotional plane. Though the vengeance is frustrated by the timely arrival of Oringle, there is no sense of an action left incomplete, for Enide's anguish here has avenged her 'parole', and the sufferings she endures at Limors are in their turn compensated for by the vengeance wrought for her by Erec (ll. 5157-59).

By far the most striking negative 'don' in the entire romance is the silence Erec imposes on Enide at the start of their joint adventures (ll. 2768-75). The psychological aspect poses no problem: it is a test that must be satisfactorily accomplished. They both want the silence to be broken and so it is. In narrative terms, the breaking of the silence is not a surprise, for the whole point of a taboo in a story is that it should be broken. Had Enide defied universal plot tradition rather than her husband, the tale would have come to a premature and absurd conclusion. Chrétien must invent the marauding knights in order to release his hero and heroine from the taboo. Arbitrary and two–dimensional though the robbers are, no reader will quarrel with the introduction of characters and action so urgently needed to advance the plot.

Although the narrative device of a 'don', which requires a 'guerredon' to complete it, is capable of considerable extension and refinement, it does not solve all problems of continuity. It provides an unchallengeable means of getting from A to B, but not of getting from B to C. True, as we have seen, the 'guerredon' does not always present itself immediately, or even first in sequence, and its artfully contrived delay can be worked into later episodes. Nevertheless, Chrétien is still frequently obliged to break new ground. Happily, the 'don' of chivalrous exploits tends to produce, apart from the 'guerredon', another device for linking episodes together simply and naturally: the transmission of news.

The technical problem raised by the diffusing of news describes a complete and interesting circle. At its most banal level, news has no structural function and represents a simple gesture of courtesy. Thus, after Erec endows Enide's parents with two fine castles, the knightly escort they have been given return to him and he quite naturally asks them for news of them and his father (l. 1913). The knights give him a good report and without more ado we are hastened forward to the wedding.

A more important kind of news, the transmission of information about the hero, is given typical expression by Yder. He agrees to submit to the queen, along with his lady and dwarf,

> "Et si li dirai la novele
> De vos et de vostre pucele."                    (ll. 1067–68)

Similarly Cadoc and his 'amie' bring news of another of Erec's victories to Arthur's court. The young squire brings Galoain second–hand news of Erec's victory over the robber knights, rousing the count to action by this "novele" (l. 3248). Likewise, the news of Erec's impressive cortège (ll. 542–44) prompts Evrain to action, though of a more courtly kind. When news of Erec precedes his appearance in the action, the recipient of the news prepares to act in accordance with it and with his own attitudes. So, when Gawain brings Arthur the joyful news that Erec is close at hand (ll. 4162–64; 4196–202), it is a measure of Arthur's esteem for Erec that he springs into action to welcome him (l. 4199) and lament his wounds and help to heal them (ll. 4218–20). Erec makes the news and Arthur gives the news significance by reacting to it.

There are several variations on the theme of the transmission of news. News can appear to arrive before it has been brought, and we have the

impression of effects preceding their cause. When Yder arrives for the
battle of the Hawk, he has heard of a challenger, though we are never
told how he received the information. When, defeated, he sets out for
Cardigan to recount the news of Erec's victory, Chrétien switches our
attention to Gawain and Kay, who happen to be "es loges de la sale fors"
(l. 1089), as if expecting an arrival they can know nothing about. On
seeing Yder approach, Kay says to Gawain

> ". . . Mes cuers devine
> Que cil vassaus qui la chemine
> Est cil que la reïne dist
> Qui ier si grant enui li fist."                    (ll. 1097-100)

The queen will identify him later, but the inspired guess of Kay comes
first. This is entirely in keeping with the speedy, impatient pace of the
romance as a whole, and establishes a basis for believing that news can
be transmitted almost of its own volition. News comes first; explanations, if any, later. When Erec crosses the bridge to Brandigan, the
inhabitants instantly assume that he has come to conquer the Joie. They
divine his intentions just by looking at him:

> A mervoilles l'esgardent tuit;
> La vile en fremist tote et bruit,
> Tuit an consoillent et parolent.                   (ll. 5501-03)

And they jump to the correct conclusion. It is paradoxical that in such
cases Chrétien, without any recourse to the "marvellous," nevertheless
conveys a sense of the supernatural by sheer narrative compression.
    The prospect of news can be projected into the future, linking it with
an episode yet to come. Erec asks Guivret not to forget him, should the
news reach him that he is in need of help (ll. 3908-12). In due course
news comes to Guivret about the drama at Limors, news that travels
without any apparent need of a human agent:

> Mout est tost alee novele;
> Que riens nule n'est si isnele.
> Ceste novele estoit alee
> A Guivret. . . .                                   (ll. 4939-42)

'Novele' is on the verge of becoming an allegorized figure. When it is
required to spread the most joyful tidings of the romance, the news of
the Joie de la Cort, it flies of its own accord: "Novele par le païs vole"
(l. 6176).
    In a more abstract romance, it would have been possible to make
'Novele' a character in her own right.[5] But *Erec* is dominated by the
exploration of human problems, so Chrétien creates human messengers. Erec sends messengers ahead of himself to his father at Carnant

---

[5]Benoît de Sainte-Maure, perhaps inspired by Virgil's *Fama*, makes Renommee an
entity capable of speech. See also Nitze, "Two Virgilian Commonplaces," 442-46.

(ll. 2329-31). With Guivret, he sends a messenger ahead to Arthur's court to announce their arrival (ll. 6424-26). These are mere extras in the drama and represent nothing more than emanations of Erec's will. But messengers are sometimes given slightly more personality, like the solitary lady who appears at the exchange of confidences between Enide and her cousin:

> Que qu'eles parloient ansanble,
> Une dame sole s'an anble,
> Qui as barons l'ala conter
> Por la joie croistre et monter.                    (ll. 6327-30)

The barons are delighted, particularly Mabonagrain,

> Et cele qui lor aporta
> La novele hastivemant
> Les fist mout liez sodainnemant.                   (ll. 6336-38)

After this brief but entirely plausible appearance she disappears. Chrétien does not let her encroach on our interest, which is kept focussed on the central characters. So news, from being first transmitted by messengers, then starts to take on a life of its own, but in the end is returned to human agents. The lady is the product of narrative artifice and Chrétien subordinates her to the needs of the narrative.

Chrétien keeps his moral, intellectual and aesthetic convictions in the background throughout the action of *Erec*. The foreground of the romance is filled with human and personal concerns, subtly reinforced by the way episodes are sometimes linked by nothing more than physical contact. Enide, whose constancy is one of the unifying forces of the romance, nearly always figures in these links. When we are first introduced to her and Chrétien holds up the narrative for a description of her beauty, he then reintegrates her physically into the narrative by making her father say:

> ". . . Bele fille chiere!
> Prenez par la main cest seignor,
> Si li portez mout grant enor.
> Par la main l'an menez la sus!"
> La pucele ne tarda plus,
> Qu'ele n'estoit mie vilainne;
> Par la main contre mont l'an mainne.               (ll. 470-76)

Her father takes her "par le poing" (l. 677) to give her to Erec, and the courteous figures of the romance repeatedly take her by the hand to draw her into their world. Just as Gawain helps Yder's damsel dismount and be made part of the Arthurian court (ll. 1177-78), so King Arthur performs this courteous act for Erec's bride and leads her by the hand into the hall (ll. 1545-51), followed by Erec and the queen, also hand in hand (ll. 1552-53). When the queen has formally robed Enide in clothes becoming her new status, they return as equals to the king's presence, hand in hand. Arthur again takes her by the hand and seats her beside him (ll. 1760–62) and the "beisier del blanc cerf" (l. 1819) sets the seal on Enide's integration into the life and customs of the court (ll. 1841–43). Gawain, Arthur and the queen all later express their desire to draw the couple back into the Arthurian world by the physical warmth of their salutations (ll. 4157–69; 4210–12).

The formal gesture of linking hands eases a difficult transition later in the romance. Cured by Guivret's sisters, Erec is impatient to continue his journey (ll. 5265–82). There is no narrative reason for his haste, but Erec's impatience is by now a fact of life, so we do not think of asking for one. Chrétien softens the blow of his abrupt departure by making him conclude his thanks with a courteous gesture in which he is partnered by Enide:

> Puis a l'une par la main prise,
> Celi qui plus li estoit pres;
> Enide a prise l'autre aprés;
> Si sont fors de la chanbre issu,
> Tuit main a main antretenu.                    (ll. 5306–10)

Evrain hastens to lend a courteous hand to Enide to help her dismount and he leads her graciously by the hand into his palace (ll. 5554–70). So, before ever Erec and Enide set foot in Evrain's court, we already know something about this new king. Because he draws guests into his ambience with the same physical gestures of courtesy as Arthur on a similar occasion, we are not surprised to learn that he behaves like Arthur in other respects. He too is a courtly ruler who passively accepts a mysterious and dangerous situation, while remaining free of the taint of evil and of the supernatural. Erec is irresistibly drawn into this last adventure by the promise of joy, but Enide draws her unhappy cousin physically into the general rejoicing that the liberation of Mabonagrain produces (ll. 6343–57). At Erec's coronation, all loose ends must be gathered together. The vavassour and his wife are summoned with all due ceremony, warmly welcomed by Enide and Erec, and then all four, hand in hand, are physically drawn into the Arthurian court (ll. 6588–602).

A more subtle form of linking is provided by temporal connectives, which can be impregnated with a sense of purpose or causality, especially when they involve a speedy and forceful character like Erec. A good example occurs early in the romance. Erec, pursuing Yder with a powerful motivation for finding him, moves with apparently more than temporal progression from one stage of his pursuit to the next:

> Erec va siuant tot le pas
> Par le chastel le chevalier
> Tant que il le vit herbergier.
> Quant il vit qu'il fu herbergiez,

> Formant an fu joianz e liez.     (ll. 368–72)

It would hardly be betraying the spirit of Erec's pursuit to render 'tant que' by "in order that" rather than "until" and 'quant' by "because" rather than by "when." The sense of purpose is powerful, even though it is not expressed and still less explained.

After his victory, Erec travels back to Cardigan with his bride. They spend the time gazing their fill at one another, but the journey is compressed and accelerated both by Erec's impatience to leave and the court's desire that they should arrive:

> Erec de son oste depart;
> Que mervoilles li estoit tart
> Que a la cort le roi venist.     (ll. 1479–81)
>
> . . .
>
> Tant ont ansanble chevauchié
> Qu'an droit midi ont aprochié
> Le chastel de Caradigan,
> Ou andeus les atandoit l'an.     (ll. 1517–20)

'Tant que' is thus placed in a context in which an action is prolonged until the desired conclusion has been reached. All intermediary considerations of time and space are squeezed out. Chrétien frequently makes this use of this temporal connective, notably at lines 321–22; 774–75; 1087–88; 3936–37; 4310–11; 5878–80; 6510–13. His emphasis on purpose and his disregard for naturalistic devices of description and local colour can give the impression that reality has been suppressed. Moreover, the absence of rational explanation tends to evoke the response proper to the "marvellous" even when the marvels have been eliminated.

The one apparently "marvellous" episode, the final adventure of the Joie de la Cort, entails the most difficult transition of the entire romance. When we look back at what precedes, we see that Chrétien has been preparing us to believe that the end of the romance is in sight. On the personal level, past wrongs have been righted and consigned to oblivion (ll. 5257–59). Erec, evidently assuming (as we must in our turn) that his quest is over, announces to Guivret with his customary impatience that he will stay with him no longer. He will leave at once, delaying nowhere unless he is captured "tant qu'a la cort serai venuz" (l. 5280). Enide is then honoured with her farewell gift of the palfrey with its magnificent trappings and Chrétien stresses that it fully obliterates her past loss (ll. 5354–56). What could more appropriately herald an imminent happy ending? They duly mount and set off speedily, and we and they expect them to travel until they reach Arthur's court for the last time. Later, when they eventually arrive at Arthur's court, Erec will relate his adventures up to and including the episode at the castle of Limors, but not further, it would seem (ll. 6471–509). The Joie de la Cort has an undoubted thematic significance, but on the level of narrative continuity it retains the air of an interpolation.

Erec, his lady and their dwarfish companion, like a courteous counterpart to the Yder trio at the beginning of the romance, ride straight
towards their goal but instead reach a destination as unexpected for
them as it is for us:

> Chevauchié ont des le matin
> Jusqu'au vespre le droit chemin
> Plus de trante liues galesches,
> Et vienent devant les bretesches
> D'un chastel fort et riche et bel.          (ll. 5367–71)

Erec stops to look at it and asks Guivret if he knows the name of the lord
of the castle "des que ci amené m'avez" (l. 5385). Yet it is not Guivret but
Erec who is responsible for bringing them there. The castle lies on the
'droit chemin' to his goal and must be part of it. It is he who is eager to
find out about it and we can only assume that it will realize some
aspiration of the hero as yet unknown to him as it is to us.

Here, more than anywhere else, we are made aware of Chrétien's
constant care to link episodes for here, by contrast, he has done
everything possible to sever them. Not only has everything said and
done at the castle of Penevric led us to believe that no further adventures
were envisaged, but even after he has confronted us with the totally
unexpected castle of Brandigan, Chrétien proceeds to detach it from
every kind of material context. The castle (or rather, the whole fortified
town) is on an island, and is independent enough to withstand assault
from a king or an emperor (ll. 5389–97). Guivret emphasizes how
entirely the island can do without outside help: it grows its own food
supplies which no siege could exhaust (ll. 5398–403). Its lord, King
Evrain, has had it fortified purely for decoration, for the deep water that
flows round it is the best possible defence (ll. 5404–14). We see in due
course that such an island is an appropriate setting for Mabonagrain's
prison–orchard, but Guivret's initial description of Brandigan is more
than a little provocative. Erec's curiosity is roused further and, with
typical imperiousness, he announces that he wishes to lodge there
(ll. 5416–18). We begin to feel that we are not on such unfamiliar
territory after all, though the transition to this episode has been abrupt
in the extreme. The scribe Guiot attempted to soften the shock by
writing that the trio rode "tant qu'il sont devant les bretesches" (ed.
Roques, l. 5322), thus making it easier to imagine a sense of purpose
behind Erec's arrival at Brandigan. The other scribes transmit a more
brutal text, as we have seen: the trio ride *and* come to the castle (l. 5370).
Erec's destination is a mystery to him and only begins to be revealed at
the end of Guivret's explanations (ll. 6466–67).

Guivret assumes a new and thankless role. He outlines an interdiction
(the unspecified danger in the castle) which, just as surely as the silence
imposed on Enide, is a taboo that demands to be broken by the rules of
narrative continuity. And, just as Enide is driven by her principal

motivation, her love for Erec, to risk infringing the interdiction, so now Erec feels impelled by his sense of chivalry to brave the forbidden danger of Brandigan. But Erec could not be as sure of Enide's reactions as Guivret is of his. His past experience of Erec's valour (l. 5249) enables him to predict the future with certainty. This is the only expressed link between the past and this strange new episode.

Guivret's frantic attempts to turn Erec away from the adventure are the author's way of making Erec and the public all the more eager and curious. Guivret pleads with great eloquence, begging Erec by the love he has sworn him, not to seek this terrible adventure,

> L'avanture, don nus n'estort,
> Qu'il n'i reçoive honte ou mort.        (ll. 5445–46)

It is almost comic to see with what instantaneous, mechanical predictability our hero reacts: "Or ot Erec ce que li siet" (l. 5447). At the beginning of the romance, Guivret's speech would have been impossible; but by this stage of the romance, Chrétien has given us enough information about his hero for another character to be able to predict his reactions.

The sum of the character established for Erec is more than the list of acts he performs. Though the movement of his progress is a forward one, Chrétien still takes care to direct our attention, however rarely and briefly, sufficiently outwards and backwards from the 'droit chemin' to give some illusion of depth in time in order to round out the portrait of the hero. Chrétien's presentation of Erec sketches out his reputation, good looks and prowess (ll. 81–104). He lets Erec fill in other details of his background as appropriate: as Enide's suitor, Erec reveals himself as the son of the rich and powerful King Lac; called Erec by the Britons, he has been three years at the court of King Arthur and will be in a position to make Enide queen of three cities (ll. 650–65). At court, we find that Erec's place in the Arthurian hierarchy is after Gawain, who is first, and before Lancelot (ll. 1691–94). Later, Erec identifies himself to Guivret as the son of a king second only to Arthur (ll. 3880–89). And again, when Gawain leads the wounded Erec to Arthur's tent, Erec, in tribute to Gawain's courtesy, reveals his identity:

> "Je sui Erec qui fu jadis
> Vostre conpainz et vostre amis."        (ll. 4155–56)

The slightly melancholy evocation of companionship in times past makes us realize that we crossed several narrative bridges without being made aware of them and that we are looking back over a considerable distance travelled since Gawain and Erec were first presented to us at Arthur's court. We have a sense of temporal transitions already assimilated, which creates a past and prepares the immediate future. The feeling recurs when Guivret pleads with Erec not to undertake the adventure at Brandigan. We have witnessed the companionship of Erec and Guivret, so Guivret's reference to "l'amor que m'avez promise" (l. 5443), however ineffective, adds emotional depth to the adventure and gives the present and future a more significant resonance by linking them with the past.

Retrospection is often used to underline the importance of an incident. Erec's first adventure is critical, so the queen repeats the circumstances of it to the court (ll. 323-32), even repeating Erec's declaration (ll. 254-56) that he will either avenge his shame or increase it. Erec recalls his shame and his vow of vengeance when he is fighting Yder (ll. 917-20); indeed, the shameful memory would have made him behead his defeated opponent if Yder had not asked for mercy (ll. 989-92). Erec's initial motivation is triply reinforced and justified by these backward glances and even Yder's unmotivated aggression acquires substance by dint of being mentioned.

At the crisis of the romance, Enide's 'parole' is provoked by retrospection, her painful reflections on the reproaches levelled at Erec. The diffused criticisms of the barons are collected from the past into the present and condensed into the anguish of the person who feels herself indirectly to blame. Enide's 'parole' has long drawn out repercussions (ll. 2487-88). She keeps on reproaching herself bitterly for it (ll. 3116-17; 4623-33). The adventure at Limors, which marks both the climax and the resolution of the personal crisis precipitated by the 'parole', is given an extra dimension by being told and retold: Guivret hears one version (ll. 4941-52) which he repeats to Erec (ll. 5066-75) before being given all the details by the hero himself (ll. 5093-106), who later tells it all again to Arthur (ll. 6493-95). The reverberations of this dramatic episode are not allowed to die away, but are preserved by being verbalized.

Looking back over *Erec*, we see how Chrétien realizes its particular ideas and themes in narrative terms. In this, his first romance, he is challenging no moral ideal: all his characters and their actions are presented in terms of an idealized rational humanism which feels no need to justify its convictions or assumptions, so there is little authorial intervention. What Chrétien challenges—and systematically rejects—is the deadening influence of the "marvellous" on the freedom of action of his heroes; hence the emphasis on will, particularly the will of the hero. He is concerned with the responsibility that is the consequence of the hero's liberty of action. Erec as a knight can only express himself in terms of chivalrous action, so physical expression and its repercussions is the principal means of ensuring narrative continuity, whether it be through sheer speed, acts of the will, the giving and receiving of 'dons' and 'guerredons', the use of messengers, the gestures of affection and courtesy, or the simple temporal links impregnated with a sense of purpose.

The movement of the narrative is always forward. Chrétien allows us a few backward glances to round out the picture, but in the main our attention is focussed on the linear progression of the hero. The lack of authorial comment and the concentration on action make *Erec* the most dramatically presented of all Chrétien's romances, marking a sharp contrast with his second romance, *Cligès*.

# CLIGÈS

# IV. The Technique of Alternation

The difference between the narrative techniques Chrétien uses in *Erec* and those he adopts in *Cligès*[1] is most strikingly displayed at the very point where the two romances offer a structural parallel. In both cases a prefatory section is divided from the remainder of the narrative by the author's intervention: it is Chrétien who tells us when we have come to the end of the first "vers" of *Erec* (*Erec*, l. 1844), and he also who informs us when the preliminary romance of Alexander and Soredamors ends and the story proper of Cligès begins (*Cligès*, ll. 2383–88). Yet the slightest attempt to press the comparison any further only throws into relief the differences between the techniques used in these two romances. The first section of *Erec* had assembled all the elements of the complete romance, that is, the situation and character of the hero and heroine and the codes of conduct of Arthurian society; the remainder of the romance develops these elements.

In *Cligès* everything is different. Here Chrétien abandons the most basic concern of conventional narrative technique, that of continuity. Instead of running the elements of his story together, as he had in *Erec*, he does everything he can to pull them apart. We know from the prologue that Cligès is to be the hero, but he is not even born until line 2382 and at that point both he and the narrative are cut off in the most summary manner from all that has gone before. His father Alexander, whose fortunes in love and war we have been following in minute detail for over two thousand lines, is eliminated from the plot with scarcely decent haste. The birth of the hero leads first to endings rather than beginnings, for the moment he appears Chrétien kills off all the characters of the first part of the romance who have no function to fill in the second part. The announcement of the birth of Cligès is followed in the very next sentence by an account of the death of his grandfather, the old emperor. Alexander has no sooner made his brother Alis promise to make Cligès his heir and recommended his son to learn prowess at Arthur's court, than he is dragged off the scene by an implacable and somewhat arbitrary "Mort" (l. 2595), quickly followed by his hapless wife Soredamors, who dies of grief and is never mentioned again.

These three deaths bring the first section of the romance to such a full stop that it is immediately apparent that whatever kind of 'bele conjointure' Chrétien has in mind as a unifying principle for his second

---

[1]Citations are from Hilka's abridged edition of Foerster; see Bibliography. For a recent general study, see Polak, *Chrétien de Troyes: Cligès*.

romance, it will not depend on the action. There is certainly no obvious conjointure in *Cligès*: on the contrary, all the elements of the narrative divide and separate, sometimes to the verge of narrative disintegration. Analysis rather than synthesis is Chrétien's aim in this romance and it will offer him the greatest challenge as a narrator.

As in *Erec*, the clues to the author's intentions are to be sought first of all in the prologue. It is clear from the first line that we will be dealing with a different kind of romance, for here we see an experienced Chrétien standing back from his earlier achievements and passing them in review, indicating an even more self-conscious approach than he had brought to *Erec*. We cannot know whether the works he lists at the beginning of *Cligès* were composed in the order named, for something may need to be conceded to the constraints of rhyme, even in as fluent a writer as Chrétien. Whether or not *Erec* was written before the lost Ovidian works he mentions,[2] it was certainly written in a different spirit. There is nothing Ovidian about Erec, no trace of the influence of the *Ars Amatoria*. There is no reference to any art of conduct designed to help a man or woman conquer love and keep it. In *Erec*, merit was enough, and the hero showed little sign of Ovidian diplomacy in his dealings with his lady. There will be a radical change of manner in *Cligès*.

Not that Chrétien abandons all that concerned him in *Erec*. The Arthurian setting reappears, though viewed from a different angle. The love interest is again considered an improvement on the Tristan model, though the contrast is more fully explored. Moreover, the final solution of the plot is tackled from a moral and social standpoint similar to what we find in *Erec*.

Nevertheless, the raw material of this new romance marks the difference between it and the earlier one. Instead of facing the practical problem of dealing with disparate fragments of narrative to be welded into a coherent whole, Chrétien has by now explored the more theoretical problems posed by Ovid. From an oral source to which he felt superior, he has turned to an authoritative literary source. The new influences are not only narrative (the *Metamorphoses*) but also didactic. It is difficult to decide whether the "Comandemanz Ovide" he translated (l. 2) refers to the *Remedia Amoris* or, redundantly, to the *Ars Amatoria*, the "Art d'Amors" mentioned in the next line. The essential point is that for Chrétien art and commandment are closely linked and this new romance illustrates an elaborate and didactic art of true love. Art, then,

---

[2]The *Philomena* by one Chrétien li Gois may be the lost Ovidian tale by Chrétien de Troyes. In the introduction to his edition, de Boer defends his attribution of this work to our author. For a more cautious acceptance, see Frappier, *Chrétien de Troyes*, 63–68. On Chrétien's debt to Ovid, see Guyer, "The Influence of Ovid on Crestien de Troyes." Guyer assumes, however, that all the Ovidian material in Chrétien was taken directly from source, and he takes no account of the influence of the romans d'antiquité in the dissemination of the Ovidian spirit. According to Faral, the Pyramus reference in *Lancelot* probably came to Chrétien through a French version (*Sources latines*, 13).

will be the matter of *Cligès*, as action had been of *Erec*. With such a change of content, a change of style is only to be expected.

For a model of true love, Ovid is a curious authority to have chosen, as he protests over and over again that he is treating only of the lighter, irresponsible, amoral side of love.[3] But Chrétien, like so many medieval writers, seized on this model with eagerness. No doubt, for an author with the idealizing tendencies Chrétien had shown in *Erec*, any systematic didacticism was to be greeted and exploited with pleasure. Yet there is no reason to suppose that he was insensitive to the tone of frivolous cynicism that pervades both the *Ars Amatoria* and the *Remedia Amoris*. Surely the casual acceptance of inconstancy in love and the portrayal of love as a power struggle must have been antipathetic to the author of *Erec et Enide*, yet he is silent about all that might displease him in his classical model.[4] Ovid could at least supply him with a methodology of behavioural observation applicable to any moral norm. Besides, the very antiquity of the poems entitled them to respect and Ovid's elegant and witty style was an aspect of the classical culture that Chrétien is so proud of seeing transmitted from Rome to France (ll. 33–39).[5] And it was the fashion: a large part of the Ovidian influence so visible in *Cligès* probably did not come directly from Ovid's works, but was filtered through the Ovidian imitations of other contemporary writers, notably the author of the *Roman d'Eneas*.[6]

Much stranger than the use of Ovid is Chrétien's claim that he had composed something "Del roi Marc et d'Iseut la blonde" (l. 5). It is understandable that he should have written about Iseut, but how can we account for the presence of her husband's name and the absence of her lover's? He is under no constraint from the verse: "De Tristan" would have scanned just as well as "Del roi Marc." Perhaps he concentrated on the marital aspect of the story, on the fate of King Mark, doomed from the start to be deceived by his wife.[7]

---

[3]His most explicit declaration is in the *Ars Amatoria*, 3, 27: "Nil nisi lascivi per me discuntur amores."

[4]Unlike Marie de France, who expresses severe disapproval of the *Remedia Amoris* in *Guigemar*, ll. 239–44.

[5]Chrétien's treatment in the *Cligès* prologue of the *translatio imperii* and the *translatio studii* has been widely commented upon. Curtius saw it as a declaration of the superiority of the moderns over the ancients (*European Literature*, 385) and he is supported in this view by Hunt, "Tradition and Originality," 324–26. Lyons, on the other hand, argues that Chrétien is led to emphasize history and tradition because his literary source is merely legendary; see her "Interprétations critiques." She was using the edition of *Cligès* by Roques, and the scribe Guiot unfortunately omits a most helpful couplet. It appears in the text of Foerster's edition: from the library at Beauvais the story was taken "Don cest romanz fist Crestiiens. Li livres est mout anciiens" (*Cligès*, 23–24). Appealing thus to his audience's belief in the antiquity of his source leads Chrétien quite naturally to his statement about the transmission of ancient materials down to his time.

[6]See Faral, *Sources latines*, 391–419, and Micha, "Enéas et Cligès."

[7]Van Hamel, "Cligès et Tristan," 488, says that "Dans ce roman, épisodique ou non, le beau rôle aura été pour le roi." If this was the case, it was diametrically opposed to *Cligès*, where the husband has the worst possible role.

The sources of Chrétien's knowledge of the Tristan story cannot be determined comprehensively. It is generally agreed that the literary version of the story he was best acquainted with was the one by Thomas.[8] Unfortunately, Thomas's text survives only in a few thousand lines of fragments. The content of the missing parts was reconstituted by Joseph Bédier by assembling the common elements in the direct derivatives of Thomas: the anonymous Oxford *Folie Tristan*, the *Tristan und Isolde* of Gottfried von Strassburg, the *Tristams saga ok Isöndar* of Friar Robert of Norway and the anonymous English *Sir Tristrem*.[9]

Given that Thomas, Beroul and Marie de France all claim acquaintance with both oral and written versions of *Tristan*,[10] it is more than likely that Chrétien too was acquainted with more than one version. Did he know any of the surviving versions of the other Tristan tradition, the *version commune*? The *Tristrant* of Eilhart von Oberg may have been written as early as 1170 and Eilhart's lord was closely allied to the court of Champagne.[11] Eilhart shows some French influence (probably indirect), for he gives his Isalde a monologue closely modelled on the Ovidian monologues of Lavinia in the *Roman d'Eneas* (*Tristrant*, ll. 2398–599). There is, however, no evidence that Chrétien knew the German poem. The Berne *Folie Tristan* is too late for Chrétien; so is the *Tristran* of Beroul if we accept that it is to be dated to the last decade of the twelfth century.[12] It is noteworthy that Chrétien is much closer to Beroul than to Thomas on one vital point: Thomas is indifferent to the isolation of the lovers from society, but Beroul regards it as the most serious effect of the adultery and, as we have seen in *Erec* and will see again in *Cligès*, Chrétien treats as incomplete any love which isolates a couple from society. In any case, the various versions of the story were so widely diffused and Chrétien's preoccupation with it so intense that he undoubtedly knew all the versions available in Champagne, though there is no doubt that for *Cligès* the most significant version is the one by Thomas.

---

[8]Chrétien's debt to Thomas was first established by Gaston Paris who showed that the pun on "la mer," "l'amer" and "amers" (ll. 549–52) must go back to Gottfried's source, Thomas ("*Cligès*," 354–57). Further parallels are explored by Van Hamel in "*Cligès* et *Tristan*" and numerous textual echoes of Thomas in *Cligès* are listed by Fourrier in *Courant réaliste*, 124–76. See also Frappier, *Chrétien de Troyes*, 106.

[9]See Bédier's discussion of these derivatives in volume 2 of his edition, 55–94.

[10]Thomas, ed. Bédier, ll. 2116–18; Beroul, ed. Ewert, ll. 1265–68 and 1789–90; Marie de France, *Chievrefoil*, ll. 5–7.

[11]Eilhart was the vassal of Henry the Lion, Duke of Saxony, whose second wife was Matilda, daughter of Eleanor of Aquitaine and Henry II and so half–sister of Marie de Champagne. See *Eilhart von Oberge: Tristrant*, ed. and trans. Buschinger, xxi. On the date of the poem see *Eilhart von Oberge's Tristrant*, trans. Thomas, 1–4.

[12]Bédier dated the Berne *Folie* to the early thirteenth century; Hoepffner confined himself to placing it after Beroul. The arguments of both sides are summarized in *La Folie Tristan de Berne*, ed. Hoepffner, 26–33. Beroul is dated on the evidence of a possible allusion to the siege of Acre which took place in 1190–91. This evidence was challenged by Whitteridge in "The Date of the *Tristan* of Beroul," but reaffirmed by Ewert in his edition of Beroul, 2: 33–36.

The Ovidiana and Tristaniana that provide Chrétien with material for *Cligès* are the common literary property of all writers of his period. Chrétien also lays claim to a more specific source for the "novel conte" he is undertaking (l. 8). He derives this new romance from an old book, a volume from the library of St. Pierre in Beauvais. He tells us nothing more about the book, except to say that its age makes it more worthy of belief than it would, presumably, have been without the support of antiquity (ll. 24–26). There is no reason to doubt the existence of a written source, though the absence of any further particulars makes us suspect that he has transformed it out of all recognition. The Beauvais story must have been some version of the legend of Solomon's wife, who pretended to be dead in order to deceive her husband. Chrétien alludes explicitly to this legend at lines 5876–78. It has also been argued that the version Chrétien read must have resembled the deception story preserved in the thirteenth-century romance *Marques de Rome*, where the hero Cligès deceives his uncle, the emperor of Constantinople, just as Chrétien's hero will deceive Alis.[13] If, as is quite possible, Chrétien's source was an earlier version of this tale, it is understandable that he was both attracted to this story on account of its similarity to the Tristan triangle, and anxious to suppress details of his source, for *Marques de Rome* has only the scope and interest of a *fabliau*, whereas Chrétien is aiming at something greater in scale and more significant in its theme.

The *Marques de Rome* story had another advantage: it was set in Constantinople. Byzantine alliances with the West were much talked of in Chrétien's period,[14] though Constantinople itself is known to Chrétien only as a distant and magnificent port. It has all the advantages of being a prestigious location about which nothing much is known. By moving away from more familiar locations with the familiar expectations they arouse, Chrétien could give himself more freedom to draw on the various *matières de France*, *de Bretagne*, and *de Rome* for the one narrative.[15]

In the presentation of his first hero, Alexander, it is the echoes of the *matière de France* that are most distinct. The heir to the empire of Constantinople frequently recalls Roland. He arrives at Arthur's court with twelve companions (l. 330); he hastens to the defence of a king threatened by the treachery of a man "qui est pire de Guenelon" (l. 1076); treachery is punished through divine intervention in the natural sequence of day and night, though instead of sunset being delayed (*Roland*, ll. 2449–50), moonrise is advanced (ll. 1700–12), and Alexander laments and avenges the death in battle of his companion Calcedor (ll. 1904–37).[16] Alexander is designed as a hero of epic rather than romance, though the reasons for this do not appear for some time.

[13]See Paris, "*Cligès*", 641–55.
[14]See Fourrier, *Courant réaliste*, 160–174.
[15]See *Jean Bodels Saxenlied*, ed. Menzel and Stengel, ll. 6–7.
[16]See Owen, "Chrétien and the Roland", 145–46.

The story of Alexander is given a very developed treatment by
Chrétien, much more substantial than that given to the corresponding
parental character in any of the Tristan romances. He is more than
Rivalin, the father of an ideal lover, for he is an ideal lover in his own
right, though he first appears in remote Constantinople like a heroic
figure from one of the romans d'antiquité. Far from plunging us into a
fairy-tale atmosphere as he had at the beginning of Erec, Chrétien opens
his new tale in the dry, detached style of a chronicle. We are informed
in the most unadorned, factual style, of the situation at the court of
Constantinople. Unlike Arthur, already familiar to Chrétien's public, the
Greek king is introduced in a formal, orderly, informative way. We are
told of his imperial status and power and the extent of his kingdom, of
his noble wife and of his two sons who were separated so much in age
that by the time the younger was born the elder was of an age to be
knighted. The names of all four persons follow in due course, but it is
significant that the description of status and circumstances was put first.
Throughout the romance the exposition of situation will take precedence
over the presentation of the individual. It is the opposite of Erec where
the hero is introduced first as an individual whose problems arise in the
course of the action. The "natural" effects of Erec will give way in Cligès
to a more artificial style and more abstract concerns.

The introduction of young Alexander contrasts with the introduction
of Erec on several significant points. We can hardly be surprised to hear
that he is "corageus et fiers" (l. 65), but his spirit does not prompt him
to proceed, like a more typical hero of romance such as Erec, from
collective to solitary action, but quite the reverse: he goes out to find
himself a lord, like a hero of epic. Chrétien must have been aware of one
drawback of innovation: in this remote spot, there was no criterion of
chivalry that was available to his hero and acceptable to his public.
Charlemagne would have drawn the hero into epic action. The only
possible alternative was Arthur, and to Arthur he goes. But not to the
Arthur of Erec. By a curious reversal, the king we met in the earlier
romance belongs to a later stage of development where he is already the
roi fainéant. In Cligès, Chrétien uses the earlier and more epic phase of
the legend, as transmitted by Geoffrey and Wace. In the introductory
scene between Alexander and his father, he makes direct use of the
passage where Wace describes how Arthur's court served as a testing
ground for all the knights aspiring to prowess and other knightly virtues
(Brut, ll. 9761–84).

Alexander, too, wishes to go there but, unlike Erec, whose first action
precedes reflection, this new hero sets out his objective with methodical
deliberation. No outrageous insult propels him into action, only his own
inner qualities. It is because he is "corageus et fiers" to begin with that
he aspires to the best, and his aspiration in turn determines his course
of action. Chrétien will not allow us to hurry into the action of the
romance. Pace is no longer a matter of prime importance for him as a

narrator. Instead, he adds emphasis to the hero's motivation by going over it twice. Alexander has heard of Arthur's reputation and he makes up his mind that nothing will stop him from going to Britain (ll. 68–77). He goes to ask formal leave from his father and Chrétien makes us stand back a moment from the encounter, while he points out to us again his hero's physical and chivalrous excellence and the firmness of his will (ll. 78–85). The speech he makes to his father bears out the decisive character Chrétien has sketched out for us:

> "Biaus pere! por enor aprandre
> Et por conquerre pris et los,
> Un don," fet il, "querre vos os,
> Que je vuel que vos me doigniez."          (ll. 86–89)

Though he does not yet know what is involved, the emperor can only accede to such a request and Alexander sweeps on, demanding abundant funds and his own selection of companions for his purpose: he means to leave his father's empire and take arms from no–one but the king of Britain (ll. 108–121). His distressed father's offer of the kingdom of Constantinople, of a coronation, of a knighthood, of the homage of all his knights, is all doomed to refusal, for this is a hero determined to rise above the tame acceptance of honours he as inherited in order to reach the level of honours he will have deserved. Alexander knows exactly what he wants and neither prayers nor flattery will turn him from his purpose (ll. 144–68). His will, though as strong as Erec's and similarly used as a device to get the narrative under way, nevertheless manifests itself very differently. The opening scene of *Erec* showed the will of the sovereign dominating the rational objections of his nephew Gawain. Here the roles are reversed, for the emperor pleads in vain against the superior will of his son. Alexander prevails because he is in the right. Given that he is asking for something that will increase his worth, he ought, says Chrétien, to be granted it by his father (ll. 94–95).

The spontaneous movement of Alexander's will towards what is right is a clear indication that he is to be a morally exemplary character, and the direction of his will towards chivalrous excellence marks him out as a hero. Though the same is true of Erec, Alexander's beginning is different in every way. Instead of being forced to set off alone and in haste into a "forest avantureuse" (*Erec*, l. 65) to avenge an insult, young Alexander sets off in good order, with twelve chosen companions, after mature deliberation, to a specific destination, for a specific purpose. Mystery and suspense are eliminated: Chrétien is holding out no carrots in this romance. We will be obliged to take the exemplary Alexander as he comes.

The one point that both departures have in common is that they both take place in spring. In *Erec*, spring is mentioned in connection with the feast of Easter and the love of five hundred ladies. In *Cligès*, the factual, expository style strips spring of any lyrical associations. April and May are mentioned as the time of the voyage (ll. 270–71), that being the earliest season it was safe to sail; even so, they suffer discomfort on the voyage and are relieved to reach land (ll. 276–85). From these unromantic experiences they progress to a very down-to-earth exploration of southern England. Here again there is a marked contrast with Erec who, propelled through Britain and Brittany by his own powerful volition, never appears to cross the Channel. Alexander, though filled with abstract ideals, functions from first to last on a specified material plane.[17] He lands at Southhampton, spends the night recovering from the voyage, enquires the next day after Arthur and is told that he is in Winchester (ll. 286–91).

Without more ado, Alexander and his companions make their way directly to Arthur's court and, before appearing in the king's presence, take off their mantles "que l'an ne les tenist por fos" (l. 316). No–one could possibly take them for fools or ill–bred young men: the barons correctly deduce at first sight that they are "tuit de contes ou de roi fil" (l. 323). A further point is made about their dress:

> Et les robes que il vestoient
> D'un drap et d'une taille estoient,
> D'un sanblant et d'une color.                    (ll. 327–29)

This echoes a passage of Wace (*Brut*, ll. 10503–08) which occurs just before the critical part describing how love, in the exemplary court of King Arthur, becomes the reward of chivalrous merit. The hint is not made explicit. Alexander has a long way to go and Chrétien declines to rush him.

The hero is installed with due ceremony at Arthur's court, ready to be trained as a knight, and he is duly initiated into the life of chivalry. He makes friends with Gawain, still the unambiguous criterion of excellence in the Arthurian world. He takes his father's parting sermon to heart and displays liberality as his rank deserves and as his heart directs (ll. 412–13). We have heard all about his natural gifts, but the high qualities he aspires to are not granted automatically; he has to strive to perfect himself: "Mout i antant et mout s'an painne" (l. 409). Eventually, however, his efforts and service are rewarded by the esteem of king, queen and barons (ll. 418–21). His story so far is certainly not as exciting as Erec's, but Alexander has not yet undertaken any adventures. He is a very young man indeed, not yet a knight and still in the process of formation.

---

[17]Fourrier, *Courant réaliste*, 111–160, accounts for this new realism in Chrétien by invoking the influence of Thomas. The military realism of the Angres episode is analysed by Shirt in "*Cligès*: Realism in Romance." On the other hand, Gaston Paris pointed out a number of oddities in the text, such as the fact that Alis can only be two years older than Cligès ("*Cligès*", 439), a fact also noted by Noble in "Alis and the Problem of Time in *Cligès*."

Then, abruptly, the narrative changes direction in the very middle of a couplet.[18] Chrétien starkly announces:

> Li rois Artus an cel termine
> S'an vost an Bretaingne passer. (ll. 422–23)

It is the first transition of the romance, and we are not prepared for it. True, Arthur had begun the story of Erec with an expression of will that was just as arbitrary and far more extraordinary. A desire to go to Brittany in no way competes in strangeness with the desire to revive the hunt of the White Deer, a hunt, moreover, immediately subjected to rational criticism. The cases are not quite comparable, though. In *Erec*, Arthur's decision is the basic narrative premise of the romance which we must accept if we are to read the story at all. In *Cligès*, Arthur is by this stage a well-established character in the story, portrayed as an excellent king, acting rationally and courteously in his reception and appreciation of the young Alexander.

Arthur's sudden departure is no doubt inspired by the *Brut*, for Wace's Arthur also sets out for the continent (*Brut*, ll. 11163–268), but there is a difference. Wace's Arthur, like Geoffrey's, sets out on a mission of war, in response to a challenge from Rome. Chrétien's Arthur sets out for no reason at all. He does nothing in Brittany once he gets there: all he achieves is to expose Britain to the treachery of Angres of Windsor. He is not criticized for his expedition, for his whole *raison d'être* in this romance is to provide the criterion of chivalrous excellence. His motives are irrelevant: Chrétien makes him cross the Channel not so that he may do or fail to do anything, but so that a new strand may be drawn into the romance.

The real reason for the move is the needs of the hero. We have just been told that Alexander has progressed as far as his aspirations and efforts can take him. He must now progress to what he can learn from other sources. When we hear that the ship that takes Arthur and Alexander to Brittany also takes the queen and a maiden called Soredamors, the sheer symmetry of the arrangement, if nothing else, signals the entrance of the new influence on Alexander's education.

In retrospect this passage makes sense thematically, but it still marks a break in the narrative sequence and in the attention focussed on Alexander. Alexander has no premonition of what is to come. He is no Guigemar, no Lanval: neither he nor we have been made conscious that there is still a lack in his life. Nor has any external pressure been brought to bear on him. It is his innate capacity for excellence and the desire to achieve it that have brought him through every event of his life so far; each part of his career has arisen in due and deliberate order from his potential for perfection. This slowly unfolding excellence poses a

---

[18]The breaking of the couplet is a feature of Chrétien's style. See Frappier, "La Brisure du couplet." The breaks in sense are more marked in *Cligès* than in *Erec*; see particularly ll. 1647–48.

narrative problem, for it makes it difficult to integrate the first external factor in Alexander's development. Here, far from hastening his narrative forward with the expectation of some want that has been felt and that must be supplied, Chrétien not only slows his story down, but teases the elements of it apart.

The new element, the heroine Soredamors, is more than a new character, she represents a new narrative style. As a character, she scarcely exists at all when we first meet her: she is introduced as the queen's companion without further detail (ll. 444–45); strange indeed, given the care Chrétien took to establish Alexander's family and background. It is only after she has played her part and fallen in love with Alexander that we are told she is Gawain's sister (l. 467). Why was this relationship not mentioned when we first met her? Chrétien has a reason for presenting his heroine in instalments, but it is not immediately obvious. Our first information about Soredamors is neither social nor aesthetic. The primary fact we are given about her is not her beauty or her status or her qualities, it is her attitude. She is

> . . . Soredamors,
> Qui desdeigneuse estoit d'amors.          (ll. 445–46)

Thus the narrative transition is even more of a break than we might have expected. Alexander, methodically striving to deserve knighthood in sight of all at the court of Arthur, is lifted clean out of this exteriorized chivalrous context, and in his place we are confronted with the means of the next stage of his development, represented by the negative state of mind of a girl.

Any expectation that love will introduce an element of the unpredictable into the narrative is rapidly dispelled by Chrétien. Before the disdainful Soredamors has had time to analyse more than the first disturbance of her feelings, before the queen can notice any change in the two young people on the ship, Chrétien intervenes to undermine all suspense by informing us that they both love and are loved as they deserve:

> Amors igaumant lor depart
> Tel livreison, come il lor doit.
> Mout lor fet bien reison et droit,
> Que li uns l'autre aimme et covoite.          (ll. 532–35)

This love would be completely "leaus et droite" (l. 536) if only each knew what the other felt, so our interest is focussed on the way they discover what we already know. The interest of the succeeding monologues of both parties does not depend on suspense, but rather on the appreciation of the connoisseur. Despite his moralizing tone, Chrétien reveals his indebtedness to Ovid: it is not the plot that he wants us to admire, but his illustration of his particular concept of the art of love. His ideals differ radically from Ovid's, but the idea of expounding a model of behaviour in love has so strongly marked Chrétien's imagination that he is content to sacrifice suspense and even continuity to explore the unfolding of his heroes' minds and hearts.

Their inner turmoil has no outwardly disruptive effect. It is remarkable how, throughout the romance, outward normality is maintained right to the last crisis. Alexander's most significant adventures are internal and never fully understood by the general public. Even in the throes of love, he and Soredamors behave in a way that is susceptible of rational, if mistaken, interpretation. The queen, a courteous and intelligent observer, attributes their pallor to sea-sickness, not so absurd when we recall the emphasis Chrétien put on the discomforts of Alexander's earlier voyage. So, though their pale faces are a symptom of love familiar to readers of Ovid (*Ars Amatoria*, I, ll. 727–36), the truth remains hidden from reasonable observation and their own consciousness until it has matured at leisure under our inspection. Chrétien may allow them to mislead themselves, each other and the queen as to the true nature of their feelings, but he has no interest in misleading us. He wants us to know just where their development is heading so that we can appreciate its gradual unfolding.

Meanwhile, what of the epic side of Alexander? It is relegated to a separate compartment. From the moment he meets Soredamors, the whole progress of Alexander's career will consist of a regular oscillation between external, collective, epic action and internal, solitary meditation. Chrétien never integrates these two sides of his hero's life. On the contrary, he deliberately dissociates them. The essence of his narrative technique in telling the story of Alexander will be to alternate from love to war, from contemplation to action, without ever giving us to understand that the two activities are in any way linked. It is an odd procedure on the part of an author who knew that love and chivalry were interdependent in Wace.

What was Chrétien's purpose in separating the two sides of his hero's life? The first clue comes in the way he introduces Alexander's meditation on love. He will not, he says, speak any further of Arthur on this occasion,

> Einçois m'orroiz dire comant
> Amors les deus amanz travaille,
> A cui il a prise bataille.　　　　　　　　　　(ll. 572–74)

It is not the fact of love that is the point of interest, but its "comant," how it develops, seen in terms of a battle between Love and the lovers. Chrétien expresses the same thought in his lyric:

> Amors tençon et bataille
> Vers son champion a prise.[19]　　　　　　　　(ll. 1–2)

---

[19]Raynaud, 121. See Brakelmann, 44–46.

Love is developed as a theme parallel to war, closely modelled on it and likewise a means of attaining personal excellence. Yet it is never exploited in a causal relationship with the virtues of chivalry. War is set aside so that hero and heroine may explore on equal terms the new element in their lives that is prompted from without, but develops entirely from within.

The progress of the hero's "conplainte" (l. 873) is marked by rhetorical self-questioning and answering, an alternation between the logical and emotional sides of his nature. The rational side of him opposes the claims of common "san" (l. 680) to the "folie" (l. 630) to which he has directed his thoughts; then another impulse makes him feel that it would be a greater folly to reject love which urges him towards a greater realization of himself. Love is a demanding master, but Alexander is an eager pupil who thrives on challenges and has a confident hope of reward:

> "S'Amors me chastie et manace
> Por moi aprandre et anseignier,
> Doi je mon mestre desdeignier?
> Fos est, qui son mestre desdaingne.
> Ce qu'Amors m'aprant et ansaingne
> Doi je garder et maintenir;
> Car tost m'an puet granz biens venir." (ll. 682–88)

The positive quality of the conclusion highlights the difference between the function of monologue in this romance and in Thomas's *Tristan*, which may have served as its model. Tristan debates within himself in order to sort out the conflicting feelings which urge him towards conflicting action. His monologue comes at a moment when the plot is already complicated, the possibilities open to the hero genuinely varied, so there is a real degree of suspense for the reader which carries him forward through the repetitive oscillations of the hero's indecisions.[20] With Alexander, we have no support at all from suspense. We know in advance what his state of mind will be. Chrétien's debt to Thomas lies rather with the authorial comment on the monologue. The Tristan poet had invited us to reflect on the weakness and inconstancy of human nature as exemplified by his hero (Thomas, ll. 285–420); Chrétien invites us to witness the development of love in an ideal lover. He is determined to improve on his model, but his method is the same as Thomas's: in each case the hero's meditations have an exemplary force mediated by the author.

Alexander's initiation into love is taken at a leisurely pace and proceeds in a curious order. He does not begin by loving Soredamors; he begins by submitting himself to Love. Only then does he become aware of her as a person, and then only in the most gradual and

---

[20]On the style of Thomas's monologues, see Jonin, *Personnages féminins*, 313.

piecemeal way. He does not perceive her directly: he reconstitutes her
from memory. He has such pleasure in remembering her beauty (l. 622)
that an awareness of her slowly disengages itself from his consciousness. He sees her first as a composite of fragments, gradually emerging
from his awareness of Love itself. Thus the dart of Love is seen as her
body, its pennon her golden hair (ll. 770–800). We now see that Chrétien
did not describe his heroine because it is part of the hero's initiation to
perceive her and thereby discover both himself and her.

Alexander's meditations swing in a slow and deliberate pendulum
movement, outwards from his own consciousness to the object con-
templated and inwards from the object back to his consciousness. He
alternates between letting the extroverted side of his nature move out
towards Soredamors and letting his introverted side return to colour his
perception of himself through his perception of her. His extroverted side
looks to simile for support: the face of Soredamors conjures up comparisons with roses and lilies, her teeth are like ivory or silver, her mouth
crystal, her breast snow (ll. 815–45). The images are banal and give us no
idea of Soredamors as an individual, but they give us an excellent
picture of Alexander's piecemeal perception of her. The introverted side
of him uses appropriately reflexive language:

> ". . . desirranz et anvïeus
> Sui ancor de moi remirer
> El front que Des a fet tant cler."                (ll. 806–08)

Then, with perfect detachment, Chrétien leaves Alexander to his
sufferings and brings Soredamors forward for our inspection. It is a
simple sideways movement; there is no sense of progression. Her
"conplainte" is described as being equal to his (ll. 873–75) and, on
analysis, also displays a remarkable structural symmetry. For the
heroine, the effects of love manifest themselves in a much more physical
way than with the hero. Soredamors alternates between sensation and
attempts at rationalization. Feeling and thought succeed each other
without her being able to dominate either:

> Et quant ele a tant traveillié
> Et sangloti et baaillié
> Et tressailli et sospiré,
> Lors a an son cuer remiré,
> Qui cil estoit et de ques mors,
> Por cui la destreignoit Amors.
> Et quant ele s'est bien refeite
> De panser, quanque li anheite,
> Lors se restant et se retorne.                (ll. 885–93)

Alexander, of course, still has an epic side to his life. He may meditate
on love all summer, but when news comes of the treachery of Angres
(ll. 1053–66), he instantly resumes his fighting role, dropping all thought
of Soredamors as if she belonged to a different world, as indeed she

does. Now his chief preoccupation is his new status as a knight, of which he never thinks of informing Soredamors. The queen, however, gets to hear of it and presents him with a shirt as a token of her regard. She shares with Arthur the education of the hero, but she never interacts with her husband. Alexander will move back and forth between military service to the king and courteous service to the queen four times before the queen finally unites him with the heroine.

The two worlds remain apart. When Alexander, fresh from his first triumph in the field, goes to present this "chevalerie" to the queen in a courteous effort to gain mercy for his prisoners (ll. 1349–62), Arthur, who is serious about the war, summons her to give them up. In her absence, Alexander and his companions remain behind with her ladies. The hero's companions profit from the occasion (ll. 1369–74), but not Alexander, for he is not yet able to integrate the demands of love and of war. It is only when the queen returns with Arthur's decision that Alexander returns to life. He fights vigorously in the ensuing battle and then returns, as is his custom by now (ll. 1554–56) to the queen's pavilion. Soredamors is happy just to contemplate Alexander and no progress would be made on either side if the queen did not recall "par avanture" (l. 1569) that the shirt she gave Alexander contained one of Soredamors's hairs. This revelation has the effect of making them even more helpless in each other's presence.

Alexander's reaction to the queen's news could hardly be more disastrous for the narrative: it makes him long to be alone, even though Soredamors is present. All he can assimilate for the moment is his good fortune in possessing so much of her. His humility is such that he never expects to possess more (ll. 1627–29) – a characteristic of the ideal lover, but a severe problem for the story–teller. Once again the narrative is threatened with a full stop. Alexander hides his feelings from everyone, only giving way to them when alone. He progresses from purely abstract meditation on Love to an extravagant worship of Soredamors's hair (ll. 1631–45) but cannot yet approach the girl herself. Once out of sight of Soredamors or relics of her, Love no longer affects Alexander. His life is even more rigidly compartmentalized than Roland's, for he has no Oliver to remind him in battle of the existence of his lady.

Chrétien is uncompromising in the way he swings the pendulum back towards the battle. The hero thinks of love: the traitors plot their next move (ll. 1645–49). The two activities overlap in time, but we are given no indication of simultaneity. We are switched from one side of Alexander's life to the other without any explanatory linking. The only case of parallel activity is when the Greeks mourn Alexander, whom they suppose to be dead, at the same moment that he and his men are trying to convey the information about their safety (ll. 2147–50). But we already know that their anxiety only highlights the approaching joy (ll. 2145–46). All suspense is eliminated. Soredamors, whose particularly great grief passes unnoticed in the general anguish (ll. 2114–29), is correspondingly all the more joyful (ll. 2238–43) and the relief of both hero and heroine is finally drawing them together (ll. 2244–48).

Yet, at the last moment, Chrétien gives Alexander a significant scruple which prevents him from asking for Soredamors in marriage. Arthur is ready to give the hero of the hour any reward within reason (ll. 2214–20). Alexander knows that Arthur would not refuse him his niece (ll. 2223–24), but neither would he consult her, and Alexander is high-minded enough to be prepared to suffer without her than have her against her will:

> Que miauz se viaut sanz li doloir,
> Que il l'eüst sanz son voloir. (ll. 2227–28)

Only the queen has the insight to grasp the situation and the power to do something about it. She is the only one who can bring the couple together and at the same time deliver a homily on the author's behalf:

> "D'amor andotriner vos vuel;
> Car bien sai qu'amors vos afole.
> Por ce vos ai mis a escole. (ll. 2290–92)
>
> . . .
>
> Or vos lo que ja ne queroiz
> Force ne volanté d'amor." (ll. 2302–03)

Alexander has already renounced "force" by refraining from asking for Soredamors as a gift that would not be refused. Nor has either attempted, like Mabonagrain's 'amie' in *Erec*, to impose his will on the other. Selfishness and a disregard for the liberty and interests of the other party are excluded from this ideal of true love, which must be a free giving of each to the other in a way that will preserve their rightful self-respect. For the queen, and no doubt for Chrétien, the solution is straightforward:

> "Par mariage et par enor
> Vos antraconpaigniez ansanble.
> Einsi porra, si con moi sanble
> Vostre amors longuemant durer." (ll. 2304–07)

In due course this model pair become the parents of Cligès who, with such a heredity, can hardly fail to become a hero. The implied contrast with the parental romance in Thomas is significant: Tristan, conceived in shameful secrecy, is born amid scenes of appalling suffering.[21] If Tristan was predestined to sorrow and premature death, Cligès is predestined to joy and success.

The happy ending of Alexander's story is certainly a problem for the continuity of the romance, but by the time we reach it we realize that Chrétien's primary concern is expository rather than narrative, and the

---

[21]See *Thomas*, ed Bédier, Vol. 1, pp. 19, 24–25; passages reconstituted from Gottfried von Strassburg and the *Tristams saga*.

more thoroughly he exposes the problems and feelings he illustrates, the more thoroughly he breaks them down into their constituent parts. He abandons the techniques he had previously used to bind his narrative together: the more he analyses his characters, the more he isolates them. The military side of Alexander's life is so completely cut off from the courtly side that he partially regresses to the earlier type of epic hero. The echoes of *Roland* help us to understand that, courteous though Alexander undoubtedly is, his career is modelled on a pre–romance pattern: love and war figure prominently in his life but they are never integrated.

Chrétien's concern with analysis affects his narrative technique. Instead of a forward movement provided by a constant concern for continuity, he presents us with a pendulum movement of alternation. Our attention, instead of following a single line, is swung back and forth between hero and heroine, action and meditation, the subjective and the objective. Even at the end, a special intervention is required to draw the strands of the story together. Now we discover that the story of Alexander is itself the first of two alternatives. From a hero of epic we now move to a hero of romance.

The change is not immediately apparent. On the contrary, we are led to expect a continuation of the epic vein, for Chrétien tells us that the main story will be about Cligès and his "vasselage" (l. 2385). Cligès is given ample scope for martial activity. He distinguishes himself on three occasions: at the skirmish at Cologne, in the Black Forest battle culminating in the duel against the Duke of Saxony and, most conspicuously, at the Arthurian tournament held near Oxford. A change of style is apparent, however, by the end of the first of these incidents, the skirmish at Cologne, which in military terms is a mere *hors d'oeuvre*.

The German emperor, father of the new heroine Fenice, first promised her to the Duke of Saxony, but then agreed to a more advantageous match with Alis, the emperor of Constantinople, who is Cligès's uncle. The Duke is naturally aggrieved and his nephew comes to court to protest. When his representations are ignored, he challenges Cligès to a skirmish out of sheer youthful thoughtlessness (ll. 2806–08). Cligès, who himself is not yet fifteen (l. 2675), responds and a skirmish of three hundred a side is organized. Before the fighting begins, Fenice, who already loves Cligès for his beauty, though she is promised to his uncle, climbs to an upper window where she can see him perform (ll. 2891–911). From the beginning, she is more integrated into the narrative than was Soredamors. She must marry Alis, but she falls in love with Cligès at first sight. She follows him with her eyes and he performs for her benefit, hoping to give her reason to value him when she hears of his feats:

> A Cligés esgarder estrive,
> Sel siut as iauz, quel part qu'il aille.
> Et cil por li se retravaille
> De behorder apertemant

Por ce qu'ele oie solemant
Que il est preuz et bien adroiz;
Car totes voies sera droiz
Qu'ele le prist por sa proesce.                    (ll. 2912-19)

At last we are back on the familiar territory of Geoffrey and Wace: the
courtly gathering at which prowess is spurred on by the presence of
ladies and where a knight may hope for love as the reward of merit. On
his victorious return, Cligès exchanges a glance with Fenice (ll. 2956-
64)—a minimal contact, but already more than anything shared by
Alexander and Soredamors. We are moving from alternation to interaction.

The new hero's first experience of war shows that he will be placed in
more complex moral situations than his father. Instead of supporting an
excellent sovereign against a villainous traitor, Cligès now finds himself
ranged on the side of his uncle Alis against the highly motivated army
of the outraged Duke. Once again, the Duke's nephew precipitates the
action by an attack on Cligès who is only out for fun with his friends.
They carry lances and shields "por behorder et por deduire" (l. 3411).
For this extremely youthful hero, war is still a game.

His military education gets under way in the long, action-packed
sequence that follows (ll. 3412-816). The battle moves to two distinct
climaxes, the first of them exclusively concerned with military activity.
In this first part, the hero's movements back and forth are a zig-zag of
ever-increasing intensity of action, quite unlike the leisurely pendulum
movements of Alexander's career. First the Duke's nephew moves far
enough towards the Greek camp to ambush Cligès; Cligès is wounded
but repulses the Saxons and pursues them back to their lines. There, a
Saxon knight pursues Cligès back to the site of the ambush. Cligès kills
him, takes his armour and hastens back again towards the Saxon army,
pursued by the Greeks who mistake him for an enemy. Cligès leads
them on "por la meslee comancier" (l. 3538). There is an epiphany of the
hero when Cligès reveals his identity by unhorsing a Saxon and
shouting to his amazed companions:

". . . Baron! ferez!
Je sui Cligés que vos querez."                     (ll. 3565-66)

The encounter that ensues is conceived in terms of collective epic action:

Des deus parz les lances aloingnent,
Si s'antrecontrent et reçoivent
Si come an tel ost feire doivent.                  (ll. 3582-84)

This impersonally expressed activity only runs to five more lines. The
epic participation of Cligès in war is very brief, just enough to establish
him in a military context comparable to his father's. The climax of this
first part is the first victory in single combat by Cligès over the Duke.

Then there is an unexpected turn of events. The powerful sweep of
Greeks and Germans into the Saxon camp has left their side vulnerable,

and the Duke succeeds in having Fenice abducted. We are now in a new phase of the conflict which has nothing epic about it. Cligès happens to be alone on a hill when he sees the abductors fleeing and follows them, knowing nothing of Fenice's plight but spurred on sufficiently by the true hero's desire to "aquerre los" (l. 3664).

We cannot doubt the outcome of the adventure: Cligès will rescue Fenice from her twelve abductors. Yet Chrétien is reluctant to ask us to believe that his hero dispatches the full dozen at one go. Instead he sends the abductors one by one down a narrow pass, which makes it impossible for those left behind to see what has become of those who went before. Cligès disposes of the first half-dozen as they ride up, one by one, mistaking him for the Duke as he is still in Saxon armour. He then moves out to tackle the remainder, sparing only the last to take the bad news back to the Duke. The mechanics of this solution are inspired by the *Roman de Thèbes*, where Tideüs kills forty-nine men in the narrow pass lately occupied by the Sphinx, sparing only the last to be the bearer of evil tidings (*Thèbes*, ll. 1483–820).

The emphasis of the episode in *Cligès* is less on the ingenuity of the arrangement than on the interaction of hero and spectator. Fenice witnesses the later part of the action and Cligès is overjoyed at the opportunity of displaying his prowess for her benefit:

> Or li est vis que buer fu nez,
> Quant il puet feire apertemant
> Chevalerie et hardemant
> Devant celi qui le fet vivre.          (ll. 3756–59)

It is the skirmish scene all over again, with the difference that the hero now knows that the heroine is watching him and needing him. Naturally Cligès sweeps all before him, having the double driving force of the hero of romance:

> Proesce et amors qui l'anlace
> Le fet hardi et conbatant.          (ll. 3804–05)

Hostilities are concluded by the duel between Cligès and the Duke, the disappointed suitor of Fenice. Though it is a critical encounter for all concerned, yet there is an element of pleasurable display about it. The Duke, confident of winning, arms himself hastily (ll. 4211–14). Cligès, impatient for the fight, is equally confident of success (ll. 4015–24). They are both eager for the joy of victory (ll. 4048–50). It is the public spectacle of romance, completed by the presence of the heroine, who sees the hero prove himself a third time in battle and can therefore be sure that he is worthy of her love.

Yet here again there is a break in the narrative. Instead of pressing his advantage with Fenice, Cligès suddenly remembers his father's command to go to Arthur's court, to complete his formation as a knight (ll. 4240–60). What narrative reason can there be for him to set off into the unknown? He certainly fulfils his promise and distinguishes himself at the Oxford tournament, but though the Arthurian court is still the criterion of chivalrous excellence, there was no need for Cligès to prove himself further to Fenice. Besides, she never hears about his triumphs. No-one ever alludes to them once he returns to Constantinople.

Cligès needed to win an identity for himself. He knew what he wanted, but had not yet proved who he was. At the Arthurian tournament, he refuses to profit from an accumulation of reputations. Having performed excellently as the Black Knight on the first day, he does not trade on that identity the second day but starts again from scratch as the Green Knight. The spectators provide a choral commentary on the admiration Cligès inspires. The second day they gaze "a mervoilles" (l. 4773) at the Green Knight who performs twice as well as the Black Knight had. When he reappears as the Red Knight, they all stare at him "a grant mervoille" (l. 4836) and after the feats of the third day, everyone finally realizes that all these strangers are one man. The essence appears through the accidents and his final armour needs no colour (ll. 4028–3; 4878–79).

The last encounter is necessarily with his uncle Gawain, and is judged by Arthur and his men to be a draw honourable to both (ll. 4951–67). Cligès receives the ultimate accolade when Gawain, at Arthur's command, invites him to come to the Arthurian court. It is only at the request of Arthur that he tells him his name, to the joy of all present (ll. 5041–61). Even this is not enough. He could return to Constantinople now, having fulfilled his promise, but he chooses instead to gain more experience on the continent (ll. 5064–69). He stays away until the following spring, when at last he thinks again about Fenice (l. 5074). He has not been shown thinking about her for nearly five hundred lines — all that time he has been living in a watertight world of pure chivalry, which made a narrative return to the rigorous alternations of his father's career.

The difference here is largely with the heroine. Fenice has had all this time to think, and there will be a great difference between the "sinple chose [. .] et coarde" (ll. 3840–41) that Cligès left behind him and the determined young woman he finds on his return. Fenice has thought long and hard and in a very different style from Soredamors. She is not concerned, as the earlier heroine was, with the birth of love and its physical symptoms. Fenice already knows that she loves Cligès and is only concerned to discover whether he loves her. All depends on how she should interpret his parting words: he took leave of her "come a celi cui je sui toz" (l. 4327). She struggles to get at the truth of the matter by arguing with herself. Her thoughts alternate between hope and fear: "he loves me" (ll. 4410–31), "he loves me not" (ll. 4432–41), "he loves me" (ll. 4442–51), "he loves me not" (ll. 4452–66), "he loves me" (ll. 4467–81), "he loves me not" (ll. 4482–89). All she is sure of is that she loves him and that he merits her love (ll. 4490–574).

There is no progression in the action, but that is not what concerns Chrétien in this romance. He is willing to hold up the narrative for another long monologue in order to show us the mind of a lover at work. At the end of each monologue he underlines the fact that the narrative has come to a full stop by inviting us, with a demonstrative adverb, to look back over the exposition of thought that he has set out for us. At the end of the first monologue of Soredamors, Chrétien says:

> Einsi a li meïsme tance,
> Une ore aimme et une autre het.                    (ll. 524–25)

At the end of the double "conplainte" of Alexander and Soredamors he says:

> Einsi se plaint et cil et cele,
> Et li uns vers l'autre se cele.                    (ll. 1047–48)

And it is exactly the same at the end of the long monologue of Fenice:

> Einsi travaille amors Fenice.
> Mes cist travauz li est delice.                    (ll. 4575–76)

It is the expository side of his narrative that Chrétien wants us to appreciate, not any suspense in the intrigue. His concern is with analysis, and his method remains substantially the same throughout the romance: he examines in alternation the contrasting factors that go to make up each phenomenon as it appears in the gradual formation of each of his heroes and heroines.

# V. The Technique of Displacement

On two parallel occasions, one at the end of the Alexander story and the other at the end of the Cligès story, the narrative falls suddenly into an anti–climax. Alexander, the hero of epic adventures in Britain, brings his career to a close in a surprisingly unheroic way. After portraying him as a veritable Roland in support of his lord, Chrétien does not permit him to fight on his own behalf. Yet Alexander has just cause to make war: his brother Alis, believing him dead, has had himself crowned emperor in his place and refuses to relinquish the crown on learning his mistake. So why does Alexander not make war? He would indeed have accepted Arthur's help and brought back a large army, "mes n'a soing de sa jant confondre" (l. 2433). Civil war is regarded with horror: Alis, for his part, is warned by everyone against repeating the tragedy of the Theban brothers (ll. 2536–43) and recommended to seek a form of peace "qui soit resnable et droituriere" (l. 2545). So the brothers agree that Alis will keep the crown, but Alexander will rule; moreover, Alis promises that he will never marry so that his nephew Cligès will inherit the empire. While this is undoubtedly the right solution morally, there is an uncomfortable effect produced in the narrative by the sudden transformation of Alexander from triumphant soldier to cautious diplomat. The "grant force" (l. 2432) he could have brought against Alis is abruptly deprived of the chance of acting, and we feel that the narrative has struck an invisible but immovable obstacle.

The other anti–climax involves Cligès. He too returns to Constantinople (ll. 5115–30) to discover that Alis has wronged him. His uncle has perjured himself by agreeing to marry Fenice. Cligès and Fenice have never loved anyone but each other: they embark on an affair and when, it is discovered, they set out for Britain, where Cligès appeals to Arthur for justice and is offered help on a grand scale:

> Et li rois dit que a navie
> Devant Costantinoble ira
> Et de chevaliers anplira
> Mil nes et de serjanz trois mile,
> Tes que citez ne bors ne vile
> Ne chastiaus, tant soit forz ne hauz,
> Ne porra sofrir lor assauz. (ll. 6682–88)

Arthur is as good as his word and raises the largest navy ever seen:

> . . . ains le paroil
> N'ot nes Cesar ne Alixandres.
> Tote Eingleterre et totes Flandres,
> Normandie, France et Bretaingne,
> Et toz çaus jusqu'as Porz d'Espaingne
> A fet semondre et amasser.                    (ll. 6700–05)

But it is all for nothing. Just as they are about to embark, news comes that Alis is dead. Some of the army are glad, but others feel an understandable sense of anti–climax:

> . . . si ot de tes,
> Qui esloignassent lor ostés
> Volantiers et mout lor pleüst,
> Que l'oz vers Grece s'esmeüst.                 (ll. 6735–38)

It is difficult for the reader not to feel let down. Why, when all the movement of this episode is towards a final military victory for Cligès in defence of his rights, is there this abrupt halt and cancellation of what we have been led to expect?

The answer must lie with the factor common to both events, that is, the identity of the enemy, the feeble Alis. He remains a shadowy and elusive figure, though he has his significance on the moral plane as the enemy of the rational good for which the lovers strive. All four heroes, like Erec before them, direct a strong will towards the accomplishment of what they perceive to be good. Alis's good intentions only pave the way to perjury and treachery, because his will is defective. He is a morally negative figure, but he is of capital importance in the narrative as his character is determined by the way Chrétien reworks the Tristan story. When Chrétien makes Fenice refuse to lay herself open to scandal like Iseut (ll. 5309–16), he shifts the balance of the plot. If, in an adulterous triangle, the lovers are to remain sympathetic, it can only be at the expense of the husband.

Chrétien clearly saw that once all the characters are shown to be acting of their own free will, then any sympathy granted to the husband will be subtracted from the lovers. Unlike Beroul, who strives to arouse our sympathy for the sufferings of the lovers and even, to some degree, those of the husband, Chrétien strives only to arouse our admiration for the moral decisions of his heroes. Suffering may occasionally bring Mark close to Tristan and Iseut, but moral integrity cuts an impassable divide between the perjured Alis, who is wholly in the wrong, and Cligès and Fenice, who are as much as possible in the right.

The position of Alis on the functional level remains the same as Mark's: he provides the obstacle to the lovers that is essential to the plot. It is in the working out of the action that the difficulties appear. For the lovers to be in the right, the husband must be in the wrong, as Chrétien has abolished the moral alibi of the potion. So he casts Alis as a weak–willed figure, who betrays his own nephew by breaking a solemn promise. Chrétien is not, however, interested in the problem of evil as such. He is much more concerned with the problem of good, in which evil, in the most orthodox Christian tradition, appears only as a negative shadow. Alis, therefore, must provide an obstacle strong enough to make the story possible without at the same time setting up an opposing pole of values.[1]

Chrétien overcomes this difficulty by using a device he has already exploited to a minor degree in *Erec*. Instead of allowing Alis to be too effectively evil on his own account, Chrétien makes him an essentially passive figure, and displaces the initiative of evil on to a minor character, arbitrarily filled with motiveless malignity. In *Erec*, it was the hideous dwarf who performed the act of aggression rather than Yder. Here, Chrétien does not allow Alis to be either a villain worthy of the hero's steel or an essentially noble character visited by occasional gleams of remorse. All positive will is drained from him and he is left with nothing more than a facile propensity for evil. So, when the plot requires him to usurp the throne, the initiative of evil is displaced on to a new, anonymous and otherwise wholly gratuitous character:

> . . . un felon, un renoiié,
> Qui amoit Alis, le menor,
> Plus qu'Alixandre, le greignor.          (ll. 2404–06)

This arbitrary villain does not even profit by the coronation of Alis. There is no logical conclusion to his treachery, or to himself. Once his lying report has put Alis on the throne, he disappears forever. He is as wholly subordinated to the presentation of Alis as Alis is to the presentation of Cligès and Fenice. In this way Alis himself can be shown acting at first in good faith. It is only when he learns the truth of the matter that his fatal moral weakness is revealed and we see him unwilling to believe that his brother is alive and clinging to the crown that he ought by right to resign.

Alis's weakness is further illustrated by contrast with Alexander's other adversary, Angres of Windsor. Angres may be a worse traitor than Ganelon, but he is a much more vigorous villain than Alis. He wants power and he goes all out to get it. His defence of Windsor is practical in the extreme (ll. 1238–55), and the abundance of material detail establishes the strength of his position. He suffers when he sees the knights he holds dear dragged to death at Arthur's command (ll. 1504–06). He is able and willing to fight to the end against impossible odds, even against God's opposition to his treachery (ll. 1676–77;

---

[1]Chrétien does not share the beliefs of dualists such as the Cathars for whom evil had a substantial reality. He follows the tradition of St. Augustine for whom evil is the absence of good: "mali enim nulla natura est; sed amissio boni mali nomen accepit" (*De Civitate Dei*, XI, 9). Even more to the point, the evil will has a negative cause: "Nemo igitur quaerat efficientem causam malae voluntatis: non enim est efficiens sed deficiens quia nec illa effectio sed defectio" (*De Civitate Dei*, XII, 7).

1702–12). Yet all this strength is only given to him to highlight the greater powers of Alexander, who is defending the rightful cause. Once Angres is defeated, he is rapidly removed from the scene in two lines (ll. 2204–05), having served his purpose. Despite his vigour, he too is only an evil shadow in the narrative and, like Alis, his function is to throw into relief the qualities and abilities of the hero. The difference in character depends on Chrétien's purpose: one villain must be physically powerful to make him a satisfactory foil to the hero's prowess; the other must be morally feeble to make him a satisfactory contrast to the hero's highmindedness.

Alis's moral weakness is apparent in the terms of peace he agrees with his brother: Alexander can have the real power provided that Alis keeps the title. From then on "Alis n'i a mes que le non" (l. 2588). Alexander has the substance and Alis is content with the shadow. It is a foretaste of the central situation in which he will have only the name of being Fenice's husband, while Cligès enjoys the reality of her love.

After Alexander's death, Alis is faithful for a time to his promise and abstains from taking a wife, but his weak will leads him inexorably into perjury and treachery. Once again, evil does not come spontaneously from within, but he falls an easy prey to it when it comes from without. This time the evil initiative is displaced, as in *Tristan*, on to the barons. By dint of sheer nagging, they persuade him to take a wife and convince him that the right bride is the daughter of the emperor of Germany, even though her father has promised her to the Duke of Saxony. By agreeing to betray his nephew, Alis abandons the most fundamental of courtly qualities, that of honour:

> Que por blasme ne por reproche
> Fame a prandre ne leissera;
> Mes s'enors an abeissera.                    (ll. 2696–98)

He is morally prepared to take his bride by force, but he does not have the courage of his convictions. It is Cligès who has to win the bride from the Duke. Alis himself never puts hand to lance. On the level of chivalry, his alliance with Fenice is invalid: Alis is incapable of winning her and he never proves himself even once in battle. Given that prowess is the fundamental quality of a noble, to displace all effective action on to Cligès is the most telling indication that Alis is so worthless as to be practically non-existent. When he discovers that his marriage to Fenice was nothing but a delusion, he cannot hope to win her back, for he lacks all effective will. So the final crisis with Cligès exactly repeats the earlier crisis with Alexander. In each case the hero has amply proved his worth before Arthur and has merited the love of the heroine. It would add nothing to his glory to crush the insubstantial Alis who could not possibly be metamorphosed into an Angres just for the occasion. Death in battle would be too positive an end for him. Instead, he dies offstage of impotent anger.

Alis's impotence is an essential feature of Chrétien's story, for it is inextricably linked to the problem of the potion, itself the key to Chrétien's remodelling of the Tristan story. The potion occurs in all the Tristan romances; accidentally swallowed by Tristan and Iseut, it produces inescapably tragic results: it forces Iseut to deceive a worthy husband, it forces Tristan to deceive a beloved kinsman who is also his lord, and it forces Mark, who loves them both and fears his treacherous barons, to be torn on a rack of suspicion, anger and eventual sorrow. It is the earliest and most powerful version of the so-called eternal triangle and yet Chrétien was dissatisfied with it. The reason, as we have seen, is set out in his lyric in which he says, speaking as a lover, that he never drank of the drink with which Tristan was poisoned

> Mais plus me fait amer que lui
> Fins cuers et bone volentez.[2]                    (ll. 30-31)

The impulse of a refined heart and a rightful will: that is what is missing from the Tristan story. Chrétien is opposed to the fundamental irrationality represented by the potion. In his ideal world, where love is based on the merits of the lover and the loved one, the potion is degrading. There is no provision for tragic passion in Chrétien's scheme of things, because there can be no question of glorifying any human behaviour that does not come under the jurisdiction of reason and free will.

Chrétien does not take exception to Tristan and Iseut as characters. We have seen how Erec is guaranteed as a hero by being compared to Tristan, and Enide exalted by comparison with Iseut. Indeed, if the couple had not made such a powerful appeal to him, he would hardly have returned to their story so insistently. There is nothing for him to blame in them as characters. They both have birth, beauty and a high sense of the dignity of their rank. The religious aspect of their adultery does not concern him. Certainly Cligès and Fenice display no purely religious scruples. Chrétien baulks only at the irrational and the scandalous, that is, at the potion and its effects. His attitude is that the story would have been vastly better if it had not been a potion that had inspired their love, but a "fins cuers et bone volentez." Once again, Chrétien is anxious to eliminate any magic interference in the motivation of his heroes. So, in his plan of Cligès, his first step was to suppress the potion.

Nevertheless, the ghost of a potion hovers over the parental romance. Soredamors is already in Arthur's entourage, she is no distant princess like Iseut for whom a sea voyage has to be made. The only purpose of Arthur's voyage to Brittany is to bring the hero and heroine together on board a ship. If Chrétien goes to such lengths to make their love begin

---

[2]Raynaud, 1664; Brakelmann, 46–48. It is noteworthy that Marie de France, who has no compunction about mixing love and marvels, nevertheless omits all reference to the famous 'boivre' from Chievrefoil.

at sea, it can only be because he wishes to evoke the Tristan model and then reject it by implication. If we are reminded of circumstances in which a potion appeared and no potion is forthcoming, then it is because he wishes us to be conscious of the fact that he has suppressed it. For a strong-willed, high-minded character like Alexander, whose career so far has been the product of mature deliberation, to descend into treachery and deceit through the accidental swallowing of a magic potion would be an indignity indeed. If his love is a "folie" (l. 630), it is a folly consciously chosen with a view to raising his life to a higher plane, not the random effect of something outside his control.

In the Cligès part of the romance, the treatment of the potion is much more complex. Cligès gets off to a much more low-key start than his father. He slips into the narrative in the company of his weak-willed uncle (l. 2689), who is about to break his promise not to marry. Cligès is not yet fifteen (l. 2765), ten years younger than Erec and more than ten years less assured; younger too, no doubt, than the determined young Alexander of the opening lines of the romance. Chrétien is even more concerned with showing us the stages of his education. He insists on the part played by a benevolent Nature in his making (ll. 2776-85). As for the practical side, he already knows more about archery "que Tristanz, il niés le roi Marc" (l. 2790). It is the first explicit allusion in Cligès to the rival story, and should prepare us to see this new hero, like Tristan, fall in love with the bride destined for his uncle. Meanwhile the Iseut figure has been introduced. Her beauty is a "miracles et mervoille" (l. 2732) which Chrétien feels he could never describe adequately if he lived for a thousand years (ll. 2735-45). His abundant accumulation of rhetorical negatives contributes to the impression that this new heroine, Fenice, is somehow to be understood in negative terms.

The physical beauty of both Cligès and Fenice together with the allusion to Tristan are indication enough to any reader of romance that we are rapidly heading towards another love story; but, in keeping with the leisurely, expository, didactic style of this romance, there is no dramatic coup de foudre. Instead, the beginnings of their love are slipped into the narrative so skilfully that it is under way before we realize it. The young pair are the cynosure of an admiring court, but while the courtiers are occupied in gazing at Fenice "a mervoille" (l. 2799),

> . . . Cligés par amor conduit
> Vers li ses iauz covertemant.　　　　　　　　　(ll. 2800-01)

Fenice's returning glances are equally discreet; nobody notices that

> Par buene amor, non par losange,
> Ses iauz li baille et prant les suens.　　　　　　(ll. 2808-09)

It is not yet a fully-fledged love, for it is based only on external appearances, vitally important indications of worth though these are. Fenice, for the moment, knows nothing more of Cligès than this; "n'an set plus que bel le voit" (l. 2813), and she would have greater cause for happiness "se seüst auques de son estre" (l. 2812). Be that as it may, she has already promised him her heart.

On the cue of that heart, Chrétien takes off on a violent tirade against the improbability of conventional love imagery. He vigorously rejects the kind of expression that others use, about two hearts being in one body (ll. 2820–24). He rejects it because it is not true and even if it were true he would still reject it as going against the appearance of truth:

> Qu'il n'est voirs n'estre ne le sanble,
> Qu'an un cors et deus cuers ansanble;
> Et s'il pooient assanbler,
> Ne porroit il voir ressanbler.          (ll. 2825–28)

It is this categoric statement that Chrétien makes on the nature of the probability that directs his narrative. Objects external to his characters can be, as we have seen in *Erec*, fantastic in the extreme, but within his characters he will tolerate only what he feels to be true. He rejects the physical absurdity of the two hearts in the one body, but only to substitute the superior intellectual reality of two wills that beat as one:

> . . . uns cuers n'est pas an deus leus.
> Bien puet estre li voloirs uns.          (ll. 2840–41)

Once he is confident of having made that vital point, Chrétien can be as extravagant as anyone else. When, well over two thousand lines later, Cligès at last declares his love, he does not hesitate to speak in terms of separating his heart from his body (ll. 5180–81). But at this critical early stage, Chrétien wants to convince us that the force that binds the lovers together is more than can be conveyed by conventional rhetoric about hearts. This love is serious because it entails an act of the will:

> . . . la volantez de chascun
> De l'un an l'autre se trespasse.          (ll. 2834–35)

The point engrosses him so much that he labours it with repetition and with the illustration of different voices singing in unison and it is only with reluctance that he brings himself back to the business of relating what happened next.

Chrétien develops the theme of love and the will when he turns his attention to Fenice. She is grateful to Love for having prompted her to love the most worthy of men (ll. 2974–86). The choice of a worthy object for her love reflects credit on both parties. The choice of a husband is not, however, in her hands:

> Mes par force avoir li estuet
> Celui qui pleisir ne li puet.          (ll. 2987–88)

She is obliged to marry the uncle rather than the nephew. It is not that Chrétien is opposing the freedom of love to the constraints of marriage.

The key phrase is "par force", precisely the factor the queen had opposed to the honour to be found in the right kind of marriage. It is not marriage that is incompatible with love, but the forcing of the will. Unfortunately, like any noblewoman, Fenice cannot choose her husband: that is the exclusive right of her father. Her will remains free, but her power of effective action is limited. Chrétien's concern for social probability makes him show us a princess who is unable to act as she pleases. His concern with true love makes him find a solution for her problem that abolishes material obstacles.

He displaces the burden of solving Fenice's practical problems on to a character specially created for the purpose, her "mestre" Thessala. He has barely finished telling us about his heroine's dilemma when he informs us:

> Sa mestre avoit non Thessala,
> Qui l'avoit norrie d'anfance,
> Si savoit mout de nigromance.
> Por ce fu Thessala clamee,
> Qu'ele fut de Thessaille nee,
> Ou sont feites les deablies,
> Anseigniees et establies;
> Car charmes et charaies font
> Les fames qui del païs sont.               (ll. 3002–10)

He then makes Thessala boast of her medical skills in these terms:

> "Si sai, se je l'osoie dire,
> D'anchantement et de charaies
> Bien esprovees et veraies
> Plus qu'onques Medea ne sot."               (ll. 3028–31)

It is astounding to find Medea and all her "charaies et charmes," implicitly rejected in *Erec* (l. 710), being openly available here. Thessala's arts are apparently limitless. Chrétien is boldly writing himself a blank cheque for means of getting his heroine out of difficulties. Chrétien, who has rejected the Tristan potion, which accounted for everything, will now let Thessala produce one potion to deceive Alis, another to make Fenice appear dead and a third to bring her back to health! Nor has there been the slightest narrative preparation for these marvels. On the contrary, it is positively provocative the way Thessala calmly tells Fenice that she has kept her magic powers secret up to now (ll. 3032–33). Chrétien is unrepentantly presenting us with a figure whose marvellous powers are got up solely for the immediate emergency.

Thessala's potions only make sense in Chrétien's narrative if we accept that she is not to be classed as a character. Despite the similarities in their situation, the relationship of Fenice and Thessala is radically different from that of Juliet and her Nurse, for the Nurse is a character in her own right. Chrétien's moral concerns are thoroughgoing but abstract. His hero and heroine will illustrate a testing art of love, but all those who surround them will be ruthlessly subordinated to the author's intentions. He is not aiming at an overall naturalism, but at depicting an exemplary ideal projected by his two main characters. The physical is so thoroughly subordinated to the mental that the different functions are allotted to different characters and the material ones delegated to figures inferior in rank and narrative importance. All the expressions of will, of principle and precept are the province of the heroes, and all the external practical details are left to Thessala, and later to the corresponding externalized support of Cligès, his serf Jehan.

The practical problems being taken care of thus, at least potentially, Fenice is free to develop her ideas of love. As she cautiously unfolds her secret to Thessala, she reclaims some of the initiative lost to the "marvellous" by laying repeated stress on the voluntary nature of her desire:

> "Mes enuiz est ma volantez
> Et ma dolors est ma santez.
> Ne sai donc, de quoi je me plaingne;
> Car rien ne sai, don maus me vaingne,
> Se de ma volanté ne vient.
> Mes voloirs est maus se devient,
> Mes tant ai d'eise an mon voloir,
> Que doucemant me fet doloir."          (ll. 3075–82)

The mechanically magical resources of Thessala's art are the price Chrétien is willing to pay for the preservation of the freedom of Fenice's will. As he displaced the initiative of wrongdoing from Alis to an anonymous 'felon', so he displaces the material aspects of problem-solving from the heroes to their subordinates. The effect, though far from naturalistic, can be defended as realistic in that it isolates what is true in true love for Chrétien. Once the correct principles have been established, the mechanical problems of their working out can be delegated to subordinates. Chrétien is consistent: Fenice wastes no time on practical matters, but she meditates exhaustively on the nature of true love. Thessala, on the other hand, gets on with the business of brewing potions and does not presume to moralize. It is a perfect division of labour.

Once the relative positions of Fenice and Thessala have been made clear, Fenice can go ahead and make her famous declaration of principle. She rejects as utterly unworthy of her the love of Tristan and Iseut—she would rather be torn apart, she says,

> "Que de nos deus fust remanbree
> L'amors d'Iseut et de Tristan,
> Don tantes folies dit l'an
> Que honte m'est a reconter."          (ll. 3146–49)

Fenice will never do anything that will bring her "honte." She would never accept the life that Iseut led, sharing her body between two men so that, as she says, Love itself was degraded in her. Fenice has a curious way of describing Iseut's behaviour:

> "Ceste amors ne fu pas resnable;
> Mes la moie est toz jorz estable."          (ll. 3157–58)

Iseut's love was not reasonable, unlike Fenice's, which is constant. This unexpected contrast is an allusion to Thomas, for whom 'reisun' is a key word. When Thomas's Tristan is tempted to share himself between two women, he refrains from being unfaithful to Iseut la blonde, despite his natural desire to consummate his marriage with the second Iseut, because at the critical moment, reason prevents him:

> La reisun se tient a Ysolt.          (Thomas, l. 648)
> . . .
> Amur e reisun le destraint,
> E le voleir de sun cors vaint.          (Thomas, ll. 653–54)

Reason is here identified with that right kind of love that gives Tristan (though belatedly) the power to be 'estable' or constant to one object. Fenice, unlike Tristan, never wavers, and her single–mindedness merits all the help she can get from Thessala.

For both Thomas and Chrétien true love is identified with the ability to be true to one's commitment, and Fenice is justifiably confident of her ability to be constant. Her truly "resnable" love involves her whole person, heart, body and honour. The extreme difficulty of reconciling the demands of all these aspects of the personality is felt by both Thomas and Chrétien, but while Thomas takes a gloomy pleasure in showing us how human beings inevitably fall short of the ideal, Chrétien takes the more optimistic view that where there's a will there's a way.

It is noteworthy that Fenice does not question the validity of her marriage.[3] All she says is that once it is consummated there will be no hope for her lover as any kind of promiscuity is intolerable to her (ll. 3142–44). She makes no appeal to our sympathy by pleading constraint, by pointing out how hard it is that though she loves one man, her father is forcing her to marry another. She does remind us that Alis cannot marry anyone without breaking his solemn oath to Alexander, but she does not use this fact to argue against the validity of her marriage to him. Both she and Cligès accept the marriage as a social fact, even though it is not based on a free choice. The Tristan model demanded that the heroine have a husband to form the obstacle, but Chrétien does everything in his power to minimize the moral obligation

---

[3]The complex legal aspects of marriage at this period are explored by Duby in *Medieval Marriage*. He stresses the difference between the secular aristocratic concept of marriage and the evolving ecclesiastical concept. Shirt gives a lucid exposition of the conflicting views of Gratian and Peter Lombard on what constitutes a valid marriage in "*Cligés*–A Twelfth–Century Matrimonial Case-book?".

that marriage places on Fenice, by opposing her particular marriage to all considerations of freedom, honour, merit and love. The effect is inevitably to weaken the force of the obstacle. The elimination of the potion and the quasi-elimination of the husband take away the fateful tragedy of the Tristan story: Fenice struggles against no obstacles other than her own scruples.

It was certainly not the tragic side of *Tristan* that appealed to Chrétien, for the most conspicuous difference between it and *Cligès* is that every version of the Tristan story ends in death and disaster while *Cligès* lives happily ever after. There is surely a link between the two principal features of Chrétien's adaptation: the potion is eliminated and free will triumphs as it had in *Erec*. It would have been quite unacceptable for Chrétien that his hero and heroine, after providing an example of true love, should not reap the rewards of their principles. *Cligès* represents, even more than the triumph of love, the triumph of honour and reason.

The husband, such as he is, still needs to be deceived and it is on this point that Alis suffers his greatest indignity, far worse than anything Mark had to endure, for the potion in *Tristan*, if it degraded the will of the lovers, at least preserved the dignity of the husband. Mark, reluctantly deceived out of fear and shame is one matter: Alis, permanently consigned to the domain of delusion is another. It is the most damning reflection of all on him that he is always cut off from reality. Chrétien expresses his contempt with rhetorical relish:

> Tenir la cuide, n'an tient mie;
> Mes de neant est an grant eise:
> Neant anbrace et neant beise,
> Neant tient et neant acole,
> Neant voit, a neant parole,
> A neant tance, a neant luite.
> Mout fu bien la poisons confite.          (ll. 3358–64)

His negative potion is a parody of the 'boivre' in *Tristan* and it is significant that Chrétien chooses to displace the effects of magic from the heroes to the most weak-willed character in the story. One might object, of course, that the potion in *Tristan* which induced love was not one tenth as improbable as this new concoction which induces delusions of love; but in Chrétien's scheme of things, it is acceptable that the least rational character should be a victim of the absurd. Alis cannot come to terms with reason at all and he dies "come forsenez" (l. 6729).

The pressure is all the greater on the main characters to act admirably. Cligès distinguishes himself in his apprenticeship with Arthur. Fenice pursues honour too, but in the only way available to her. For a man, honour derives from his capacity to act, but for a woman it derives only from the will to resist dishonourable action. Fenice cannot promote her honour positively, she can only resolve to avoid 'blasme'.

Just as the concept of chivalrous honour depends upon the assumption that chivalry is excellent and a source of excellence, so honour in the conduct of love depends on the belief that love is noble. Iseut's shameless conduct was subversive as well as disgraceful, for Love was degraded in her, "Amors an li trop vilena" (l. 3152). Fenice will not offer such a scandalous model of behaviour for, as she tells Cligès:

> ". . . ja nus par mon essanpleire
> N'aprandra vilenie a feire."                        (ll. 5251–52)

Their love would be devalued if it were exposed to blame like the love of Tristan and Iseut:

> "Se je vos aim et vos m'amez,
> Ja n'an seroiz Tristanz clamez,
> Ne je n'an serai ja Iseuz;
> Car puis n'an seroit l'amors preuz."                (ll. 5259–62)

Unless Cligès can devise a way whereby she can be his without anyone being able to blame them (l. 5270), he will never become her lover. But Cligès, though his own code of chivalry is rigorous, fails at first to understand Fenice's scruples, for he suggests that they simply run away together to distant Britain, where she would be received at the court of Arthur with as much joy as Helen was at Troy (ll. 5292–308). Joy, though, is not enough for Fenice. All that this plan would achieve, she fears, would be to dishonour them in the eyes of the world and get them talked about like the unacceptable Tristan and Iseut la blonde (ll. 5310–14). Everyone would blame them, for no-one would believe the improbable truth:

> "Et ci et la, totes et tuit
> Blasmeroient notre deduit.
> Nus ne crerroit ne devroit croire
> La chose si come ele est voire."                    (ll. 5315–18)

This is a perfectly reasonable supposition, though, when it comes to the crisis, the truth of the situation imposes itself without difficulty. The serf Jehan, dragged before Alis to corroborate Bertrand's sensational discovery of the lovers, delivers a scathing public denunciation of the emperor's betrayal of his nephew and reveals the truth about his delusory marriage and Fenice's faithful and courageous love for Cligès (ll. 6534–626). Alis, though enraged, accepts the truth of the matter. Some of his subjects are even prepared to hide the lovers, rather than pursue them as Alis commands (ll. 6654–57). In Britain, Arthur accepts everything Cligès tells him and at once sets about raising a huge naval force to uphold his claim. In the end, Fenice emerges with her reputation unblemished, but she was right to take no chances. Her concern for her reputation is as honourable as Erec's, because she too shares the values of her society.

Fenice is fully aware that others may take example from her conduct and she is prepared to forego her private happiness rather than provoke public scandal among those who cannot be expected to know the extraordinary circumstances of her marriage. She is aware that St. Paul recognized that celibacy is not for everyone, but adapts his recommendation to fit the social context she lives in, saying "those who are not chaste should take care to avoid scandal" (ll. 5324–29). Fenice is not trying to have her cake and eat it. She is prepared to make sacrifices. If it is to preserve her honour, she is ready to give up all the benefits of rank and wealth for the rest of her life. Living with Cligès, she says,

> "Uns povres leus, oscurs et sales,
> M'iert plus clers que totes cez sales."          (ll. 5355–56)

Her vision of love in a cottage may strike a modern reader as naïve, but no writer of twelfth–century romance speaks disparagingly of the splendours of the noble life that Fenice is ready to abandon for her principles. When, for example, remorse at last strikes the Tristan and Iseut of Beroul, they both bitterly regret the loss of their life at court (Beroul, ll. 2161–216).

Once Cligès understands what is at stake for Fenice, he is happy to agree to whatever she wants. Once again, however, she is unable to effect a practical solution. But this time, too, once the problem has been solved morally, the material details of the solution are displaced on to subordinates. Fenice knows she can count on Thessala (ll. 5366–69), and Cligès has a parallel support:

> "An ceste vile a un ovrier,
> Qui mervoilles taille et deboisse:          (ll. 5378–79)
> . . .
> Jehanz a non, si est mes sers."          (l. 5383)

He will construct anything they need. On the level of the narration, Jehan is more disconcerting than Thessala, who at least doubled in the role of confidante and had produced herself and her potions decently early in the story. It is much more daring to introduce a new figure five–sixths of the way through the romance, and then only after the need of such a person has been expressed. Produced at a snap of the fingers by Cligès, Jehan appears more contrived than Thessala. He is an undisguised prop to the plot and, arriving on the scene with all the requisite marvellous powers at the crisis of the story, he has irresistibly the air of a magician *ex machina*.

Is he in fact so indispensable? Could the lovers not have escaped to the kind of retreat Thomas appears to have envisaged for Tristan and Iseut, an ideal combination of nature and art?[4] Chrétien has a different purpose in view. In contrast to *Erec*, nature has played little part so far in the plot of *Cligès*. All the purposes of love are carried out through art.

---

[4]*Thomas*, 1: 234–39 (ed. Bédier); reconstituted passages.

Jehan's palace, too, had no previous function beyond being his own retreat as a solitary artist (ll. 5444–53). There is even a retreat within this retreat, its entrance so cunningly concealed that no-one could find it (ll. 5576–610). It contains, as he says, everything a lady might need: baths, hot and cold water, underfloor hot pipes (ll. 5628–31). As he tells Cligès, one would have a long way to go to find a place so eminently suitable "por s'amie metre et celer" (l. 5633). Chrétien does not alleviate the improbability of a serf just happening to have prepared the ideal retreat for a prince's mistress. On the contrary, he insists on the ingeniously artificial aspect of the tower. Artifice is the province of subordinates, and the distinction between the principals and the supporting players is maintained. Fenice undergoes the ordeal of her false death, and then the two subordinates deal with the practical consequences:

> Thessala panse a li garir,
> Et Jehanz vet la tor garnir
> De tot quanque il i covient. (ll. 6317–19)

Once installed in their tower the lovers are happy, but Chrétien devotes a bare ten lines to describing their joy (ll. 6332–41) and even then betrays a certain ambivalence towards it. On the one hand, he harks back to Fenice's fear that love might be degraded in them, and takes care to assure us that this is not the case:

> Certes, de rien ne s'avilla
> Amors, quant il les mist ansanble. (ll. 6336–37)

Then he sows doubt in our minds about the effect of their love:

> Car a l'un et a l'autre sanble,
> Quant li uns l'autre acole et beise,
> Que de lor joie et de lor eise
> Soit tot li mondes amandez. (ll. 6338–41)

Their joy may seem to them to improve the whole world, but the complete social isolation that makes their love possible without scandal at the same time makes it impossible for anyone else to be improved by it. It is a difficulty that Chrétien sees and does not want to be pressed on: "Ne ja plus ne m'an demandez," he says (l. 6342). He has gone to endless trouble to portray a pair of lovers superior to Tristan and Iseut and yet, when he finally brings them together, it is in a retreat as isolated as anything in his rejected model. Worse, it recalls the isolation of Mabonagrain and his 'amie' in *Erec*. For exemplary lovers like Cligès and Fenice, their forced isolation cannot last, and Chrétien releases them from it in due course.

Art has taken them as far as it will go. They are now ready to hand over to Nature. They have been a long time proving themselves, but once their love reaches the stage of physical realization, then nature can

take over. It is remarkable how simply the story of Alexander and
Soredamors ended: after the long drawn-out anguish of the birth of
their love, the birth of their child was surprisingly straightforward and
natural:

> Ainz que fussent passé cinc mois,
> Soredamors se trova plainne
> De semance d'ome et de grainne,
> Si la porta jusqu'a son terme.
> Tant fu la semance an son germe
> Que li fruiz vint a sa nature.          (ll. 2374–79)

If love is a complicated art, sex is simple and natural. Fenice's case,
being much more difficult, is resolved more gradually, but to the same
effect. She is content for a time with her "reclus" (l. 6398), but the
reawakening of Nature in the spring reawakens her to natural life. She
hears the song of a nightingale, which makes her long for the sun and
the moon and an orchard (ll. 6351–69). The wish is instantly realized by
Jehan, who opens a mysterious door into an orchard already waiting for
her (ll. 6376–92). When Fenice sees the sun shining, she is ecstatic: "De
joie a tot le sanc meü" (l. 6396) and says that now she seeks nothing
more (l. 6397). It is a shadow cast in retrospect on her time of seclusion,
since she acknowledges that something had been lacking in it.

Nature and art combine in the orchard. The branches of a pear tree
have been trained downwards so as to form a pleasing shade for Fenice
to sleep under and no-one, says Chrétien, could get over the high wall
around it if he did not pass through the tower (ll. 6402–24). But the
prospect of discovery is in the air. The spectacle of the escaped lovers
sleeping under a tree with the hero's sword laid close by (ll. 6450–79) so
inevitably evokes the discovery of Tristan and Iseut in the forest that we
cannot be surprised at the appearance of an intruder. But how did
Bertrand succeed in intruding? How did he get over the insurmount-
able wall? We are reminded of the mysterious wall of air surrounding
the orchard in *Erec*, which had so mysteriously expressed the desire of
Mabonagrain's 'amie' to cut her lover off from society. Fenice has
certainly not been guilty of forcing Cligès's will, but she was content to
live in artificial isolation for a time. Then, just as the song of the
nightingale prompted Fenice to return to Nature, so the flight of the
hawk over the wall destroys the garden's artificial immunity from the
outside world. Where his bird has led, Bertrand can follow. Nature
encroaches at last on the artificial paradise. The excellence of their
hearts and wills have enabled Cligès and Fenice to perfect themselves
in the art of love, but the realization of the ideal has only been achieved
by displacing all blame on to Alis and all the practical problems on to
subordinates until at last, at the end of the initiation of the lovers,
nature takes over from art.

# VI. The Silence of Soredamors

Towards the end of her second interior monologue, when, after much mental and emotional turmoil, Soredamors finally acknowledges to herself that she loves Alexander, a new moral concern is voiced in a way that is not easy to account for. Her problem now is to know what she should do next, and she recoils in horror at the idea of speaking her love. The categorical revulsion she expresses is quite new in the sharpness of its tone, and the repeated stress she lays on her objection is surely more than is called for:

> "Comant? Proierai le je donques?
> Nenil. Por quoi? Ce n'avint onques,
> Que fame tel forsan feïst,
> Que d'amor home requeïst,
> Se plus d'autre ne fu desvee.
> Bien seroie fole provee,
> Se je disoie de ma boche
> Chose, qui tornast a reproche.
> Quant par ma boche le savroit,
> Je cuit que plus vil m'an avroit,
> Si me reprocheroit sovant,
> Que proiié l'an avroie avant.
> Ja ne soit amors si vilainne,
> Que je pri cestui premerainne,
> Des qu'avoir m'an devroit plus vil."      (ll. 997–1011)

Soredamors's modesty is so acute as to be almost aggressive. Why is she so emphatic about it? There are plenty of cases in romance where a woman asks a man for his love without being reproached for it. Marie de France, for example, does not at all share this idea that it is degrading for a woman to take the initiative in love, as we find in *Lanval, Milun,* and *Eliduc.*

Some clue to the attitude of Soredamors can be found in the monologues of Lavinia in the *Roman d'Eneas,* which are certainly the model for Soredamors's style of meditation and to some degree for its content. Lavinia, having fallen in love with Aeneas, and with no possibility of speaking to him, first contemplates finding a messenger to take him word of her feelings, but fears that Aeneas will think her accustomed to making offers of her love (*Eneas,* ll. 8362–74). She

---

[1]Frappier, *Roman breton,* 2:70.

recognizes that it is not quite the thing for a princess to offer herself to a total stranger (ll. 8720–24) but, realizing that knowledge of her love may tip in Aeneas's favour the balance of the duel with Turnus, she takes parchment and ink and writes him an eloquent letter in the best manner of Ovid's epistolary heroines.

Why cannot Soredamors follow where Lavinia has led? The heroine of the *Roman d'Eneas* comes across as a much livelier character, very much mistress of her fate, and she helps on the narrative by her enterprising declaration. Its effect on the duel and on other events all follow as natural consequences of her action. Lavinia's love keeps the story on the move, whereas Soredamors's love brings her story to a full stop, for she is ready to suffer in silence. The very little that she is prepared to convey to Alexander "par sanblant et par moz coverz" (l. 1041) is quite ineffectual and had the queen not intervened, the silence of Soredamors would have silenced the narrative.

Why is Chrétien so emphatic on her behalf? Part of the reason is that having set up a partner for his exemplary hero, it will not do for her to behave in a way that is anything less than exemplary either, and he will not arrange for her the convenient kind of emergency that let Lavinia infringe the proprieties. But why exactly is it so improper for a woman to take the initiative? The reason is set out in the *Roman de Thèbes*. Antigone meets Parthenopeus and it is a case of love at first sight on both sides (*Thèbes*, ll. 4129–38). Parthenopeus takes the initiative: he wastes no time in asking Antigone to be his "amie" (l. 4612), to which she haughtily replies that he is addressing a princess as if she were a shepherdess; but she goes on to say that if he addressed himself formally to her mother and brother and if it were arranged that she were to be given to him in marriage, then she would respond to his love. Parthenopeus can and does move easily from asking for love to asking for marriage, but Antigone has no such freedom. She owes it to her rank to reject facile and dishonourable love, but she cannot herself offer marriage.

Chrétien's emphasis is unmistakable. Jean Frappier thought that there must be a literary reason for it: "Chrétien insiste, semble critiquer ici d'autres héroïnes de roman". [1] Which heroines? But we have no indication that he knew of the heroines of Marie de France, Lavinia is excusable and Antigone impeccable. There remains the constant irritation of the Tristan model. The counterpart to Soredamors in the Thomas *Tristan* plays a part that is far from exemplary in this respect. Friar Robert, the most faithful witness to the lost parts of Thomas, shows us Markis's sister Blensibil falling in love at first sight with Kanelangres, whom she sees jousting. She realizes that it would be more seemly for him to request than for her to offer love, thereby bringing shame and disgrace on herself and her family, yet her greatest fear is the same as Lavinia's, that the man she loves will reject her, thinking her accustomed to making such offers. She goes ahead, nevertheless, addressing him with words that are hardly "coverz". He responds and they embark on a

clandestine love affair, though Markis would have been glad to give her
to him in marriage. Only when she is pregnant and in great danger from
Markis does Kanelangres finally offer to marry her.[2]

Chrétien may also have had in mind the unfortuante Medea of the
*Roman de Troie,* who is alone among these heroines in her attempt to take
control of the social bond of marriage. She offers Jason her love and her
help on condition that he marries her (*Troie,* ll. 1407–18). Jason eagerly
accepts, as he knows he needs her help in order to win the Golden
Fleece, but he simply exploits her. All she can do is put him through a
form of private marriage before they consummate their love
(ll. 1619–34) but this in no way prevents Jason from deceiving and
abandoning her (ll. 1635–42; 2030–44).

Quite apart from their subsequent misfortunes, the disregard of both
Blensibil and Medea for their good name makes them examples that
Soredamors would naturally wish to avoid, given that she is a heroine
who is intent, not on instant gratification, but on submitting herself to
being taught by Love. The difficulty is that Love does not teach her how
to make the next move and no narrative progress could be made if it
were not for the eventual intervention of the queen.

The same problem recurs with Fenice, though it is differently
resolved. When Cligès dispatches the last of the abductors to take back
the bad news to the Duke of Saxony, he is left alone with Fenice
(ll. 3806–18). It is a promising opening, but he does not take advantage
of it. If Fenice is unable to take the initiative, says Chrétien,

> N'est mervoille; car sinple chose
> Doit estre pucele et coarde.                    (ll. 3840–41)

Chrétien's heroine has maidenly modesty to account for her reticence,
but his hero is a different matter. Yet Cligès is silent too. Chrétien puts
the question for us: "Mes cil qu'atant et por quoi tarde?" (l. 3842). He is
conscious of the problem, for he expatiates with much rhetorical
repetitiveness on the unnatural nature of his hero's fear, comparing it to
hounds fleeing before the hare and so on for a good dozen lines
(ll. 3845–58).[3] He then settles down to explain at leisure the 'reison'
which makes 'fins amanz' hold back and appeals directly to those
members of his public who have always maintained the highest standards in love:

> Vos qui d'Amor vos feites sage
> Qui les costumes et l'usage
> De sa cort maintenez a foi,
> N'onques ne faussastes sa loi,
> Que qu'il vos an deüst cheoir,

---

[2]The Saga of Tristram and Isönd, trans. P. Schach, 7–17. According to Bédier (*Thomas,*
2:64), "La *saga* est notre témoin le plus sûr du poème de Thomas."

[3]The topos of "the world turned upside down" is treated by Curtius, *European Literature,*
94–98.

> Dites moi, se l'an puet veoir
> Rien, qui por amor abelisse,
> Que l'an n'an tressaille et palisse. (ll. 3865–72)

Fear is inevitable in those for whom love is a source of moral improvement. Chrétien expands on the theme by the use of a feudal analogy: a 'sergenz' who does not fear his lord has no right to follow in his train, for fear presupposes respect and respect goes with a proper sense of value. Anyone who puts himself under the authority of Love must realize that such a service will inspire fear (ll. 3879–92). He sums up the principle thus:

> Qui amer viaut, doter l'estuet,
> Ou se ce non, amer ne puet. (ll. 3901–02)

He adds a significant rider for a hero such as Cligès:

> Mes seul celi qu'il aimme dot
> Et por li soit hardiz par tot. (ll. 3903–04)

At the end of sixty lines of explanatory justification, Chrétien at last feels free to declare:

> Donc ne faut ne ne mesprant mie
> Cligés, s'il redote s'amie. (ll. 3905–06).

Nothing could be further from his earlier style, the rapid, unjustified narrative of *Erec*. This didactic interlude is part of Chrétien's purpose in writing *Cligès*, but it contributes enormously to his problems of narration, for if his hero is silenced through respect and his heroine through modesty, then the progress of their relationship is going to be difficult.

The situation is complicated by the introduction of a third factor. After explaining why it was so right of Cligès to fear Fenice, Chrétien adds, as a brief postscript, that he would nevertheless have asked for her love if she had not been married to his uncle (ll. 3907–11). After all the talk of love, it comes as something of a jolt to be reminded of the marriage, even in this marginal way. Why does Chrétien make so little of marriage here, when he had earlier been at pains to make the queen praise it as the best means of preserving love? In neither passage, it must be said, is Chrétien talking of marriage as the moral absolute. For Alexander and Soredamors, who have completed their formation, and who are both perfectly free, marriage is the obvious way forward. Fenice, though her story will end with a happy marriage, is for the moment bound to the perjured Alis. Though the validity of the marriage is never questioned, yet if its claims were too heavily emphasized, Fenice's love would scandalize and alienate the public. Chrétien only mentions it here when he is gathering up all the obstacles, even the least weighty ones, which prevent, or at least postpone, Cligès's declaration of love. The essential point is that the declaration should be postponed. Both hero and heroine have still to develop further before they are allowed such a serious commitment.

Once Chrétien has justified the complete silence of the couple, he picks up the story line again in a way reminiscent of *Erec*. They ride back fast to the Greek camp where there has been much mistaken sorrow on their account. The couple hasten forward: the whole army come to meet them and sorrow is turned into joy (ll. 3918–35). This rapid reabsorption of the characters into their social context certainly promises more in the way of narrative progress. The progress of love, however, remains in suspense until Cligès returns from proving himself at Arthur's court and Fenice has had the opportunity to meditate in solitude and silence.

Even when he returns, Cligès cannot advance the narrative. Chrétien tells us at length about his overwhelming impatience to rejoin Fenice (ll. 5070–98) and about their almost incontrollable emotion on seeing one another again (ll. 5125–31). Yet Cligès has still the same reasons for remaining silent, although he has several occasions to speak (ll. 5149–56). Fenice, who holds the secret of her illusory marriage, is now forced to take the initiative. Even now, there is no unseemly haste; she has to wait quite some time for a suitable opportunity. When at last an occasion arises, she approaches the subject with the most cautious discretion, starting off with safe, neutral small-talk about Britain and polite enquiries about his uncle Gawain (ll. 5166–67). She then moves to asking him if he was in love with any lady or maiden in Brittany, to which he responds cryptically:

> "Dame!" fet il, "j'amai de la,
> Mes n'amai rien qui de la fust." (ll. 5178–79)

He waxes eloquent on the theme of the separation of his heart from his body, and assures her that he is unwilling and unable ever to reclaim it, but then returns to the tone of polite conversation with the words:

> "Je ne vos doi de plus anquerre
> Fors tant, se li païs vos plest." (ll. 5196–97)

This is discretion indeed. Fenice, once again forced to take the initiative, admits that her heart has been in Britain. Even then Cligès will jump to no helpful conclusions and presses her further about the exact time of her heart's absence, adding with repressive politeness:

> "Se c'est chose, que par reison
> Puissiez dire moi ne autrui." (ll. 5211–12)

Fenice bravely perseveres, but it is only after several more exchanges that Cligès is finally brought to the point of admitting that his heart is hers.

Here Fenice frankly takes over. Instantly replying that he has her heart too, she tells him everything about her circumstances and her scruples and he acquiesces in everything:

> Quant Cligés ot sa volanté,
> Si li a tot acreanté.                    (ll. 5281–82)

Why this sudden reversal of roles? What has become of the invincible hero of the Arthurian court? And what indeed has become of the "sinple chose [. . .] et coarde" of the lovers' last meeting? Chrétien's preoccupation with female modesty has undergone considerable modification. Impossible to imagine the passive Soredamors speaking thus to Alexander. Once again, there is no principle of morality at stake. Fenice must act differently because she is in a different situation. There was no reason for Soredamors to settle for anything less than the ideal solution of marriage; all she had to do was be sufficiently self-controlled to refrain from asking for love, which would have devalued her, and wait until the queen arranged her marriage.

Fenice is in a different position. Having been already married against her will, there is no straightforward honourable solution to her love problem. She could not refuse the husband she was given or ask for the one she wanted. Cligès's belief that she is a real wife to his uncle is the deciding factor that keeps him silent. So there can be no solution if Fenice does not take the initiative. But Chrétien does not allow her to rush into it. On the contrary, she thinks long and hard during Cligès's absence in Britain. Her thoughts, as we have seen, are principally composed of efforts to understand the true meaning of his parting words and to submit herself to being taught by Love. The effect, appropriate in a woman of such clearly-enunciated principle as Fenice, is cerebral rather than sensual. Fenice sustains her existence on nothing more material than the happiness of remembering that Cligès said that he was all hers:

> . . . ele ne vit d'autre deintié,
> Ne autre chose ne li plest.
> Cist seus moz la sostient et pest
> Et tot son mal li assoage.
> D'autre mes ne d'autre bevrage
> Ne se quiert pestre n'abevrer.                    (ll. 4378–83)

She is alone in a foreign land with no queen to look to for help and the object of her love is far away in Britain. It is this solitude that gives Fenice her independence.

All the main characters of this romance have a penchant for solitude. They all withdraw when they can from an outer to an inner world. Silence is broken when it must be, but restored whenever possible. The movement from outward to inward action is reflected by Chrétien's interventions in the narrative. He gives us none of those rhetorical descriptions of magnificent occasions that gave visible splendour to *Erec*. Of the first event that offers a similar opportunity for description in *Cligès*, Chrétien remains silent: Alexander is knighted with his companions and all the author says is: "Chevalier sont, a tant m'an tes" (l. 1209).

If it was odd in a fast-moving romance like *Erec* that he should pause for descriptions, it is doubly odd that in a slow and deliberate romance like *Cligès* he should deny himself the indulgence. But *Cligès* is a romance about people's hearts and minds, so he suppresses all unnecessary externals. But not all description: the details of the siege of Windsor help us to understand Alexander's heroic honour and the tower built by Jehan is a manifestation of Fenice's moral honour.

Festivities, on the other hand, are all rapidly passed over. Alexander's wedding is left undescribed by Chrétien, though it is astonishing to see the author of *Erec* renounce the rhetorical possibilities of such a splendid occasion. He claims that he has refrained from description because his public might not appreciate it:

> Por tant qu'as plusors despleüst,
> Ne vuel parole user ne perdre.                    (ll. 2357–58)

It is not impossible that some of his audience had found his longer descriptions tedious, but here he is principally preoccupied with moving toward a definite goal, for he adds: "a miauz dire me vuel aerdre" (l. 2360).

When it comes to describing his principal character, that is another matter: beauty is an essential indication of worth and to leave Cligès undescribed would risk equating him with his undescribed and unworthy rival Alis. Chrétien feels thematically justified in describing him, though he does so with a placatory gesture towards the more impatient of his audience:

> Por la biauté Cligés retreire
> Vuel une descripcion feire,
> Don mout briés sera li passages.                  (ll. 2761–63)

On the other hand, there is no problem when it comes to the wedding of Fenice and Alis. If Chrétien will not describe the wedding of a hero, he will certainly not waste time over the wedding of a villain. Indeed, he sounds irritably anxious to get it over with:

> Que vos iroie je contant?
> Lor afeire ont aprochié tant
> Li dui anpereor ansanble,
> Que li mariages assanble
> Et la joie el palés comance.
> Mes n'i vuel feire demorance
> A parler de chascune chose.                        (ll. 3241–47)

We might expect something more on the occasion of the Arthurian tournament, especially since Chrétien tells us that the occasion brought together "li plus de la chevalerie" (l. 4635), but he quickly and sharply adds:

Ne cuidiez pas que je vos die
Por feire demorer mon conte:
Cil roi i furent et cil conte
Et cil et cil et cil i furent.                              (ll. 4636–39)

It is paradoxical that in *Erec*, which is all speedy, forward movement, he paused twice to make just such a list, while in *Cligès*, which is so slow as to be almost static, he rejects any expectation that he will string out the story with picturesque details. The tournament is for the hero's education, not to gratify our curiosity. When we reach the triumphal banquet, Chrétien refuses to say anything more about the food than that it was abundant (ll. 5038–40). Nor, when Cligès returns to Constantinople, will the author indulge himself or us with any description of the festivities of welcome:

De la joie qui la fu feite
N'iert ja ci parole retreite.                              (ll. 5137–38)

All exterior ornament is renounced in favour of interior exploration, and our attention is focussed on individual feelings rather than on social relations. Alexander's desire to prove himself at Arthur's court sprang from a spontaneous inner impulse towards perfection. His father's response is significant in the light of later developments: the "joie et pesance" he experiences (l. 170) mark the first occasion on which Chrétien depicts warring feelings within the one character, and it is the first clue that the romance will treat more than the prowess of young Alexander. The emperor goes on to supply a moral complement to his son's motivation. Functionally, it is unnecessary: once he has given his consent, Alexander is ready to go. But here, as throughout the romance, Chrétien, while eager to shear superfluous ornament from his story, is even more willing to sacrifice narrative movement to thematic completeness. He holds up the tale, scarcely yet under way, so that the emperor can deliver a formal encomium of the virtue of liberality. His homily is not linked with his natural grief at losing his son (ll. 173–74); he does not infuse any emotional appeal into his speech. Instead, he sets out in a detached way to prove a case:

"Biaus fiz!", fet il, "de ce me croi,
Que largesce est dame et reïne,
Qui totes vertuz anlumine,
Ne n'est mie grief a prover."                              (ll. 192–95)

The proof is that liberality makes a "prodome" (l. 201), as no other quality can do, and he goes on to list all the qualities of a 'prodome': courtesy, knowledge, nobility, wealth, strength, prowess, lordship and beauty, all qualities which the young Alexander duly manifests. There is nothing in the content of this to surprise us. The importance of 'largesce' had been noted in *Erec*, illustrated, as it happens, by reference to the exemplary generosity of Alexander the Great.

The position of the emperor's speech is remarkable. The liberality he recommends gains in disinterested moral emphasis by having no narrative necessity. The emperor appeals to the universality of the esteem in which liberality is held. It is a general truth worth reaffirming in solemn detail (ll. 192–217) in order to set the moral tone of the romance.

There is something else new in the presentation of this royal figure. The emperor agrees to let his son go, because he has given him a promise and "anperer ne doit mantir" (l. 178). There is nothing new in the principle: it echoes what the Arthur of *Erec* had already told us: "Je sui rois, ne doi pas mantir" (*Erec*, l. 1793). The difference lies in the method of informing the reader. Arthur, though a less active character in *Erec* than in *Cligès*, at least speaks for himself. The same principle, evoked in connection with the emperor Alexander, is mediated through the author. Chrétien tells us how emperors ought to behave before he allows this particular emperor to speak. This is a hint that the action of the romance will be less dramatically presented than in *Erec* and that we will have more explicit direction from the author.

The hint is further developed when we meet Arthur in *Cligès*. The young Alexander had made Arthur's worth clear to us—it is what prompted him to seek Arthur out (ll. 68–73). Nevertheless, when he reaches his goal, Chrétien allows neither side to speak before he has impressed on us once again, in his own name, that the young Greek nobles stood before

> . . . le meillor roi del mont,
> Qui onques fust ne ja mes soit.                    (ll. 310–11)

This is a change of style for Chrétien. Like the emperor, Arthur is guaranteed by favourable authorial judgment before he is allowed to act or speak. When Arthur answers Alexander we know that he will not, indeed cannot, say anything to surprise us.

The weight of Chrétien's authority is most distinctly felt on the character of Soredamors. Alexander, as we have seen, is not portrayed as feeling the lack of love—there are no empty spaces in his life. So, when Chrétien introduces love into Alexander's experience, he has to create a special kind of heroine. Soredamors will not be like Enide, a heroine with a well-rounded social context and a well-rounded personality. Enide has individual and social substance, to counterbalance Erec. Soredamors, on the other hand, is parallel to Alexander (ll. 441–45), who is not driven by an individual purpose, but following in Arthur's wake without any immediate object or desire. The woman Chrétien invents as a counterpart is designed to fill a need that has not yet been felt.

Chrétien's ingenious solution to the problem of finding a mate for a hero who apparently needs no-one is to create the necessary vacuum not within the man, but within the woman he is destined to love. For once, the beauty, rank and other merits of the heroine are put into second place. The first description we get of Soredamors is negative. She is

> . . . Soredamors
> Qui desdeigneuse estoit d'amors.                    (ll. 445-46)

Here is a vacuum that calls out to be filled. When Soredamors finds someone worthy of her love, she will love with exemplary constancy. For Chrétien's purpose, this will highlight the excellence of his hero. Given that Soredamors

> Onques n'avoit oï parler
> D'ome, qu'ele deignast amer,
> Tant eüst biauté ne proesce
> Ne seignorie ne hautesce,                          (ll. 447-50)

to show her falling an instant victim to the merits of Alexander is praise indeed. It is also a subtle way of drawing him into the narrative. Her disdain of love, though it proceeds from admirably high standards, provokes revenge from Love (ll. 456-59). So she pays dearly for her pride (ll. 468-69), recognizing the effects of "Amor, qui justisier me viaut" (l. 487) and struggling in vain against this power that has vanquished her through her eyes (ll. 474-89). We are led to demand a response from Alexander and Chrétien keeps us, unlike his lovers, in no suspense, for he tells us at once that though neither of the pair knows it, each is thinking in the same way of the other (ll. 530-40).

Love is not introduced into Alexander's life as light relief from heroic activity. Love of Soredamors of a serious part of his education, as he is part of hers. She is a promising pupil, being

> . . . tant avenanz et bele,
> Que bien deüst d'amors aprandre.                   (ll. 452-53)

Like Alexander, she has within her all the requisite qualities which only need to be drawn out and developed. When she overcomes her initial resistance to love, she has still much to learn and her development cannot be rushed. She poses the same narrative problem as Alexander does: if we are to witness all the stages of development of an ideal pupil following an ideal programme of education, we cannot expect speed or suspense. Moreover, while Alexander could at least alternate between love and war and participate in some external action, the silent Soredamors is confined to private meditation. As in his monologue, 'folie' is one of the key words of her inner conflict, but not so much in opposition to common 'san' as to her previous calm. She describes herself as "fole" (l. 897), "esgaree" (l. 919) and "esbaië" (l. 934) under the disturbing effects of Love. This turmoil is left behind once she accepts Love and what Love has to teach:

> "Or vuel amer, or sui a mestre,
> Or m'aprandra Amors. — Et quoi?
> Confeitemant servir le doi."                        (ll. 946-48)

She knows the disposition Love requires:

> "Amors voldroit, et je le vuel,
> Que sage fusse et sanz orguel."        (ll. 953–54)

She knows too that Love teaches her to be gracious to all but to love only one (ll. 955–56) and that in short: "Amors ne m'aprant se bien non" (l. 961).

The release of a wrongful inhibition on her impulses and the whole-heartedness of her response to the teachings of Love quickly bring to the surface a new knowledge of herself. She suddenly realizes that there is a reason "que Soredamors sui clamee" (l. 963). This sudden awareness of true identity is a foretaste of *Perceval*. Her understanding has the spontaneity of intuition but, characteristic of this romance, she places the knowledge in the context of moral obligation and rational proof:

> "Amer doi, si doi estre amee,
> Si le vuel par mon non prover,
> Se la reison i puis trover."        (ll. 964–66)

Admirable though her soul-searching is, it produces another problem for the narrative. The more profoundly Soredamors explores her true nature, the less she is concerned with Alexander as an individual. Nothing indicates more clearly how deeply Chrétien's style of story-telling has undergone the influence of Ovidian theorizing. Enide knew nothing about Love an an entity. She responded to Erec as a person and the story of their love has a simplicity and directness absent from this new romance. Soredamors had not only disdained men, she had disdained Love which becomes personified and takes on a nebulous character of its own, mediating between the lover and the loved one. Chrétien is not concerned here with love as a relationship between a man and a woman. Nowhere in *Cligès*, for example, will either Alexander or his son be able to read their loved one's thoughts as Erec can read Enide's as they approach Evrain's orchard (Erec, ll. 5827–67). Alexander and Soredamors are concerned with themselves rather than each other—not in any shallow and selfish sense, but because their experience of love is, in the first instance, a way of realizing their own innermost being. Each is primarily for the other the instrument whereby they become aware of another dimension of life; and this essential separateness of the lovers has its effect on the narrative, for they both remain unaware of each other's love, and even heedless of the other's presence.

This isolation of the lover is most strikingly displayed in Alexander. Chrétien introduces his 'conplainte' by telling us:

> Amors celi li represante,
> Por cui si fort se sant grevé
> Que de son cuer l'a esgené.        (ll. 618–620)

It is to the picture projected by Love that Alexander turns his thoughts, not to a direct perception of Soredamors. He duly acknowledges himself bound to a new service, not a service to her, but to Love, which he recognizes as a "mestre" (l. 684). Chrétien does not use the word "god" in speaking of love, but he is clearly basing himself on the Ovidian divinity. Ovid's task was easier than Chrétien's. Amor was a not too seriously sacred god, so Ovid could appropriately use him in a frivolous poem. Chrétien's Amors, who demands such exacting service is, on the other hand, an invisible interior force, only perceptible to the finest hearts. Moreover, the only religious language available to Chrétien was the language of a religion that was taken seriously; to use it, as he proceeds to do, for non-religious purposes must have surprised his contemporaries much more than anything Ovid could do with the Roman god Amor.

The use of religious language isolates Chrétien's heroes further in an impenetrable inner life. Alexander, when the queen obliges Soredamors to tell him that one of her hairs is sewn into his shirt

> . . . a grant painne se retarde,
> La ou il le chevol esgarde,
> Que li ne l'aore et ancline.          (ll. 1617–19)

Though Soredamors is present in person, Alexander longs to be alone with his relic of her and when he is sure of his privacy "mout an fet tote nuit grant joie" (l. 1635). He withdraws from possible contact with Soredamors as a person and retreats into solitary contemplation of a reminder of her.

The religious language causes another difficulty. The second love story, no matter how it is justified by Fenice, is based on an extra-marital love that would certainly never have been sanctioned by the Church. Yet Chrétien shows us in his prologue to the romance that he considers himself to be working in a tradition that depends for its continuance on divine favour (ll. 30–44). He is not anti-religious, but his specific moral concerns are secular and aristocratic. The first love story in Cligès has an easy moral solution. The second one is a much harder case. Chrétien takes pleasure in devising the particularly difficult circumstances that test to the utmost the principles of characters with a high idea of love. But their love remains exceptional from first to last. They are not allowed to give a bad example to a society that could not understand them. Up to the moment of discovery, all external appearances remain correct, so that society cannot be scandalized. In the final crisis, the whole truth of the matter imposes itself so imperatively that all moral indignation is directed against the treachery of Alis. Treachery is the most serious of sins in the feudal context. The only time God intervenes in this romance is to punish the traitors who rebel against Arthur (ll. 1702–12).

Chrétien is extremely careful in the way he uses religious language with reference to the special case of Fenice's love. The common people underline her value by lamenting her supposed premature death, but they do not bring God into it directly. Instead they blame Death, to whom God has given too much power (ll. 5791–809). Inside Fenice's mind, however, Chrétien pushes the use of religious analogy as far as he can. Fenice does not conclude her interior monologue, as Soredamors did, with a declaration of service to Love. She is much more a heroine of romance and her love less isolated from the hero. Her service is given directly to Cligès, for she regards him as worthy of such devotion:

> "Qu'an lui n'a rien a amander.
> Por ce vuel que mes cuers le serve."          (ll. 4570–71)

Fenice does not think of love as separate from the man who has inspired it in her. Love with her is never reduced to an abstraction. It is the problem of moral behaviour that she thinks of as an abstract matter of principle. So in her mind it is possible to merge Cligès, love, the God of Love and even God. When, during her feigned illness, she tells Alis that her life is in the hands of the one she is wholly submissive to, the public put a mistakenly pious construction on her words:

> De De cuident que ele die,
> Mes mout a autre antancion;
> Qu'ele n'antant s'a Cligés non.
> C'est ses des qui la puet garir
> Et qui la puet feire morir.          (ll. 5714–18)

Fenice's esteem for Cligès is such that she can idolize him thus privately, but Chrétien will not allow her to scandalize the public.

The appalling sufferings Fenice endures at the hands of the physicians of Salerno are the climax of a long series of sufferings in the romance. From the beginning, love is bound up with suffering. Alexander must wait for the gratification of knowing that Soredamors loves him, not until he has proved himself as a knight, but

> De ci a tant qu'il an avra
> Maint mal et maint enui sofert.          (ll. 578–79)

To make love the reward of suffering rather than action is to cut off the characters even further from the possibility of social interaction and simple narrative progress. The end of the monologue of Soredamors is inevitable: she will be silent and suffer and prepare for more suffering: "Ancor n'ai je gueires sofert" (l. 1014). Her final line is the acceptance of painful solitude if that is demanded of her: "S'il ne m'aimme, j'amerai lui" (l. 1046).

Fenice is in a different position. She knows from an early stage that Cligès has at least some regard for her and Chrétien has allowed them some interaction of a conventional romance kind. Yet even here, suffering has played a vital part. In the course of his combat with the Duke of Saxony, Cligès is dealt such a fierce blow by his opponent that he is brought to his knees (ll. 4088–94). Fenice, who is watching, is terrified and cannot refrain from screaming "Des! aïe!" and then falling in a faint so that she wounds herself in the face (ll. 4099–107). As always, the general public takes Fenice's private motivation for a laudable public one. Cligès, hearing her voice, is reinvigorated (ll. 4120–30) but the others are content to praise Fenice's sensibility, believing that she would have done as much for any champion (ll. 4114–19). It is generally accepted that it is the man's part to act and the woman's to suffer.

Readiness to suffer is a guarantee of the genuineness of love. Fenice is ready to endure poverty for Cligès, but when instead she is to be offered Jehan's luxurious tower, then Chrétien makes her suffer to the utmost before she can enjoy it. If he wants to spare his lovers the social degradation of a life of savage outlawry in a desert like the forest of Morrois in *Berouil*,, he nevertheless obliges them to merit the happiness they attain, for fear of devaluing it. Cligès has merited Fenice by action. Now it is her turn to merit him by suffering. He acknowledges that the sufferings she endures are for his sake, for he suffers himself when he hears of

> La grant angoisse et le martire
> Que s'amie a por lui sofert.                    (ll. 6056–57)

She is willing to endure the appearance of death, and makes no complaint when the consequences are so severe that the second magic potion Thessala brews to induce this appearance has to be supplemented by a third call on "marvellous" resources to revive her (ll. 5450–65; 6296–304). Magic is the province of unreality: the death is a delusion, though the sufferings are real enough. Fenice embarks on her dangerous deception by claiming that she suffers from an illness "Don li cuers li diaut et li chiés" (l. 5673). Heart and head are what make Fenice suffer: love and will drive her to suffer anything for the man she loves and the principles she believes in. Her martyrdom in the cause of love is made explicit by Chrétien. Not only does she "sofrir martire" (l. 6025), but Jehan asks the emperor for permission to bury her in a tomb he had designed as a reliquary, for the empress is "mout sainte chose" (l. 6096).

The men who bring about her martyrdom, the three suspicious physicians from Salerno, introduce a jarring note. Chrétien has done everything he can to impress us with the nobility and dignity of his heroine, but for her sufferings he turns back abruptly to his source. When everyone believes that Fenice is dying and they are honouring her with their lamentations, suddenly

> Antre les lermes et les criz,
> Si con tesmoingne li escriz,
> Sont venu troi fisiciien
> De Salerne . . .                               (ll. 5815–18)

Everything about the physicians is unfortunate. We cannot be interested in them as characters, even as villains, as they only appear near
the end of the story. On the functional level they play the role of the
three hostile barons in the Tristan story, determined to do the right
thing for the wrong reason and convince a ruler that his wife has been
deceiving him. The barons, though more positively evil, have a more
justified existence on the level of the narrative: they have political
reasons for wanting to destroy the hero who has shown up their
cowardice. The physicians, on the other hand, enter the story in a
wholly arbitrary way and distort its tone. They brutalize Fenice so
thoroughly that they nearly reduce her to the status of an inanimate
object (ll. 5959–6025). Their punishment is far from dignified: they are
given their just deserts by the ladies of the court who fling them out of
the window (ll. 6042–50).

The difficulty with this episode is that the sources are showing
through. Both the Solomon's wife story (which the physicians recall at
ll. 5876–78) and the Marques de Rome story were tales in a well-defined
anti-feminist tradition, in which the point of the story was to illustrate
the endless wiles of women, and the moral of the story was that
husbands cannot be too suspicious. Several such tales, introduced with
reference to Solomon's warnings on women, are to be found in Petrus
Alfonsi's *Disciplina Clericalis*, a work certainly known to Thomas and
possibly to Chrétien.[4] In this episode Chrétien is not entirely successful
in his attempt to transform a pre-established plot where the woman is
the villain into one in which she is the victim. He acknowledges the
effect of the Solomon story at the very end of the romance: his own
heroine's exceptional merits are duly rewarded, publicly and personally,
but the ordinary run of women who succeed her are all the more closely
guarded on account of her false death.

As soon as the physicians are disposed of, Chrétien regains control of
his narrative. Fenice's dignity is re-established by the grief of Cligès, the
attentions of Thessala and the other ladies of the court, the universality
of the lamentations for her supposed death and her interment in Jehan's
splendid tomb (ll. 6051–162). Her sufferings, however, have been so
intense that Chrétien redresses the balance by making Cligès suffer too.
His anguish on her behalf is extreme: it is a marvel that he does not kill
himself (l. 6143). He is only restrained by thinking of the moment when
he will disinter her and know whether she is really alive or dead. The
sheer momentum of lamentation is such that when he finally lifts her
body from the tomb, he believes at first that she really is dead and adds
his lament to the sequence before his grief is turned to joy.

The preoccupation with suffering as an integral part of true love,
developed to a degree that is quite gratuitous on the narrative level, is

---

[4]See *Die Disciplina Clericalis*, ed. Hilka and Söderhjelm, and Hilka's article "Der
Tristanroman des Thomas und die *Disciplina Clericalis*."

certainly derived by Chrétien from Thomas. It is remarkable how, in the surviving fragments of his *Tristan*, Thomas never once mentions the joy of love without at once reminding us of its sorrows. No fewer than twenty-eight times, in the course of the few fragments that we still have of his poem, Thomas rhymes "amur" with "dolur," perhaps most notably in his concluding couplet. He reproaches Tristan for his inability to suffer, to remain constant to Iseut in absence and isolation and to reject the temptation of physical satisfaction with another woman. He admires Iseut for her capacity to suffer voluntarily; Eilhart's heroine had put on a hairshirt to do penance for her unjust suspicions of her lover (*Tristrant*, ll. 7127–444); the Iseut of Thomas is a "veire amie" because, though she committed no wrong against her lover, she puts on a "bruine" simply so that she may in some way share his suffering (Thomas, ll. 2028–35).

The sufferings of Cligès are modelled on the Ovidian source used by Chrétien in *Erec*: the lover who laments, mistakenly believing that the loved one is dead, is borrowed from the story of Pyramus and Thisbe.[5] As with Enide's lamentation over the supposedly dead body of Erec, the point of the episode is to emphasize both the sincerity of the one who laments and the value of the one who is lamented. Here again, the tragic outcome of Ovid's story is averted. At the critical moment, Fenice recovers just enough strength to tell her lover that she is not dead (ll. 6266–80). To highlight the qualities of his lovers, Chrétien may put them through the sufferings of Tristan or bring them to the brink of Ovidian tragedy, but at the crisis he still displays the same optimism that he had in *Erec*. His characters may suffer in solitude and even in silence but in the end high principles are rewarded, true love triumphs and collective joy prevails.

If Chrétien's outlook remains the same as in *Erec*, his techniques of narration have changed. *Cligès* is not a *conte d'aventure* but a serious initiation story in which the four central characters, starting from excellent beginnings, are shown to develop to maturity. The core of Chrétien's reworking of the Tristan story is that all Chrétien's characters have control of their will. Alis, the King Mark figure, is devalued to the point of absurdity, but the 'bone volentez' of his heroes succeeds in bringing their stories to a happy conclusion. The narrative style of the romance is the exact opposite of that of *Erec*: it is slow and deliberate and Chrétien more than once brings the narrative to a full stop to illustrate or underline a point. He analyses his characters so thoroughly that he is willing to sacrifice synthesis to analysis in the Alexander story and suspense to exposition throughout the romance. Chrétien's manner is more detached and didactic than in *Erec*. We know a great deal that the

---

[5]For Chrétien's exploitation of the Pyramus and Thisbe theme, see Lyons, "La Fausse Mort dans le *Cligès* de Chrétien de Troyes." She accounts for the ambiguous tone of the feigned death sequence by showing that Chrétien superimposed the tragic theme of supposed death (the Pyramus story) on the burlesque theme of feigned death (the Solomon's wife story).

general public within the romance never learn and we even know things before the main characters do. We watch the two couples learn to love and merit love but we are never carried away by adventures. On the contrary, we are constantly lectured, either by the characters or by Chrétien, on the nature of true love and the means of realizing it.

*Cligès* is a less accessible romance than *Erec*, but it is perfectly intelligible. In recent years, however, many scholars have felt it impossible to accept it on the literal level and have preferred to understand it as an example of sustained irony.[6] It is true that almost everything in this romance is alien to modern sensibilities. Instead of being offered the exciting adventures of a hero with properly "human" failings, like Erec and Yvain and Perceval, we are asked to attend to the unfolding of four admirable natures who afford us no relief from their relentless excellence beyond the faults of their exemplary virtues. Worse, all possible suspense about them is undercut by the author. Worse still, they do not act themselves to solve their problems, but have the practical solutions of their difficulties displaced on to convenient subordinates. Worst of all, the dramatic style of *Erec* is abandoned and Chrétien concentrates on telling rather than showing, and telling with a distinctly didactic tone.[7] But if Chrétien meant us to take this story seriously, then we must. And he surely is serious. He set out to write a better version of the Tristan story and not merely a parody of it. He shows us heroes who love of their own free will and who achieve the rewards of love through merit and suffering. There can be no doubt that Chrétien is seriously concerned with exploring the nature of true love. It is the theme he will investigate at length in the *Chevalier de la Charrette*.

---

[6]Bertolucci, "Di nuovo su 'Cligès' e 'Tristan'," sees it as a comedy with no serious moral implications. Haidu, *Aesthetic Distance*, 112, believes that both young couples are foolish, weak and self-deluded and that Chrétien is constantly ironic at their expense. Owen, "Profanity and its Purpose," argues that the religious language used of Fenice's sufferings denotes a burlesque intent. Lonigan, "*Cligès* and the Tristan legend," believes the whole romance is composed in a mode of comic irony.

[7]For an unusually sympathetic treatment of "telling" rather than "showing," see Booth, *Rhetoric of Fiction*.

# LANCELOT: LE CHEVALIER DE LA CHARRETTE

# VII. Internalizing the Narrative

**B**efore the destruction of the villain at the end of the romance, the hero makes an incognito display of prowess at a long Arthurian tournament; so far, this piece of plot summary applies equally well to *Cligès* and to *Lancelot*.[1] We are now, however, in a different world. *Cligès* leaves the tournament at Oxford in a blaze of glorious recognition and returns to the heroine and a happy ending. The nameless Red Knight at Noauz begins by covering himself with glory, but then, at the behest of the queen, covers himself with shame. On the second day, he again agrees to fight "au noauz" (l. 5862) and then accepts the contradictory instruction to fight his best. The damsel who conveys the queen's messages is amazed at his reactions, or rather at his lack of reaction, for as she says to her mistress:

> ". . . se le voir m'an demandez,
> Autel chiere tot par igal
> Fet il del bien come del mal."                    (ll. 5932–34)

Lancelot has no mind of his own in the matter, no personal feeling, no preference for praise over scorn. It is scarcely credible that the creator of Erec should produce a hero so wholly indifferent to chivalrous reputation and so unquestioningly submissive to his lady's will. Lancelot's position echoes that of the unfortunate Mabonagrain, condemned to social isolation by the caprice of his 'amie.' Indeed, Lancelot displays even less "human" interest than Mabonagrain, for he betrays neither anxiety nor relief. It is as if all personal feeling has been drained from him, making his reactions those of an automaton. At the tournament of Noauz he appears as little more than a marionette with Guinevere pulling the strings.

There is certainly a case to be made for seeing Lancelot as an anti–hero.[2] To begin with, his love for Guinevere is adulterous and in both of Chrétien's previous romances, as we have seen, he gives ultimate preference to married love. Marriage has obvious social advantages over secret liaisons: for Chrétien, it is the most effective means of preserving love with honour and for the benefit of society. Marriages last and married couples fulfil their obligations to society openly and

---

[1]Citations are from Foerster's 1899 edition; see Bibliography.
[2]The case was first made by Foerster (*Lancelot*, lxvi–lxxvii), who considered that the inconsistencies in the text indicated Chrétien's reluctance to treat the subject. Other hostile criticism of the *Charrette* is reviewed by Kelly in *Sens and Conjointure*, 4–21. For a survey of more recent scholarship, see Shirt, "Chrétien's *Charrette* and its Critics 1964–74."

honourably, as we see with Erec and Enide, Alexander and Soredamors. Liaisons are discovered and have to be transformed into a relationship which takes account of society. Cligès and Fenice marry and Mabonagrain and his 'amie' are forced to leave their orchard.

Second, if Mabonagrain cuts a poor figure, there are those who think that the figure Lancelot cuts is downright comic, revealing the antipathy Chrétien feels for the role his hero plays.[3] It is very difficult for a modern reader not to laugh at Lancelot's misadventure at the ford. Absorbed by thoughts of love, the Knight of the Cart fails to hear the challenge that is shouted at him three times by the knight who is guarding the ford (ll. 734–63). Lancelot's horse heads for the water of its own accord and begins to drink. The knight, furious at the way his challenge is being ignored, gallops up and knocks Lancelot into the water, sending his lance and shield flying. It is only when he hits the water that Lancelot comes to his senses and looks around him with a bewilderment that strikes us as comic: the perfect example, one might say, of a Bergsonian *distrait*.

Moreover, Lancelot's behaviour during his first combat with Meleagant seems to illustrate the very essence of Bergson's concept of the comic: it is such a startling example of "du mécanique plaqué sur du vivant." Guinevere's damsel calls on him to turn and see who is watching him (ll. 3680–84). Lancelot turns, but once he sets eyes on the queen he will not look away and goes on defending himself from behind. His opponent takes all possible advantage of the situation, the people of Gorre rejoice and the prisoners from Logres display horrified anxiety (ll. 3695–705). The damsel, reproaching him for acting "si folemant" (l. 3709), tells him to turn so that he is facing the queen. Thus instructed, Lancelot leaps backwards and manages to place his adversary between himself and his view of Guinevere, so he eventually overcomes him. The automatism of his reactions to the queen is a momentary weakness. At Noauz, as we have seen, he carries automatism to the limit. In contrast to the free movements of the others, Lancelot alone is lifelessly and perhaps laughably mechanical.

We naturally look to the prologue for enlightenment about Chrétien's intentions, but the prologue to the *Charrette* is notoriously ambiguous.[4] It is possible to interpret his compliment to his patroness as a desire to disclaim responsibility for the theme of his romance:

---

[3]This is the position of Benton, "The Court of Champagne," 352, and Owen, "Profanity and its Purpose." There is a more mixed response from Bogdanow, "Love Theme in the *Chevalier de la Charrette*," and from Topsfield, *Chrétien de Troyes*, 124.

[4]Controversy has focussed particularly on ll. 26–27. Rychner interprets these lines as little more than "The countess inspires him," whereas Frappier defends the traditional interpretation "The countess gives him the matter (of this new romance) and its meaning." See Rychner's four articles in our bibliography; Frappier, "Le Prologue du *Chevalier de la Charrette*"; Hunt (supporting Rychner), "Tradition and Originality"; and Burgess (supporting Frappier), "*Sen(s)* 'Meaning' in Twelfth-Century French."

Des que ma dame de Chanpaingne
Viaut que romanz a feire anpraingne,
Je l'anprandrai mout volantiers                    (ll. 1–3)

. . .

. . . tant dirai je que miauz oevre
Ses comandemanz an ceste oevre
Que sans ne painne que j'i mete.
Del Chevalier de la Charrete
Comance Crestiiens son livre;
Matiere et san l'an done et livre
La contesse, et il s'antremet
De panser si que rien n'i met
Fors sa painne et s'antancion.                    (ll. 21–29)

Does this mean that he was working under constraint on a subject that was uncongenial to him?

The epilogue only adds to the uncertainty. In the last lines of the romance, we discover that it was completed by "Godefroiz de Leigni, li clers" (l. 7124), with Chrétien's consent. Godefroi tells us that he took up the story

. . . des la an ça,
Ou Lanceloz fu anmurez.                    (ll. 7130–31)

Is it a sign of distaste that Chrétien abandoned his romance unfinished?

The *Charrette* raises many unanswered and unanswerable questions. It is a disconcerting story, but one thing about it is certain: nowhere in the text does Chrétien give us any indication that the subject of the romance is distasteful to him. On the contrary, all the indications are that this story, extraordinary though it is, is to be taken seriously. The problems of interpretation are there, as we have seen, but they are not insoluble.

The adultery is much less of a problem than might appear. No doubt Chrétien gives preference to marriage, but it is not an absolute for him. His preference is based on social pragmatism rather than on religious principle. He never speaks of the sanctity of marriage or the sinfulness of adultery. The liberated Mabonagrain does not hasten to the altar with his 'amie'. Cligès and Fenice are perfectly happy for a long time to live in a situation which enables them to enjoy extra-marital love without social dishonour. Adultery, as such, is never condemned. Marriage is certainly preferable from the point of view of society, but it has one serious drawback from the point of view of love. The whole progress of Erec's sentiments, for example, is to be traced from a love indulged to the exclusion of all else, to love reconciled with more public concerns. We take leave of Erec as he is crowned king: love will never come first with him again. This may be inevitable, even admirable, but it cannot give us an illustration of human love in its most absolute form. The complete lover cannot allow any rival claims on his attention. The simplest solution is to cut him off from all demands of society, including the demands of marriage, which always ranks as a major social commitment in Chrétien's romances.

Chrétien was, of course, familiar with the idea that love and marriage might be considered incompatible. He tells us that he translated the *Ars Amatoria* and Ovid is categoric in excluding marriage from his treatment of love (*Ars Amatoria*, II, 153–58; III, 585–588). In the Christian tradition, even the sacramentalization of marriage had not yet led to its being highly regarded: it could still be seen as only a concession to the weakness of the flesh. In *Cligès*, lines 5324–29, we find a garbled version of St. Paul's dictum that it is better to marry than to burn.[5]

The most startling expression of the low esteem in which marriage could be held in the twelfth century is that formulated by Heloise. Abelard, in his *Historia Calamitatum*, tells us how Heloise brought forward every argument she could think of to dissuade him from marrying her, citing numerous authorities to show how incompatible marriage was with their ideal of the philosophical life and also with love. As she puts it in a letter: "Si uxoris nomen sanctius ac validius videretur, dulcius mihi semper extitit amice vocabulum [. . .] Amorem conjugio, libertatem vinculo preferebam." Abelard quotes her as saying that to be called mistress rather than wife would be dearer to her and more honourable for him; free inclination should keep him for her, and he should not be constrained by the bond of marriage; and if they were to be separated for a time, the joys of being together would be all the more pleasing the rarer they were: "Tanto [. . .] gratiora [. . .] gaudia, quanto rariora."[6]

This is a sentiment that undoubtedly had some significance for Chrétien, as it so closely echoes a line of one of his lyrics: "Bien radolcist par delaier."[7] No doubt this is why adultery seemed more appropriate than marriage to Chrétien for a romance in which the joys of love are given their most extreme expression and concentrated in the rarest possible gratification of a single night. It is not impossible that Chrétien had access to the *Historia Calamitatum*, or that some echo of its

---

[5]There was certainly some theoretic upgrading of marriage in the twelfth century by theologians such as Hugh of St. Victor; see Chydenius, *Love and the Medieval Tradition*, 16–24. Canon lawyers such as Peter Lombard and Gratian raised the moral seriousness of marriage by their insistence on the free consent of the contracting parties; see Shirt, "*Cligès*—A Twelfth-Century Matrimonial Case-book?" Nevertheless, marriage was always considered vastly inferior to the religious life.

[6]*Historia Calamitatum*, ed. Monfrin, 78, 114. See also Laurie, "The 'Letters' of Abelard and Heloise," 124.

[7]Raynaud, 1664. Brakelmann, 1. 43. See Zai, *Chansons courtoises*, 93–95, for a discussion of the troubadours' use of the theme of *carestia*, the delay that will make them more worthy of their lady's mercy. Zai claims Ovid as the source for this theme. The citation from the *Ars Amatoria* (II, 579; 603 is a misprint for III, 579; 603) comes, however, from a different context: Ovid is cynically reminding women that it is sometimes a good tactic to play hard to get. The asceticism implied by the troubadours is closer to Heloise's ideal of love.

sentiments reached him (the Paraclete was not far from Troyes). In any case, Chrétien is not the only twelfth-century romancer to believe that the absence of easy satisfaction increases love. We find, for example, in the twelfth-century French adaptation of Pyramus and Thisbe (the tale Chrétien most frequently uses from the *Metamorphoses*) that the hero and heroine become more eager in their love for one another once they have been forbidden to meet.[8]

Other than Ovid, however, only one relevant author positively declares that love and marriage are incompatible and that is Andreas Capellanus. We have, unfortunately, no certain information about Andreas at all. His *De Amore* may have been written as early as 1186; Chrétien's *Charrette* may have been written as late as 1187-88; Marie de Champagne may have been Andreas's employer as well as Chrétien's patroness, so the possibility that Andreas influenced Chrétien cannot be ruled out.[9] It is not easy, however, to make valid comparisons between a vernacular work of the imagination and a laborious treatise in Latin prose. Andreas has the didacticism of Ovid, but none of his light touch and certainly none of his wit. Nor does he have anything like as generous a concept of love as Heloise. Nowhere throughout his first two books, devoted to instruction in love, does he allow women any good qualities. For him, it is merely the accident of sexual attraction that gives women their power over men, a power they can and do abuse. In his final book, devoted to the rejection of love, Andreas abandons himself to a violent anti-feminism which, though it reveals no originality, nevertheless makes explicit the attitudes implied in the first two books: once a man can do without what these creatures have to offer, he says in effect, then he need have no more pretence of respect for them. One cannot help wondering if Marie de Champagne saw this last book, and if so, how she took it.

There is at least one notable difference between love as depicted in the *De Amore* and Lancelot's love for Guinevere. Andreas's lovers pursue their object without any of the humility that is so essential to Chrétien. Lancelot, having passed through unequalled perils to rescue Guinevere, is received by her with inexplicable coldness. Like King Bademagu and the reader, Lancelot is taken aback, but he behaves with what Chrétien describes as the humility of the true lover:

> Ez vos Lancelot trespansé,
> Si li respont mout humblemant

---

[8]*Piramus et Tisbé*, ed. de Boer, ll. 113–16.

[9]On the date of the *De Amore*, see Walsh, *Andreas Capellanus on Love*, 2; on the date of the *Charrette*, see Luttrell, *Creation of the First Arthurian Romance*, 32; on the slightness of the evidence connecting Andreas with Marie, see Benton, "The Court of Champagne," 578–82. For a sympathetic presentation of Andreas, see Lewis, *Allegory of Love*, 32–43. His possible influence on Chrétien is studied by Zaddy in "*Le Chevalier de la Charrette* and the *De Amore* of Andreas Capellanus." Many of the parallels cited are in fact derived from Ovid, the common source of these writers.

A maniere de fin amant:
"Dame, certes, ce poise moi,
Ne je n'os demander por quoi."                    (ll. 3978–82)

Not so the would-be lovers of Andreas, who pay their court by means of verbal bludgeoning, seeming to feel that they can win love by winning their argument.

The conflation of two distinct genres of imaginative literature causes the principal difficulty in the interpretation of *Lancelot*. The similarity between some of the themes of the romance and the themes of lyric poetry has often been remarked. Chrétien gave a lyric formulation to the most important of them in *Amors tençon et bataille:*[10]

Nuls, s'il n'est cortois et sages,
Ne puet d'amor rien aprendre;
Mais tels en est li usages,
Dont nuls ne se set deffendre,
Qu'ele vuet l'entrée vendre
Et quels en est li passages,
Raison li covient despendre
Et mettre mesure en gages.                    (ll. 17–24)

. . .

Molt m'a chier amors vendue
S'onor et sa seignorie
Qu'a l'entrée ai despendue
Mesure et raison guerpie.
Lor consals ne lor aïe
Ne me soit jamais rendue,
Je lor fail de conpaignie,
N'i aient nule atendue.                        (ll. 33–40)

Such extravagance is permissible in a brief lyrical outburst, but the literal acting out of the abandonment of reason and moderation in a narrative context is another matter.[11] The same is true for the lyrical commonplace whereby the lover declares himself to be thinking only of his mistress.[12] When this is translated to a narrative plane, we get the scene in which Lancelot's exclusive preoccupation with Guinevere causes his mishap at the ford.

It is nothing more than an effect of generic transference if we laugh at Lancelot being lost in thought. By transferring the theme of his lyric to

---

[10]Raynaud, 121. See Brakelmann, 44–46.

[11]This problem is studied by Ferrante in "The Conflict of Lyric Conventions and Romance Form." Diverres argues that the rejection of moderation and reason is acceptable in a lyric context but not in a chivalrous one and that Lancelot's extravagant behaviour as a knight is an indication that Chrétien was criticizing him; see "Some thoughts on the *sens* of *Le Chevalier de la Charrette*," 35.

[12]The lover's absorption in the thought of his lady is a frequent theme in Bernard de Ventadour; see *Bernard de Ventadour*, ed. Lazar, nos. 13, 18, 20, 24, 38 and 42. For a discussion of the *Charrette* in the context of the troubadour love lyric, see Lazar, *Amour courtois et "fin'amors,"* 233–43.

the more substantial genre of romance, Chrétien gives it a more complete expression. There is not the slightest evidence that he saw Lancelot's abstraction as ridiculous. No-one laughs in the romance, least of all the Knight of the Ford, who is defeated by Lancelot and then courteously released by him. The spectacle of preoccupied love clearly took Chrétien's fancy, for he develops it with unequivocally serious intent in *Perceval* (ll. 4171-671). Nor is there anything laughable in Lancelot's behaviour in his fight with Meleagant. His automatic and extreme reaction to Guinevere puts his cause in danger, but the danger is needed in the narrative: the fight takes place at a point in the story when Lancelot's prowess has been so repeatedly proved to the reader that the critical conflict of the entire quest will appear a foregone conclusion unless the hero is handicapped. What follows is that Lancelot actually turns his obsessive gazing at the queen to advantage and ends up playing with the hero at will (ll. 3763-75). As for his extraordinary indifference to glory at Noauz, Chrétien tells us what to think through the intermediary damsel. She returns to the queen amazed, but her admiration is unambiguous:

> ". . . Dame, onques ne vi
> Nul chevalier tant deboneire,
> Qu'il viaut si outreemant feire
> Trestot quanque vos li mandez." (ll. 5928-31)

As for the prologue, the most straightforward interpretation is, as always, the most probable. Chrétien sets about writing the romance "mout volantiers" (l. 3). His stated rejection of hyperbole in the compliment addressed to his patroness has been plausibly interpreted as a criticism of his fellow-romancer, Gautier d'Arras,[13] and an indication that Chrétien felt confident of his greater ability to handle his romance. His "sans" and "painne" are flatteringly subordinated to the "commandemanz" of the countess; he then abandons the tone of eulogy to say:

> Del Chevalier de la Charrete
> Comance Crestiiens son livre. (ll. 24-25)

Marie de Champagne may have suggested the theme and the general bias to be given it, but it is to be his book. Anyone who had read *Cligès* might easily have suggested that Chrétien should progress from showing novices in the art of love to showing a master. Whatever the countess's part, Chrétien takes responsibility for the realization of the book through his skill as a writer, "sa painne et s'antancion" (l. 29).[14] It

---

[13]See Fourrier, *Courant réaliste*, 205-07. It is even possible that Chrétien is making a counter-attack: in his *Eracle*, Gautier makes what may be a disparaging reference to Fenice; see *Gautier d'Arras: Eracle*, ed. Raynaud de Lage, ll. 2259-361.

[14]Lyons, " 'Entencion' in Chrétien's *Lancelot*," 429, suggests that 'antancion' should be rendered as "effort and careful attention."

is a considerable part of the labour for a romancer like Chrétien who, as we saw in the prologues to *Erec* and *Cligès*, willingly works on existing material. What he can do with it is what interests him and *Lancelot* no doubt cost him plenty of the twice-mentioned "painne" (ll. 23, 29), as it is a highly unusual narrative.

We have no information at all as to why he left the romance unfinished. Douglas Kelly has pointed out that there are no grounds for assuming any quarrel with Marie de Champagne.[15] The most plausible explanation is that Chrétien, a tireless innovator, was impatient to get on with his next idea, a romance of yet another sort. In any case, everything he leaves us of *Lancelot* indicates that he intended us to take it seriously. But seriously as what? Lancelot is quite unlike the serious and socially conscious Erec; nor is he an exemplary novice like Alexander or Cligès. He is not like any of Chrétien's previous heroes insofar as he has no social dimension to his background and no social aspiration in his future. He is an isolated figure who will never be integrated into society by the bonds of marriage. He is, in every sense, a thoroughly exceptional character, for he is not a "character" at all, being entirely absorbed by one function. Lancelot is an illustration of the complete lover, what Chrétien calls the "amis antiers" (l. 3818), who has no other claim on his attention beyond obedience to the commands of love. Lancelot is far from being a representative knight or a realistic hero. On the contrary, Chrétien emphasizes over and over again that his performance as a knight verges on the supernatural. Moreover, we are invited to marvel as Lancelot explores, to the full extent of its heroic limits, the perfect service of love. External, material reality all but ceases to exist as our attention is focussed insistently on the hero's exceptional motivation. What goes on in Lancelot's mind is the subject of the romance and everything else will be internalized accordingly.

The full extent of the change in Chrétien's narrative technique is not immediately apparent. If the Noauz episode has some structural echoes of *Cligès*, the opening scene of the *Charrette* is a return to the manner of *Erec* and even to some of its matter: at one of the important Christian feasts celebrated in the spring, Arthur holds court at one of his strongholds. A threat is made to the order of the Arthurian world and Arthur makes no move to counteract it, in spite of the rational reproaches of his nephew Gawain. Then the court is left behind and a hostile figure is pursued into the forest. So far, the pattern is recognizable.

There are differences. *Lancelot* is in every respect more extreme than *Erec*. Meleagant is the most complete villain we ever meet in Chrétien and his arbitrary irruption into the Arthurian court poses a far more serious challenge to the order of the kingdom than the custom of the White Deer, for he holds prisoner many of Arthur's subjects (ll. 53–55).

---

[15]Kelly, *Sens and Conjointure*, 71.

Erec pursued Yder into the forest to avenge an indirect insult to the queen: Kay, Gawain and Lancelot will pursue this new adversary who succeeds in abducting the queen.

Arthur was inflexible in *Erec* but in Lancelot he is shockingly weak. Meleagant tells him that he does not have the strength to free his people from the land where they are held prisoner, and Arthur is never more colourlessly static, more completely the *roi fainéant*, than in his reply:

> Li rois respont qu'il li estuet
> Sofrir, s'amander ne le puet;
> Mes mout l'an poise duremant.                    (ll. 63–65)

Chrétien is relentless in his depiction of Arthur's helplessness. The hostile stranger is shown making a calculated and rather theatrical exit: he pretends to depart and then, just at the moment of exit, he turns and proposes a *jeu-parti* (ll. 66–81). Even then, we are shown no reaction from Arthur. Our attention is switched to Kay, and when Arthur grants the boon rashly promised to the seneschal, Gawain's reproaches are much blunter than anything he had said in *Erec*:

> "Sire", fet il, "mout grant anfance
> Avez feite, et mout m'an mervoil."                    (ll. 228–29)

What has become of the energetic Arthur of *Cligès*? The answer can only be that he is now cast in the unfortunate role of Alis. King Arthur cannot be eliminated but he is very effectively neutralized. He fails his wife and Chrétien will manipulate us into thinking that the man who saves her life merits her love.

The opening scene remains shorn of all explanation. Meleagant appears, issues his challenge and vanishes, all within the space of thirty-six lines (ll. 46–81). We never discover how he has taken Arthur's subjects prisoner, or why no-one in Logres missed them. Instead of explaining, Chrétien causes a diversion, focussing our attention on the much milder mystery of Kay's strange behaviour. Every member of the court is shown to be fully occupied, first with anxiety over Kay's declaration that he will leave Arthur's service, then with greater anxiety about the safety of the queen under his escort. By the time Lancelot joins the quest for the queen (l. 272), the hostile action of the strange knight is a *fait accompli* that we no longer think of questioning.

So far, there has been nothing in the narrative manner that we might not expect from the author of *Erec*. It has all been an intensification of the same technique. Even the entrance of the hero does not immediately strike a new note. Gawain leaves behind all the other members of the Arthurian household who had joined in the pursuit of Kay, the queen and the strange knight, and sees a knight approaching on an exhausted horse (ll. 270–75). It is only in retrospect that we are surprised by the low-key entrance of the hero; there is nothing surprising about it at first sight, for it is not immediately obvious that he is the hero. Nothing stands out except his sense of urgency, which has cost him the life of his horse. As an acquaintance of Gawain (l. 280), joining in a pursuit that has mobilized the whole court, he blends in with the direction of Gawain's movement and of our interest. Gawain is outstripped but follows on behind, finds the horse he had given as a replacement lying dead and catches up with the new knight who has just caught up with a cart.

It is at this point that the narrative technique changes. Chrétien breaks the flow of the story not, as in *Erec*, to indulge in splendid descriptions nor, as in *Cligès*, to justify behaviour but, for the first time, to explain at length the key dakum of the plot. The Arthurian court can by now be taken for granted. If the static quality of Arthur and the rational responses of Gawain needed no justification in *Erec*, still less do they need it—or get it—in this later romance. The cart, however, is a different matter. It is the object which will provide the hero with the opportunity of displaying his special kind of heroism. It is through the cart that we learn of the motivation that furnishes the hero the dynamic energy to carry him through the romance. By providing in inseparable combination both the means of proving love and enduring dishonour, the cart is a very economical device. Chrétien makes sure that no–one can underestimate the significance it has in his story by devoting twenty–four lines to describing its dreadful purpose. He begins:

> De ce servoit charrete lores,
> Don li pilori servent ores.                          (ll. 323–24)

By distinguishing the "ores" of the time of telling the story from a "lores" when customs were unrecognizably different, Chrétien changes the style of his narrative. The immediacy of the first part is lost. Chrétien has now introduced himself as the mediator of his tale: it is a change from the manner of *Erec* to that of *Cligès*—from showing to telling. Gawain or the dwarf who drives the cart could have been used to tell us about it. The fact that Chrétien intervenes here indicates the direction in which he is moving the narrative. We are being moved from action to discourse, as a prelude to the analysis of Lancelot's mind and the subsequent internalization of his adventures.

Later, just before we are plunged again into Lancelot's mind, Chrétien inserts a similar explanatory discourse. The Hospitable Damsel insists on accompanying Lancelot and demanding his protection. The decision is not a difficult one for Lancelot to take: he has already protected her against her own household. Yet Chrétien stops the narrative for twenty lines (ll. 1314–33) to explain exactly what the custom of this protection will involve. Once again it is a matter that is unknown to Chrétien's public and placed in the distant past. This time the past is distant even from the characters in the story, as we learn from the damsel herself when she asks Lancelot if he will escort her

> "Par les us et par les costumes
> Qui furent ainz que nos ne fumes
> El reaume de Logres mises."          (ll. 1311–13)

This is very far back to be taken for such a digression. It not only holds up the narrative, but serves to distance us from it. Lancelot's world is emphatically remote from us, as he is from those who surround him. On this occasion he falls into ecstatic contemplation of the hairs left in Guinevere's comb and the damsel cannot hope to penetrate his meditations.

To return to the cart, which is of capital importance as it leads directly to the central crisis of the romance. Lancelot (as yet nameless) goes up to it, sees a dwarf riding on it and asks him if he has seen the queen (ll. 348–55). It is our first indication that Lancelot knows, inexplicably, that she has been abducted.[16] The dwarf tells him that if he gets into the cart he will find out what has become of her before the next day. The unknown knight hesitates to get into the terrible cart, but only briefly:

> Tant solemant deus pas demore
> Li chevaliers que il n'i monte.          (ll. 364–65)

It is here that he marks himself out as the hero, and a hero unlike any Chrétien has yet shown us. Up to the moment of his decisive act we know nothing about Lancelot. Erec's name, age, social status, reputation and assured position at Arthur's court are all spelled out for us when we are first introduced to him. We have full details about Alexander's family and we know Cligès literally from the cradle. But we get no information about Lancelot, we are told nothing of his position at court or even about his family. Very much later (ll. 2354–62) we are told that he was brought up by a "fee." A Lanceloz del Lac already figures in *Erec* and *Cligès*, though without the fairy foster-mother. Some Lancelot tradition already existed and, if the fairy is part of the tradition, as seems likely, then she may have been the deciding factor which made Chrétien choose Lancelot to play the role of an "amis antiers" (l. 3818). He needed a hero with no human ties. Chrétien presents him to us as a knight with no social background and with scarcely any physical being. Chrétien never describes him and keeps his very name from us for half of the romance.

Erec establishes his identity by prompt and rapid action in his pursuit of Yder. Lancelot, introduced in the course of a pursuit, establishes his identity by making a particular decision from which all his other actions will stem. The focus of the narrative is moved from the external to the internal. The opening sequence of the *Charrette* proceeds from action to discourse and then to allegory. Alexander and Soredamors had

---

[16]Lancelot appears to respond, as if by telepathy, to the queen's words at ll. 211–13. For a discussion of these lines, see Kelly, *Sens and Conjointure*, 105–106 and Frappier, "Remarques sur le texte du *Chevalier de la Charrette*," 317–31.

submitted themselves to Love. Lancelot is torn between the conflicting claims of Love and Reason. There is a brief but telling psychomachia. Reason is only in his mouth: Love comes from deeper within him, from his heart, seat of his true wishes. Lancelot obeys his deepest desires in obeying the imperious dictates of Love. Yet Reason is never dislodged: he will always consider it his duty to have a reasonable regard for the demands of chivalry.

Lancelot's inner debate lasts only a dozen lines (ll. 369–81), but it is enough to make clear the peculiar quality of his love. What saves him as a hero, and what saves his submission to Guinevere from becoming despicable abjection, is that the initial submission he makes to Love is a voluntary one and that this submission and the service it entails are only accessible to the highest natures. This is the real significance of Lancelot's hesitation in mounting the cart. It provides an important twist to the plot later on by provoking Guinevere's anger; it also prompts a reaffirmation of Lancelot's prowess in the episode of the Flaming Lance and in the combat with the Arrogant Knight. First and foremost, however, it shows us Lancelot's will at work. The hesitation is described for us in two lines; the mental balancing of alternatives takes twelve. Realistically enough, the choice is not made in an ethical vacuum. Lancelot knows what his values are. It is not, so to speak, that he loves honour less, but that he loves Love more. If Love is already in the deepest part of his being, his decision is perhaps inevitable, though it is only at the moment of choice that he becomes aware of the greater value he gives it. He submits his own will to the will of that power that he acknowledges as even greater than Reason:

> Amors le viaut, et il i saut;
> Que de la honte ne li chaut
> Puis qu'amors le comande et viaut.          (ll. 379–81)

After such a decision, formalized by such an action, Lancelot will never be his own man again. After sacrificing all worldly considerations to the interests of love, he will never again hesitate to do what Love commands. After he gets into the cart, he becomes lost to all considerations of selfish interest and is no longer any freer with regard to Love than a serf with regard to his lord's wishes.

Lancelot's love comes close to resembling servitude, an idea abhorrent to twelfth-century feeling. We recall how eager the serf Jehan was for his master to make him free (Cligès, ll. 5491–505). Secular vernacular literature was composed for the glorification of a free class. The imperious quality of Erec's will is a characteristic of such freedom. References to the lower, less free estates are always derogatory, as we see at the beginning of the Roman de Thèbes, the end of Erec and throughout Guillaume d'Angleterre. The peculiar horror of serfdom, as R. Southern has pointed out, was due, not to the subordination of one group to another, but to its arbitrariness. The higher one rose in the social scale towards freedom, the more one's life was ruled, not by the arbitrary will of one's superior, but by rationally justified laws. What gave the free man his dignity was not that he could do what he liked, but that he could choose what law to submit to. The logical conclusion of this attitude is not difficult to imagine:

The highest law of all was that in obedience to which a man stripped himself of this world's goods and subjected himself to religious poverty and obedience. But this state had nothing in common—as the writers of the period were almost too anxious to point out—with that of ordinary poverty, the common lot of the majority of men who of necessity were poor. The monk had chosen his poverty and servitude.[17]

Chrétien borrows some of the marks of the service of divine love for his depiction of the service of human love carried to an almost superhuman extreme. For Lancelot, the abnegation of the self is the voluntary means of attaining a level of experience inaccessible to ordinary men. The terms in which his interior debate are couched are significantly non-personal. He does not say, for example, "I love Guinevere, so I will have no selfish concern with my own honour." No reference is made to any personal element at all, not even to a name. It will not be a relationship between two individuals. Even after their night of love, Lancelot and Guinevere never have the individual-to-individual relationship of Erec and Enide. We know nothing about the relationship of Lancelot and Guinevere before the abduction. All we know is that the queen, when she is being led off by Kay, murmurs an appeal (ll. 211–13); to whom, we are not sure, but apparently to the absent Lancelot and he, as if telepathically informed of what has happened, appears out of nowhere, motivated by a love already "anclose" in his heart (l. 376). Yet it is a love that is not in the first instance described as being attached to Guinevere. The Amors which dictates its commands to the hero has an abstract flavour which blends in well with Lancelot's quasi-religious vocation. Once he has committed himself to this way of life, nothing remains for him to do except to perfect his submission. "Mout est qui aimme obeïssanz," as Chrétien tells us (l. 3816). When the queen, at the intercession of Bademagu, expresses a wish that the combat between Lancelot and Meleagant should be halted, Lancelot obeys instantly, in spite of the danger he puts himself in from his unchivalrous opponent, who continues to fight. At Noauz, as we have seen, Lancelot obeys a much more difficult command with equally unquestioning readiness. By her alternation of imperious commands, Guinevere elicits more than Lancelot's name, she causes him to reveal his full identity. If perfect obedience is the sign of a perfect lover, then the harder the command, the more credit accrues to the one who obeys it. Chrétien is not concerned that what Lancelot

---

[17]Southern, *Making of the Middle Ages*, 107.

gains by his act of submission is paid for by an increase in imperiousness in the character he confers on Guinevere.

Lancelot is not only committed to obedience. His way of life entails something of the poverty and even of the chastity of a religious vocation. Material goods are used only as a necessary means to an end: he does not wait to choose between the relative merits of Gawain's spare horses (ll. 292-97); he accepts even unwelcome shelter (ll. 966-69); he reproaches his fellow fighters of Logres for wasting time over choosing his lodging (ll. 2470-81); the horse he is given by the Second Hospitable Vavassour he gives away to one of his young companions (ll. 3002-11); the horses he wins at Noauz he also gives away (ll. 6002-03). Lancelot's exceptional love for Guinevere even makes him relatively chaste: he is astonishingly self-controlled in the face of the quite sensational attempts of the Hospitable Damsel to arouse his interest in her (ll. 1092-98). The quasi-religious tone is carried into the very expression of Lancelot's love. Like Alexander, he treats his lady's hair like a holy relic (ll. 1472-90), but he goes much further: as he enters and leaves Guinevere's bedroom, he genuflects before her bed as if it were an altar (ll. 4669-71; 4734-36).

We might think that such apparent blasphemy indicates that Lancelot's love is excessive, but Chrétien tells us explicitly that we are to understand it as the privileged constraint of a rare soul:

> Tot le fet an un leu ester
> Amors qui toz les cuers justise.
> Toz?—Non fet, fors ceus qu'ele prise.
> Et cil se redoit plus prisier
> Que Amors daigne justisier.
> Amors le cuer celui prisoit
> Tant que sor toz le justisoit.                    (ll. 1244-50)

Constancy such as Lancelot's is only available to those who are highly valued by Love and the more a lover is dominated by Love the more he is to be valued.

Chrétien is clearly not aiming for realism, in the sense that the love he describes is by definition wholly exceptional and far removed from the representative lovers of his society. Lancelot is exceptional in every way. Frappier noted the strange duality of the character Chrétien gives him, the contrast between his complete self-abnegation as a lover and his lucid deliberation in dealing with the people he meets on his quest.[18] Yet Lancelot is no Erec in his dealings with the outside world. He is deliberate, but his deliberateness serves primarily to give dignity to his commitment to love. The ecstatic lover must be capable of self-possession in his dealings with others if he is to be taken seriously. It is

---

[18]Frappier, *Chrétien de Troyes*, 139.

Lancelot's calm competence that saves him from becoming a Don Quixote.

Once this new and as yet nameless hero springs into the cart, he acquires an identity, but not a character. On the contrary, the abnegation of his will deprives him of anything a modern reader can recognize as a personality. He withdraws from the outside world in which people converse about mundane matters into the world of meditation where no-one can follow him. Besides being the Knight of the Cart, he becomes identified, after his first adventure, that of the Flaming Lance, as the abstracted knight, the "chevaliers pansis." He thinks while Gawain talks:

> As fenestres devers la pree
> S'assist li chevaliers pansis,
> Cil qui sor la charrete ot sis,
> Et esgardoit aval les prez.
> A l'autre fenestre delez
> Estoit la pucele venue,
> Si l'avoit a consoil tenue
> Mes sire Gauvains . . .                                    (ll. 544–51)

When he and Gawain part company on the quest, Lancelot, the moment he is left alone, becomes lost in a thought which deprives him of all consciousness of the outside world and even of his identity:

> . . . cil de la charrete panse
> Con cil qui force ne deffanse
> N'a vers amor qui le justise;
> Et ses pansers est de tel guise
> Que lui meïsmes an oblie,
> Ne set s'il est ou s'il n'est mie,
> Ne ne li manbre de son non,
> Ne set s'il est armez ou non,
> Ne set ou va, ne set don vient.                          (ll. 715–23)

Here is the greatest narrative challenge we ever come across in Chrétien's works. The focus of our attention has been drawn back into the hero's mind, but this time there is nothing there that we can have described to us, the description proceeds almost entirely by negatives. There is no mental conflict which might provoke an allegorical dramatisation. Even the object of this intense meditation remains elusive. Guinevere becomes the nameless, de-individualized "she" of a single, unchanging, undeveloping thought:

> De rien nule ne li sovient
> Fors d'une sole, et por celi
> A mis les autres an obli.
> A cele sole panse tant
> Que il ne voit ne il n'antant.                            (ll. 724–28)

Perceval will at least have the blood on the snow to remind him of the associated characteristics of Blanchefleur. Lancelot is absorbed by a vision left undescribed and wholly devoid of any personal or material associations. Chrétien concentrates our attention on the singleness of his hero's thought. Everything else is subordinated to it: the whole narrative is made to simulate the state of Lancelot's mind. His physical self, the outside world and even the people he meets are reduced to a marginal, dreamlike existence on the fringes of Lancelot's consciousness.

Lancelot himself has no external character. Now that he has committed himself whole-heartedly to love, he has no more decisions to make and can make no kind of psychological progress. We are not dealing with a socially anchored, psychologically rounded character at all. The *Charrette* is a radically different kind of narrative from *Erec*. No doubt Erec was far from being just another knight: we see him distinguish himself publicly as early as the Tournament of Tenebroc. But he is only the first among equals, or at least among comparables. He and Yder are equal in combat: Erec's only superiority is that of rational motivation. Over and over again, Chrétien emphasizes how truly human Erec is in contrast to the world of the "marvellous." His heroism is in principle available to anyone who wishes to imitate him. If he momentarily cuts himself off from society, it is only to reintegrate himself into it all the better later on. He separates himself from Arthur's court at the beginning only to return to it with his bride; he leaves his own future kingdom only to return to it with a confident equilibrium established between love and chivalry and ready to take his place as its king.

Lancelot's case is a complete contrast. Arthur again sets the stage for the action by holding a great court, but this time the hero is absent, and his absence remains unexplained. Nameless and unannounced, he appears as if out of thin air at a particular point of the quest, pursues the queen and her abductor to the land from which no-one returns and is abandoned by Chrétien in an isolated tower. Even in the quest section a large part of the action takes place in an area that it is impossible to identify. The Damsel of the Crossroads declares that the entrance to Gorre is by means of the two perilous bridges (ll. 657–59), yet days before Lancelot reaches his bridge he is told by the First Hospitable Vavassour that he will never get back to Logres but be condemned to exile like him (ll. 2087–116). The boundaries shift and the significant dividing lines of the story are determined only by the successive phases of the quest.

The queen is led off by Kay, and Gawain persuades Arthur to follow them; Arthur, who cuts a very poor figure here, agrees and even leads the expedition, but almost at once disappears from it. Everyone sees Kay's horse return alone from the forest and understands that he has lost the queen to Meleagant. Arthur is mentioned no more and it is his nephew who takes the lead:

Bien loing devant tote la rote
Mes sire Gauvains chevauchoit:
Ne tarda gueires que il voit
Venir un chevalier . . . (ll. 270–73)

Within the space of five lines the husband's place has been taken over by
the lover. The Arthurian court and its king are silently left behind and
no backward glances are ever cast in their direction. Gawain is marked
out from the others by being alone in the lead. It is at this point that the
kingdom of Logres effectively disappears along with its king. All that
lies before Gawain is the long road of the quest on which he will have
no support from the Arthurian world, and no protection from its ruler.
Between the vanishing figure of King Arthur at this point and the
sudden appearance of King Bademagu on the other side of the Sword
Bridge, there lies the limbo terrain of the quest which is controlled by
neither.[19]

Gawain, left alone, is almost immediately joined by the nameless
knight who will be the true hero of the quest. The discreet separation of
husband and lover, the silent obliteration of Arthur before the introduction of Lancelot is the first significant dividing line of the romance and
it is bridged only by Gawain. We have moved away from the magnificent
assembly of Arthur's court (ll. 31–42), which always constitutes the focal
point of Chrétien's fiction and a level of social normality, across an
invisible frontier into a world where little is social and nothing is normal.
Nevertheless, from Lancelot's first appearance to his crossing of the
Sword Bridge the narrative has a unity of manner which derives entirely
from Chrétien's concentration on what goes on inside his hero's mind.

The division between Arthur's world and Lancelot's is unique in
Chrétien's works. All the other heroes either start out from Arthur's
court, like Erec or Yvain, or look to it to validate their chivalrous
aspirations like Alexander, Cligès and Perceval. The reason is, of course,
that Lancelot, inasmuch as he loves the queen, is setting himself up as
a rival to Arthur, and Chrétien avoids giving this rivalry any social
dimension. He isolates Lancelot from Arthur's world and even deprives
him of the remotest prospect of a domain of his own like those heroes
who are destined for marriage. Lancelot must be kept well away from
Arthur in order to minimize the wrong that is done the king. Chrétien
certainly does not show us an adulterer who is bent on irresponsible
pleasure: the adultery is as minimal as possible and takes place in the
remote and mysterious kingdom of Gorre long after Guinevere's husband has dropped out of sight and in circumstances, moreover, in which

---

[19]Kelly argues that the boundary of Gorre is at the Future Cemetery; see "Two Problems
in Chrétien's *Charrette*." It is true that the cemetery marks the end of the first phase of
Lancelot's quest, but he does not arrive in Bademagu's kingdom until he crosses the Sword
Bridge, the frontier indicated by the Damsel of the Crossroads.

it is portrayed as the reparation of an injury and the merited reward for an incomparable service.

For a character who is hardly ever alone, Lancelot is remarkably isolated. It is not only the circumstances of the adultery that isolate him; Chrétien constantly underlines the solitude of his all but superhuman hero. Ordinary people will never understand him. The moment after he gets into the cart, Gawain hastens up and looks at him in amazement. Gawain too asks the dwarf for news of the queen and is told to get into the cart if he hates himself as much as the knight who is there already. Naturally Gawain rejects the suggestion as madness: he is sensibly equipped with a spare horse. He will never be so intent on his object as to disregard the means to the end: he will never wear out his horse and still less will he dream of getting into the infamous cart. Neither the evil dwarf nor the reasonable Gawain ever understands what goes on in Lancelot's mind. From the moment he gets into the 'charrette', he is a being apart.

Once alone and plunged in thought, Lancelot is inevitably even more isolated, for the quality of his thought withdraws him from the physical world. He thinks of Guinevere in a way in which it is not possible to imagine Erec thinking of Enide. True, Erec gives himself up to love even too exclusively, but it is to the physical person of Enide, not to an abstract meditation on her. Lancelot's thought is so devoid of all immediate cause, all personal detail, all specific feeling, hope or anxiety that it becomes an isolating force. His kind of love is an end in itself. It will have its moment of physical realization, but it does not depend on physical satisfaction. Lancelot loves Guinevere whether she is absent, angry or unreasonably demanding and even when he thinks she is dead. Inevitably, the depersonalization of love affects our understanding of Guinevere, who remains remote. We can learn nothing about her from Lancelot, who cuts himself off from all social intercourse in order to commune with an ideal inaccessible to everyone else.

The intense, but undifferentiated quality of Lancelot's thought affects the narrative. Lancelot may be unconscious of where he is heading, but such is the force of his aspiration towards Guinevere that it appears to be communicated to his horse:

> A cele sole panse tant
> Que il ne voit ne il n'antant;
> Et ses chevaus mout tost l'an porte,
> Qu'il ne vet mie voie torte,
> Mes la meillor et la plus droite.                    (ll. 727-31)

His thought has the effect of compressing distance. Though he rides absorbed in this single thought from shortly after prime when he and Gawain meet the Damsel of the Crossroads (l. 609) to "pres none basse" (l. 739) when he reaches the ford, the whole external activity for the day is condensed into those three lines describing what his horse did.

Though he is almost magically propelled by the force of his thought, it is not because of any sense of material urgency. The thought is a source of pleasure in itself and he means to punish the Knight of the Ford for depriving him of it (ll. 894–97). Later on, he is displeased when the Hospitable Damsel insists not only on foisting her company on him, but also her conversation, when all he wants to do is resume his meditation (l. 1347). She can even lead him astray for a time, because he takes such intense pleasure in feeding on his thoughts that it excludes all external observation (ll. 1373–74).

A profound meditation which cannot be particularized tends to condense the narrative; deliberative thought on the other hand is expanded in the narrative to take up far more time than can possibly coincide with the time of the deliberation. So we saw Lancelot hesitating for the space of two steps and deliberating for the space of a dozen lines, at the occasion of entering the cart. With even more exaggeration, Lancelot deliberates over coming to the help of his hostess, the Hospitable Damsel. He sees her apparently on the point of being raped and with six men blocking his way to the rescue. "Deus," he says, "que porrai je feire?" (l. 1109) and he embarks on a twenty–nine line soliloquy in order to prove to himself that any display of cowardice will make him liable to fail in his quest, that honour, which he values more than life, bids him accept the challenge, that obstacles only increase the honour to be gained and that therefore he should come to her rescue. She cries for help at line 1091 and he makes no move to respond until line 1138, yet he is still in plenty of time. External action is suspended while we are switched to the different time scale of deliberation. Similarly, when the Avenging Damsel asks Lancelot for the head of the Arrogant Knight, he is torn by conflicting impulses. On the one hand, he wishes to show pity to the knight and on the other, he wishes to show liberality to the damsel. These two chivalrous virtues, each very much a part of his personality (l. 2854), struggle for victory in his mind and we are given another allegorized psychomachia, this time between Largesce and Pitiez (ll. 2852–79). It is not his victory over the Arrogant Knight that is significant, but the elaborate deliberation over a moral choice.

Time and space can be abolished altogether when it comes to transmitting information. The queen murmurs an appeal as she is led off by Kay and a few lines later Lancelot rides up, fully aware of her abduction. The knights and ladies in the meadow know instantly that Lancelot has been in the cart, though they know nothing of his identity and still less of his chivalrous qualities (ll. 1675–84). The Arrogant Knight also knows that Lancelot has been in the cart and, much more mysteriously, the queen knows that he hesitated for two steps to get into it. As the story is concentrated on Lancelot, naturally all the information is about him, but however rapidly or mysteriously it flies, Chrétien only lets it travel in one direction. No news of Lancelot moves back across the no-man's-land of the quest to Arthur's court. When the

Knight of the Ford is defeated in fair combat, he is not sent back to
Arthur's court to increase Lancelot's fame. Chrétien makes the knight's
lady intervene and have him granted not only mercy but complete
release (ll. 922–934). It is no part of Chrétien's purpose to use Arthur's
court as the touchstone of the hero's qualities. On the contrary, he has
every reason to dissociate Lancelot from Arthur and to concentrate our
attention on the forward movement of the quest. The deliberateness of
Lancelot's progress is counterbalanced by the speed at which news of
him flies ahead.

At first the news is hostile. When Lancelot arrives in the cart at the
town of the Damsel of the Tower, the people in the streets do not fail to
shout insults at him (ll. 406–13). The Damsel thinks that he wants to
commit suicide in order to prevent the terrible news of his disgrace
becoming known (ll. 579–86). But an intuition of Lancelot's heroic
qualities soon flies ahead of him too. Even the Damsel of the Tower,
when she has finished reviling him, ends by giving him horse and lance
"par amor et par acordance" (l. 594). The Hospitable Damsel, who is told
nothing by Lancelot, nevertheless jumps to the correct conclusion:

> ". . . si con je pans et devin,
> Il viaut a si grant chose antandre
> Qu'ains chevaliers n'osa anprandre
> Si perilleuse ne si grief.                                    (ll. 1286–89)

In the same way, the Old Knight of the Meadow instantly divines the
quality of Lancelot's prowess and forbids his son to fight with him, a
command that amazes their inferiors (ll. 1750–54; 1827–40).

The most extreme projection of information takes us out of the
narrative altogether. In a cemetery he enters on his way to Gorre,
Lancelot sees the signs of the end of the whole Arthurian world in the
predestined tombs of Gawain, Yvain and others, and discovers that the
tombstone he succeeds in lifting, thereby confirming his predestined
role as the liberator of the peoople of Logres, will one day cover his own
tomb (ll. 1875–948). After this critical revelation, news spreads rapidly of
the arrival of the liberator. When the First Vavassour hears how
confident Lancelot is that he will return from Gorre, he remembers:

> Qu'an li avoit dit et conté
> Qu'uns chevaliers de grant bont'ace
> El païs a force venoit
> Por la reïne . . .                                            (ll. 2129–32)

His sons pass the information to their fellow fighters from Logres
(ll. 2425–33). Meanwhile, the squire of Gorre warns the Treacherous
Host that the people of Logres have attacked with the help of a leader
who, they say, sweeps all before him, and for a purpose:

> Et dïent an cest païs tuit
> Que il les deliverra toz.                                     (ll. 2312–13).

None of this can surprise us, as we know all about Lancelot's exploits, but it has no rational explanation on the level of the narrative. There were no witnesses to the episode of the Flaming Lance, or to the defeat of the Knight at the Ford, other than the knight's lady, or to the rescue of the Hospitable Damsel beyond her own household, or to the adventure of the Stony Gap, other than the two young men who have not left Lancelot's side since. The intense concentration of Lancelot's mind projects his purpose into the minds of other people. When he finally crosses the Sword Bridge, we find that not only does news of the hero spread instantly throughout the kingdom (ll. 3505-13) but that the maidens from Arthur's kingdom have already been fasting for three days in anticipation of the arrival of this predestined liberator (ll. 3540-47).

The characters who so mysteriously receive and transmit news of Lancelot have a disconcerting insubstantiality which contributes to the elusive, dreamlike atmosphere of the quest. The reason is not to be found in these characters, but in the way Chrétien chooses to depict his hero. Lancelot saps all life from the other characters. His attitudes to both love and reason are incomprehensible to anyone who has not seen inside his mind as we have, and they are not described in detail even to us. The characters in the story cannot hope to understand Lancelot and he, lost at every opportunity in profound and ecstatic meditation, scarcely notices them. We are not invited to survey the narrative from a position superior to the superhuman hero. Instead, the action is internalized in Lancelot's mind and the other characters are only allowed to have for us the marginal reality they have for him.

The split between Lancelot's world and the world outside is first indicated after his adventure with the Flaming Lance. Next morning, no comment is made about his heroic sang-froid of the previous midnight. Lancelot sits alone at a window, the "chevaliers pansis" (l. 545). The Damsel of the Tower is engaged in conversation by Gawain, a normal courtly event that Chrétien will allow us to glimpse, but not participate in. They spoke, he says,

> . . . ne sai de quoi:
> Ne sai don les paroles furent.                    (ll. 552-53)

When all three see a procession made up of a knight on a bier, three lamenting damsels, and a company led by a tall knight escorting a lady, Lancelot is singled out in his response:

> Li chevaliers de la fenestre
> Conut que c'estoit la reïne.                       (ll. 564-65)

His recognition goes far beyond the merely physical, for he ignores the limits imposed by his material circumstances in his overpowering desire to follow the queen:

> . . . quant plus ne la pot veoir,
> Si se vost jus leissier cheoir
> Et trebuchier a val son cors.                    (ll. 569–771)

The reasonable Gawain hauls him back and reproaches him for so
hating his life. The damsel thinks it is perfectly understandable that a
man who has been in the infamous cart should want to end his life.
Their suppositions are logical but wrong. They have no access to
Lancelot's mind.

One of the characteristics of Lancelot's thought is that it makes him
forget his identity and even his name (ll. 718–21). Chrétien incorporates
this point into the narrative: as if we were part of Lancelot's mind, we
are left ignorant of his identity until the source of his abstraction, the
queen, finally reveals it (l. 3676). This anonymity is transmitted to the
other characters for, of all the principal characters in the plot, only two,
Meleagant and Bademagu, are named newcomers. Arthur, Guinevere,
Kay, Gawain and Lancelot have already been named in other romances.
In the *Charrette*, the hero's name is held in suspense and the villain's is
not revealed until long after he has disappeared from Arthur's court.

The romance gives the impression of having a teeming cast of
characters. Lancelot is endlessly meeting new figures, but they are never
given that essential mark of identity, a name. Chrétien never names the
Dwarf of the Cart (l. 349), the Damsel of the Tower (l. 435), the Damsel
of the Crossroads (l. 611), the Knight of the Ford (l. 736), his lady
(l. 737), the Hospitable Damsel (l. 943), her suitor (l. 1521), the Old
Knight of the Meadow (l. 1661), the Hermit of the Cemetery (l. 1885),
the First Vavassour (l. 2028), his first son (l. 2185), his second son
(l. 2192), the Watchman of the Stony Gap (l. 2113), the Knight of the
Stony Gap (l. 2124), the Treacherous Host (l. 2269), the Squire of Gorre
(l. 2296), the Hospitable Lady (l. 2525) and her husband, the Second
Vavassour (l. 2554), the Arrogant Knight (l. 2581), the Avenging Damsel
(Meleagant's sister) (l. 2795), Guinevere's Damsel (l. 3651), the Treach-
erous Dwarf (l. 5078), Meleagant's Seneschal (l. 5445), the Seneschal's
Wife (l. 5457), the Herald (l. 5556) and Guinevere's Messenger (l. 5657).

All these twenty–six characters make at least one speech, but they are
never distinguished by name. It is not impossible that the two evil
dwarves are one, or that Guinevere is twice attended by the same
damsel. All but the Seneschal speak directly to Lancelot or, like the Old
Knight or the Squire, speak in his presence about him. They all exist
only in function of the hero and are granted no naturalistic autonomy.
The subsidiary characters of *Erec* and *Cligès* were drawn with a concern
for consistency. Not so the minor figures of the *Charrette*. Here Chrétien
focusses our gaze so intently on the central character that the marginal
figures are distorted into insignificance.

The secondary figures can be both insubstantial and inconsistent. The
most striking example is the Hospitable Damsel, who is consistent
neither in her character nor in the function she fulfils on Lancelot's

quest. We see her first in a positive role: beautiful and well-bred, she appears at nightfall offering the shelter Lancelot needs (ll. 942–52). As she seems to have no other object but to welcome Lancelot, and as she tells him that her lodgings are made ready for him, one might think that she was expecting him. Yet this cannot be the case, as she does not know who he is and torments him in vain next day to find out his name (ll. 2009–19). Her house is deserted, yet someone has lowered the drawbridge, lit the candles and filled the basins with water. The water is hot, though no servants are visible (ll. 981–1009). They eat, then the damsel tells him to go outside and amuse himself for a while until he thinks that she may be in bed. He does so, and comes back to find that she is apparently on the point of being raped. This sensational spectacle fails to excite him (ll. 1095–98), but he duly rescues his hostess, who then dismisses her attackers as members of her household (ll. 1194–1203). Honour makes Lancelot fight for her, but Love prevents him from making love to her. Eventually she gives up and goes off to sleep on her own, guessing neither Lancelot's identity nor, surprisingly, the state of his affections, but only the fact that he is bound on some significant mission; she ends by asking God to grant him success (l. 1290).

The next morning, however, she does her best to hinder his mission by asking him to be her escort and defender against any knight they may meet on the way. When they reach the fountain with the queen's comb on its ledge, she does not want Lancelot to see it and takes him out of the right road of his quest (ll. 1369–95). Why? It cannot be jealousy, because she has given him up with good grace and she has guessed nothing of his love for Guinevere. She tells him without very much pressing who the hair in the comb belongs to and is surprised when he betrays strong feeling over it (ll. 1414–68). An unwelcome admirer of hers appears and is only dissuaded from attempting to take her by force from Lancelot when the newcomer's father, the Old Knight of the Meadow, intervenes. She pays no attention, but stays with Lancelot until after his adventure at the Future Cemetery and then, having failed to find out who he is, takes her leave, to his relief. She appears out of nowhere when Lancelot needs shelter and disappears into nowhere leaving no trace of her passage. She is with Lancelot for longer than any other character in the romance (ll. 942–2022) but she has neither future nor past in the narrative. She is an odd mixture of power and weakness, knowledge and ignorance, and positive and negative feelings towards the hero, and she moves from helping to hindering his mission and back again without any motivational coherence.

She is clearly a woman to be contrasted with Guinevere, to whom Lancelot shows such admirable fidelity, but she is very different from Mabonagrain's 'amie', who is also contrasted with the heroine, who also remains anonymous and who also functions in mysterious surroundings. The differences are radical. The girl in *Erec* is motivated in an entirely coherent, if unsympathetic way and her fate is to be drawn willy–nilly out of her "marvellous" isolation and integrated into courtly society. Nor is the Hospitable Damsel to be compared with Thessala, though she does help the hero to some extent. Thessala is the heroine's right arm and she is available to help Cligès and Fenice to the very end. If her potions are somewhat mechanically produced, the consistency of her loyalty gives her substance.

Thus a character who has some importance in the story and whom Chrétien was perfectly capable of turning into a coherent and consistent minor figure disintegrates as soon as we try to analyse her. In *Erec* and *Cligès* the secondary characters are all perfectly plausible. They are more individualized in *Erec* which is more concerned with a social context than *Cligès*; no-one, for example, would confuse the vain Count Galoain with the brutal Count Oringle, though the roles they play are very similar. *Lancelot*, on the contrary, is the romance of a highly exceptional and isolated individual. The Hospitable Damsel can have no other fate but to vanish, nameless, into nothingness because Lancelot's will, the centre of the action, is pulling against her all the time. She cannot impinge on his thought whether she helps or hinders him. She, like the other anonymous characters, has the shadowy quality of something seen out of the corner of the eye. If we were allowed to look at her fully and understand what makes her act as she does, she would distract us from concentrating on Lancelot, who will never have a social context into which she could be drawn and who must continue, uninterrupted, his meditation and his quest. He pulls away from her both physically and mentally: he will not speak to her on their journey and is glad when she leaves him; even on their first meeting, he is relieved when he does not have to have contact with her to the degree of helping her to dismount (ll. 1016–18); he sweats with anguish as he undresses to get into bed with her in order to fulfil their bargain; he keeps as far away as possible from her in bed, turning his back on her and refusing to speak to her. We are at the opposite pole of those physical links which help to bind the elements of the social romance of *Erec*.

# VIII. The Manipulation of Obstacles

Despite his strong will and the urgency of his mission, Lancelot moves less rapidly and less directly than Erec. This change is undoubtedly due to the change in the content of the narrative. Once Erec sets out on his particular quest, all is grist to his mill: every obstacle overcome advances him, every new challenge urges him on. His quest is centred on his own problems and is an end in itself. Lancelot is out to rescue the queen and though he, like Erec, is concerned with both love and honour, they manifest themselves very differently in him. Love provides such a powerful motivation that at the critical episode of the cart it takes precedence over Lancelot's concern with reputation. Yet it is chivalrous prowess that makes it possible for Lancelot to serve Love successfully, even when the occasion of exercising this prowess has no causal connection with the rescue of Guinevere. He is explicit on this point himself. When he is faced with the prospect of fighting six armed men in order to rescue a hostess who is doing all she can to distract him from his preoccupation with Guinevere, he realizes that his mission requires that he act courageously even here, and indeed on all occasions:

> "Meüz sui por si grant afeire
> Con por la reïne Guenievre.
> Ne doi mie avoir cuer de lievre
> Quant por li sui an ceste queste.
> Se mauvestiez son cuer me preste
> Et je son comandemant faz,
> N'ateindrai pas la ou je chaz."  (ll. 1110–16)

Chivalrous worth is essential to the service of Love, and it is Lancelot's worth as a knight that guarantees his worth as a lover. After the episode of the cart, he is to some extent in Erec's position, having lost his honour in the sight of everyone. His quest is divided: the pursuit of love requires prowess, yet causes chivalrous dishonour. Pursuing love and regaining honour will not be connected as they were for Erec, but on the other hand love and prowess will not be rigidly separated as they were for Alexander.

Lancelot moves more slowly and deliberately than Erec for two reasons. First, his love, as we have seen, is of such an exceptional kind that Chrétien must explain it and demonstrate its effects on him. It cannot be taken for granted like the more "normal" love of Erec which, even when it became too exclusive, had nothing superhuman about it.

137

Second, his reputation, once destroyed, must be restored, not for his own glory as with Erec, but in order to convince Chrétien's public he is a worthy follower of Love.

As regards the narrative, the demands of love and of prowess are neither integrated as they were with Erec nor alternated as they were with Alexander. Instead, the first part of Lancelot's quest is pursued in a zig–zag movement, as the hero veers from actions that demonstrate his love to actions that demonstrate his prowess. His first and decisive action is to get into the cart, thus showing his love; the next action must show us his chivalry. So when the Damsel of the Tower forbids him to sleep in a particular bed precisely because of his disgrace in the cart, he accepts the implied challenge instantly, insists on sleeping in it and achieves the adventure of the Flaming Lance, which has no direct link with his quest for the queen but demonstrates that his prowess has not been adversely affected by his disregard for honour. His desire to efface the shame of the cart makes him superior in daring at least to his companion Gawain. Next morning we are given a second demonstration of love: the 'chevaliers pansis' is ready to fling himself out of a window in order to follow his view of Guinevere. This is balanced by a second demonstration of prowess: he accepts the most perilous road to Gorre, the one that will lead him later to the Sword Bridge. There quickly follows a third demonstration of prowess when he is interrupted by the Knight of the Ford, whom he duly defeats in single combat.

Love is now put to a direct test: the amorous Hospitable Damsel tries to oblige him to sleep with her, but he is "trestoz nerciz" by the invitation (l. 958). Nevertheless, he displays the prowess he knows to be essential to his quest by responding bravely to her cries for help. In bed, he rejects her resolutely and she in return recognizes his great worth as a knight. Next day, he falls into a trance while contemplating the hair Guinevere had left in a comb, but he shows himself ready to respond to the aggressive challenge issued by the damsel's unwelcome admirer. These five demonstrations of love alternating with five demonstrations of chivalry are brought to a conclusion by the Old Knight of the Meadow, who mysteriously recognizes Lancelot's worth, though no demonstration of it has been made to him. The prophetic episode of the Future Cemetery marks the turning point of the quest. Love and reputation having been established and reconciled, Lancelot is ready to receive prophetic confirmation of his mission, and the last part of the quest will be devoted to rallying the people of Logres and overcoming the last obstacle, that of the Sword Bridge.

On three occasions the obstacles are combined in a curious and original way to test Lancelot's courage and to show how the exterior world is subordinated to his heroic mind. The usual way of testing heroes is by straightforward fighting, and Lancelot has his quota of all its varieties: five single combats, of which one is with the Knight of the Ford, one with the Arrogant Knight and no fewer than three with

Meleagant; he also takes part in a general mêlée in which large numbers of the people of Logres fight the people of Gorre, and he distinguishes himself at a tournament. But on three occasions his display of prowess takes a turn particularly appropriate to such a pensive hero. He goes unarmed to the rescue of the Hospitable Damsel and, by dint of courage and dexterity, puts himself in an advantageous fighting position: he is about to take on all that remain battleworthy of her attackers when the damsel simply dismisses them as members of her household and they vanish without a murmur and without a trace as if they had never existed outside his imagination (ll. 1138–203).

Much later, Lancelot is making his way to the Sword Bridge by the shortest route, which leads through the Stony Gap. It is so narrow that only one man at a time may pass through and it is well guarded. It is an admirable test of a single, exceptional knight and Lancelot loses no time in getting there. The watchman of the Gap warns the knight on guard who at once charges out to attack Lancelot. But he breaks his lance and drops the pieces and Lancelot makes short work of him. The men at arms in attendance on the knight then leap forward

> Mes a esciant a lui faillent,
> Qu'il n'ont talant de feire mal
> Ne a lui ne a son cheval.          (ll. 2242–44)

With no warning, no further fighting is necessary. Lancelot does not even bother to draw his sword against them. He has faced the Knight of the Gap and all the accompanying dangers melt away.

The third case is the most striking. Having at last reached the Sword Bridge, Lancelot and his two young companions think they see two lions waiting at the other side; the two young men tremble with fear on Lancelot's behalf and do their best to dissuade him from facing two such terrible adversaries (ll. 3046–91). Lancelot goes ahead regardless; he makes his painful and bleeding way across the bridge and successfully reaches the other side. Then he remembers about the lions and looks and sees nothing there to harm him. It seems, once again, that it was enough for him to face this danger to make it disappear.

The material world dissolves before Lancelot's determined courage. At the Sword Bridge, Lancelot realizes that he has been deceived and enchanted, in other words deluded (ll. 3132–48). It is not only that Lancelot's world is drained of those rounded characters and socially integrated actions that make the background of Erec's adventures so solid and convincing but, withdrawn into his preoccupations as he is, Lancelot can draw after him even material reality, or what appears as reality to others less inspired and therefore less intrepid. Danger from man or beast, once dismissed by Lancelot's mind, ceases to exist and those who threaten him disappear likewise. The only true reality of the romance is what goes on in the hero's mind.

In the *Charrette* as in *Erec*, Chrétien rejects the "marvellous," but with some interesting new variations. Lancelot, far from having Erec's well-anchored family ties, was brought up by a fairy, as we discover in the second half of his quest (ll. 2357-59). He calls confidently for her help, but not to avoid danger or obtain any unfair advantage. She gave him a magic ring, but it does not solve his problems in the way that Thessala's potions solve the problems of Cligès and Fenice. On the contrary, it is a touchstone to show him the difference between appearance and reality. When the portcullises of a castle crash down unexpectedly and trap Lancelot and his two companions, they fear that they may be the victims of a hostile enchantment (ll. 2330-46). Lancelot's ring has only a negative function: he is enabled to tell the delusions of magic from the reality of a treacherous trap. All that the ring tells him is that the trap is real: he gets no supernatural help in battering down the postern gate to escape. The ring tells him that the lions were unreal but it is love, not magic, that enabled him to face the obstacle and cross the Sword Bridge (ll. 3127-29).

There is no magic at work in the *Charrette*, but there is an acute sense of the "marvellous." Throughout the quest section of the romance, all marvelling is withdrawn from the extraordinary people and obstacles Lancelot encounters, and is directed at Lancelot himself. Before the quest begins, Gawain marvels at the behavior of Arthur (l. 229) as he might have marvelled in *Erec*. But once Lancelot appears, the only marvel is the hero himself. In *Erec*, people marvel at all sorts of people and things. In the *Charrette*, Chrétien's use of the term is much more rigorous. Gawain marvels when he catches up with Lancelot and finds that he has just mounted the cart (l. 385). He cannot comprehend such an action, having himself no reason to commit such 'folie'. As soon as they arrive at the town of the Damsel of the Tower, all the people marvel (l. 407) and make no secret of their scorn. The Hospitable Damsel marvels (l. 1441) when she sees Lancelot so wholly overcome at the contemplation of the hairs in the comb that she thinks he has fainted.

The marvelling takes on a more positive note of approval at the Future Cemetery. The Hermit almost collapses with surprise when he sees Lancelot perform the marvel (l. 1929) of lifting the prophetic tomb cover; and he recounts the marvel (l. 1980) to the Old Knight of the Meadow and his son. When Lancelot announces himself to the First Vavassour as being newly arrived from Logres, his host is duly amazed:

> Si s'an mervoille duremant
> Et sa fame et si anfant tuit.                    (ll. 2096-97).

When Lancelot is victorious at the Stony Gap, his two companions are awestruck and one says to the other:

> "Don n'a il feite grant mervoille,
> Qui par ci est passez a force?"                    (ll. 2254-55)

Lancelot plunges into the mêlée between the men of Gorre and those of Logres, and though there are a thousand on either side he fights so remarkably that "cil de Logres s'an mervoillent" (l. 2421) and, on hearing that he has come to liberate them, fight all the better themselves. When the household of the Second Vavassour discover that their guest has been in the infamous cart, they marvel exceedingly (l. 2619), unable to reconcile Lancelot's excellent appearance with such a dishonour. And when at last he reaches the Sword Bridge and his companions are weeping with distress and fear, Lancelot performs a very strange marvel (l. 3110), actually disarming himself, so that he may the more surely, if the more painfully, cross the perilous bridge; Bademagu, from the other side, describes the feat he has just witnessed as a "mervoile" (l. 3209).

Only once does Lancelot do the marvelling. Sunk in thoughts of love, he fails to hear the Knight of the Ford's challenge and is knocked into the river. At the contact of the water, he comes back to himself, or rather to the outside world:

> Quant cil sant l'eve, si tressaut,
> Toz estordiz an estant saut,
> Aussi come cil qui s'esvoille,
> S'ot et si voit et se mervoille,
> Qui puet estre qui l'a feru.          (ll. 777–81)

The "marvellous" is the point of contact between Lancelot's interior world and the material world outside it. The quite conventional spectacle of a knight defending a ford becomes a cause for marvelling when seen from the point of view of someone withdrawn from the material world.

From the moment Lancelot meets the object of his thoughts, however, the focus of the "marvellous" changes and is concentrated for a time on the queen. Chrétien shifts our attention to Guinevere, and Lancelot loses the position of absolute centrality that he occupied all during the quest section of the romance. He achieves his purpose, defeats Meleagant and liberates the queen. He begs Bademagu to take him to the queen but she, against all expectation, far from welcoming her liberator, declares that she does not wish to see him. "Mout me mervoil," says the bewildered Bademagu to Lancelot (l. 4000). Kay is equally baffled; he cannot imagine why Guinevere is angry with Lancelot and marvels strangely (l. 4093). Lancelot no longer holds the heart of the mystery: he is as mystified as anyone else. When she finally relents, he dares to say

> ". . . Dame, mout me mervoil
> Por quoi tel sanblant me feïstes."          (ll. 4490–91)

It is only on their night of love, after all misunderstanding has been abolished between them, that they achieve a joint marvel:

> . . . il lor avint sanz mantir
> Une joie et une mervoille

Tel qu'onques ancor sa paroille
Ne fu oïe ne seüe.                                    (ll. 4694-97)

Marvels decrease in intensity once Lancelot returns to the more
conventional world of chivalry, and marvelling comes to mean nothing
more than a twist of the plot that will soon be elucidated. Lancelot is
surprised to see blood on his hands when he gets home (l. 4742). The
queen is surprised to see blood in her bed (l. 4797). Meleagant reports
this marvel to his father (l. 4821). The Seneschal's Wife cannot be
surprised that Lancelot wants to go to Noauz (l. 5467) and Lancelot
cannot be surprised if she fears Meleagant (l. 5486). Of course not: these
are quite understandable feelings. The horse she gives Lancelot is
"marvellously handsome, strong and brave" (l. 5520). There is such an
assembly of ladies at Noauz that it is a marvel (l. 5545), and they marvel
that the disgraced Red Knight should come back on the second day
(l. 5881). When he then distinguishes himself, the ladies "gaze on him
with marvellous intensity" (l. 6014). It is all conventional, not to say
banal.

Godefroi de Lagny understandably continues this conventional use
(ll. 6467; 6481; 6506; 6563; 6573; 6810; 6813). There is just one variant
that occurs when Meleagant attempts to impress his father:

Devant lui, por ce que il pere
Qu'il est preuz et de grant afeire,
Comança un sanblant a feire
Et une chiere merveilleuse.                           (ll. 6250-53)

It is hard to say what Godefroi means by "marvellous." Boastful?
Impressive? Intimidating? Chrétien never used the word in this context.

Godefroi's concluding uses are interesting, however. Meleagant,
thinking that he has Lancelot safely incarcerated in the tower, is
astounded when his prisoner appears out of the blue at Arthur's court
to answer his challenge:

A grant mervoille l'esgardoit
Por ce que si soudainnemant
Est venuz; et se je ne mant,
Mervoilles li sont avenues
Aussi granz con s'il fust des nues
Devant lui cheüz maintenant.                          (ll. 6810-15)

Here once more Lancelot makes another character marvel, but very
differently from in the quest section. Here we know from the inside all
the events that led up to the hero's sudden apparition. Only Meleagant
has cause to marvel, and he only marvels at the fact of Lancelot's
presence, not at his motivations, which remain hidden from him though
they are by now familiar to us. We know so much more than Meleagant
that, far from sharing his amazement, we are prompted to laugh at it. If
Lancelot has lost the superhuman aura of his quest, Meleagant is

degraded even in his villainy from the nameless challenger who paralysed the Arthurian court at the beginning of the romance.

In the course of such a story it is inevitable, as we saw in *Erec*, that a hero who continually confronts armed opponents must, sooner or later, suffer serious injury. If we are to believe in the gravity of the obstacles overcome by the hero, we must see their effect on him. In Lancelot's case, as in Roland's, the chief wounds he receives are not inflicted by another person, which might diminish his superiority. Instead, he receives them in accomplishing the marvel that no-one imagined possible, the crossing of the Sword Bridge. No magic protects him. All that makes this feat possible is Lancelot's rejection of fear and his confidence in divine protection for his mission. He reassures his young companions by saying

> ". . . j'ai tel foi et tel creance
> An Deu qu'il me garra par tot.
> Cest pont ne ceste eve ne dot
> Ne plus que ceste terre dure,
> Ainz me vuel metre an avanture
> De passer outre et atorner.
> Miauz vuel morir que retorner."          (ll. 3098–104)

If God protects him from death, Love protects him from unbearable pain:

> . . . tot le rassoage et sainne
> Amors qui le conduit et mainne,
> Si li est tot a sofrir douz.          (ll. 3127–29)

These are not arbitrarily external agents. They are effective only because of Lancelot's will, and though they make possible a feat which no-one on either side of the bridge imagined possible, they do not save Lancelot from the physical effects of conquering this last and greatest obstacle. The courteous Bademagu notes that he has been badly injured (l. 3366) and will need to have his wounds tended to for two or three weeks (l. 3415) before he can think of meeting his son Meleagant in single combat. Bademagu does not have any of the "marvellous" ointments prepared by Arthur's sister Morgan, but he offers a similar style of remedy. His "oignemant as trois Maries" (l. 3374) is not exclusive to himself or to Chrétien; it is also mentioned in the *Mort Aimeri de Narbonne*[1] and perhaps its religious tone is not fortuitous, for Bademagu also supplies Lancelot with

> . . . un cirurgiien,
> Leal home et buen crestiien.          (ll. 3497–98)

It is only what is appropriate for a saviour figure.

---

[1] See Foerster's note to line 3374 for this reference and a discussion of the three Marys in the New Testament.

Lancelot, in true heroic style, will not hear of accepting the weeks of inaction that Meleagant's father thinks essential to prepare him for this critical encounter. He agrees to one night's rest, and that more out of courtesy to his host than consideration to himself (ll. 3429-32). The surgeon does his best (ll. 3502-03), but there is no magical cure. On the contrary, in the battle with Meleagant, Lancelot's wounded hands tell against him (ll. 3638-41). Only the sight of the queen will make the vital difference.

Of all the anonymous women Lancelot meets on his quest and whom he sees, as it were, only out of the corner of his eye, none is more devoid of character, more undisguisedly functional than the Damsel of the Crossroads. She appears, gives Lancelot and Gawain directions for finding Gorre, and vanishes. She does nothing that would not have been done just as efficiently by a signpost. She is even placed like a signpost. They arrive at the Crossroads to find her there (l. 610) and they leave her there when they part. Once they have accepted her help, they give her no further thought. Yet, even though this damsel helps them, she too is a subtle form of obstacle in the narrative.

When she tells them that she can give them the information they require, Gawain offers her his services in return (ll. 625-30). Lancelot, however, goes much further. He does not prudently promise her "everything in his power" as Gawain had but, as one whom love makes supremely rich and powerful, promises to grant her anything she desires without restriction or delay (ll. 631-38). Love gives him far greater resources than Gawain and he is generous, even reckless, in offering them to one who helps in the service of Love.

It is not understood as an empty gesture of politeness either. The damsel leaves them with a reminder:

> ". . . Chascuns de vos me doit
> Un guerredon a mon gre randre
> Quel ore que jel voldrai prandre.
> Gardez, ne l'obliez vos mie!"                    (ll. 708-11)

It is a deliberate evocation of the world of *Erec*, where Arthurian society is bound together by such ties of obligation. But like all the other anonymous characters in the romance (with the single exception of the Avenging Damsel, who reappears as Meleagant's sister in Godefroi's conclusion to the story), the Damsel of the Crossroads is never heard of again. She ceases to exist as soon as she has performed her narrative function and neither Gawain nor Lancelot are ever shown remembering their debt of gratitude. What she achieves on the level of the progress of the narrative is that she balances her positive help with a negative condition. At any moment of the quest we can expect Lancelot to be confronted with the obstacle of a 'guerredon' to be granted at the arbitrary choice of the damsel. But this *Erec* type of obstacle is only evoked in order to be rejected. Everything in this hero's quest that is not drawn into his thoughts is pushed outwards into oblivion. Lancelot will never be made to look back and he pursues his goal unbound by any social ties, even those of the return of remembered services.

Similar loose threads hang at the end of the episode at the ford. Having defeated the knight, Lancelot grants him mercy on condition that he will constitute himself Lancelot's prisoner when called upon to do so. Then the knight's lady comes up to beg Lancelot to grant him full liberty, promising him in return a 'guerredon' some time in the future (ll. 929-31). Lancelot grants her request. He recognizes her, which is what she fears. Why? If they know one another, then they must both belong to the Arthurian court, but that is a world Chrétien is moving Lancelot away from. This lady is in a similar position to the two accompanying 'amies' in *Erec*, but while the ladies attached to Yder and to Cadoc go with their defeated knights back to Arthur's court to spread the fame of the hero and be received into Arthur's kingdom, this lady and her knight vanish into thin air. The point of the lady's embarrassment is to provide a pretext for them not to return to Arthur; it would be embarrassing for Guinevere's husband to receive proof of his rival's prowess. Lancelot is cut off from the social recognition that is such a vital part of chivalrous reward. Since the knight does not go back, his lady's promise directs our attention forward, giving a prospect of future help to balance the future demands of the Damsel of the Crossroads. But this 'guerredon' never materializes either. The lady never crosses his consciousness again and he finishes his quest without any help from anyone.

The whole movement of the quest is, naturally enough, forward-looking. Chrétien makes Lancelot veer from demonstrating his qualities as a lover to demonstrating them as a knight, but neither he nor anyone else looks back. Arthur and his court are silently dropped from the quest at line 269; Gawain, who is out in front, never looks back and we hear no more of the others. When Lancelot gets out of the cart in the town of the Damsel of the Tower, the dwarf goes off, no-one knows where (l. 448). The same is true for all the anonymous characters. Even the two sympathetic young men whose company Lancelot welcomes (ll. 2196-98), who leave the home of their father, the First Vavassour, and stay with him until he crosses the Sword Bridge (l. 3147) are left behind there without a backward glance. They rejoice at Lancelot's success at the bridge, though they are unaware of the extent of his injuries. Lancelot binds his wounds ready for the next encounter and gives them neither a thought nor a glance and they too fall into oblivion.

At first, Lancelot may appear a solitary hero, given that no-one can fully understand his high level of motivation and given that he is typically sunk in a thought that cuts him off from all human inter-change. Yet in fact Lancelot is much less alone than Chrétien's other heroes. It is true that he is alone when we first meet him, and that after Gawain leaves him at the crossroads, he falls into a meditation which lasts till he meets the Hospitable Damsel. When she leaves him, he rides on alone until he meets the First Vavassour, but from thereon he is never alone again until he is imprisoned in Meleagant's tower. Except for these two brief and undescribed intervals, Lancelot is never on his own.

It is not difficult to discover why Lancelot is so much less solitary than Erec, Alexander or Cligès. Erec's first quest is a response to a direct personal challenge; on the second, he and Enide form a kind of *solitude à deux* of a couple temporarily estranged from their normal position in society. As for Alexander, part of his education is carried out through his long, solitary monologues. Cligès has his name to make and everything to learn and he only establishes his chivalric worth by going off alone and fighting incognito at the Arthurian tournament. Lancelot, on the other hand, takes his one vital decision privately and the effect is so exceptional that we continually need to be impressed with it through the reactions of marvelling intermediaries. Nor is he given only individual commentators. Lancelot, more than any other hero, is supplied with a background chorus.

Erec, setting out on his quest, arouses the anxiety of his father's court; setting out to achieve the Joie de la Cort he receives warnings from all the townspeople as well as Evrain. Naturally the hero is the one who rises above the fears and anxieties of ordinary men. Lancelot, however, is in a different category. Besides provoking onlookers to marvel, singly or collectively, he is provided with no fewer than eleven choral commentaries. When he is still in the cart, the people of the Damsel of the Tower revile him in chorus (ll. 406–21). The knights and damsels of the meadow do likewise (ll. 1675–84) but then, seeing the respect with which their lord treats Lancelot, change their collective tune (ll. 1827–39). The household of the First Vavassour break out in choral lamentation over Lancelot whom they fear is condemned to a fate like theirs (ll. 2095–103). After their victorious attack on the men of Gorre, the captives of Logres welcome Lancelot and clamour in conflicting chorus for the honour of lodging him (ll. 2451–69). At the house of the Second Vavassour all the household lament the misadventures of the cart for which the Arrogant Knight reproaches Lancelot. They puzzle in chorus over the reason why Lancelot was driven in the infamous cart (ll. 2625–26) but they never find out. It is a problem to which no public answer is ever given. No–one ever understands why Lancelot undergoes such shame. The dwarf goes off into the unknown, refusing to speak to anyone (ll. 422–23; 445).

The extremely long warning given by the two young men at the Sword Bridge is perhaps a duet rather than a chorus and is delivered in the first person. Still, it expresses in concerted voice the fears of those who, though not cowards themselves, are paralysed with fear at the sight of the final obstacle to be overcome by the hero. As might be expected, Lancelot is acclaimed with choral joy by the people of Logres after he liberates them from their exile in Gorre (ll. 3924–30). At Noauz, his disgrace provokes two collective condemnations (ll. 5756–76; 5881–87) to be changed once again to collective marvelling (ll. 6005–12).

Nothing more clearly marks Lancelot's exceptional character than the way he treats the opinion of the multitude: praise, blame and warnings are all equally indifferent to him as he pursues his heroic way, thereby highlighting still further his isolation from the common run of humanity. He ignores the taunts of the 'janz' of the Damsel of the Tower as he ignores the taunts of the damsel herself. In the meadow, he pays no attention to the comments of those present, favourable or unfavourable. He stands by in silence while the father and son wrangle at length, and in his silence impresses the old and wiser knight with his power. To the incredulous enquiries of the First Vavassour, he replies that he expects to return from Gorre if God wills it (ll. 2120–21) and asks the way with the utmost calm. When the people of Logres almost come to blows for the honour of lodging him, he firmly reproves them for such useless strife (ll. 2470–502).

He is never carried away by the emotion of the moment, he never participates in the feelings of the multitude. When the Arrogant Knight insultingly reminds him of the cart, Lancelot does not deign to answer a word (l. 2616), though everyone else breaks out in choral horror. He does not respond to the grateful joy of the people of Logres (ll. 3931–35); his "joie" (l. 3951) is reserved for the prospect of seeing Guinevere. At Noauz, when the assembled throng see him perform first well and then badly, they imagine, reasonably enough, that his good performance is to be accounted for by recklessness or beginner's luck. They have no inkling of the real reason and there can be no question that Lancelot will enlighten them. They acknowledge their mistake when the Red Knight vanquishes all, but they never have the slightest clue as to why there have been such dramatic changes in his performance. Lancelot shares his thoughts with no-one. By this stage, he does not even speak to the queen. After their single night of love, they never speak together again in private and communicate only through intermediaries.

The only incidental characters Lancelot shows some human awareness of are the two young men who accompany him to the Sword Bridge. They beg him to have pity on himself and not attempt to cross it and he, for once, does not disdain to reply:

> Et cil lor respont an riant:
> "Seignor, merciz et grez aiiez
> Quant por moi si vos esmaiiez:
> D'amor vos vient et de franchise."            (ll. 3092–95)

He can appreciate the concern of men whose company he has agreed to accept. It is paradoxical that Lancelot has his most "human" emotion on the occasion of overcoming the most superhuman obstacle. If the hero were to be permitted any social ties, it would surely be with these young men. Yet even these apparently harmless links are severed once Lancelot crosses the bridge. His companions go wild with joy at his success (ll. 3144–46), but he never spares them a thought or a backward glance.

The conflicting claims made on Lancelot as the "amis antiers" (l. 3818) on the one hand and the supreme knight on the other inevitably have a slackening effect on the pace of his pursuit of Meleagant. Lancelot's extravagance in love is given seriousness and dignity by his calm deliberation in respect of all decisions. His absorption in thoughts of his lady leaves him with no surplus emotional energy to invest in the external events of his quest. Inside Lancelot's mind no progress is made at all: he is statically ecstatic. So Chrétien is obliged to mark the progress of his quest from without. He will not distract us with characters who have no interest for his hero. Instead, he emphasizes the progress made in terms of space and time.

Lancelot rides undeviatingly towards his goal, following the 'droit chemin'. The Damsel of the Crossroads promises to set him and Gawain "el droit chemin" (l. 619). Lancelot, absorbed in thought, is carried on swiftly by his horse, who does not take any indirect route "mes la meillor et la plus droite" (l. 731). The second time he is plunged into meditation, the direct route all but takes on a life of its own. He and the Hospitable Damsel pursue their path "si con li droiz chemins les mainne" (l. 1357). Lancelot protests when the damsel tries to take him out of it, insisting that the direct path is easily visible and that he will not be turned from it (ll. 1390–93). It is his decisiveness rather than any hastiness that ensures his progress.

When he asks the First Vavassour to tell him how to get to the Sword Bridge, he is warned that he is on a dangerous road, but that it leads straight to the bridge. He offers to show Lancelot a safer way, but when Lancelot discovers that it is not quite so direct, he will have none of it. The straight road is the right road. Once he has made the right decision, Lancelot does not rush recklessly ahead but waits for the next day and sets out in orderly fashion. When his grateful fellow fighters from Logres clamour to lodge him, Lancelot sternly tells them that the only important point is that he should be lodged on his "droite voie" (l. 2481). The morning after he defeats the Arrogant Knight, Lancelot and his companions take a duly ceremonious leave of their host (ll. 2999–3016) and set off on the last leg of their journey. They pursue the straight way all day without interruption:

> Lor droit chemin vont cheminant
> Tant que li jorz vet declinant.                    (ll. 3017–18)

There are no longer even any obstacles on the way.

Similarly, given that Lancelot's state of mind is unchanging and unaffected by the passage of time, and that when he is absorbed in thoughts of Guinevere he can ride for hours at a time without noticing it, Chrétien takes care to punctuate the course of his pursuit with a far greater number of references to time than we get in *Erec*. Erec rides from one place 'tant que' he gets to the next: Lancelot's timeless preoccupation is articulated from without by regular references to the passing hours. Still in the cart, he arrives "de bas vespre" (l. 402) at the town of the Damsel of the Tower. Next morning, she has mass said "au point del jor" (l. 539) and they set off through the forest and ride until "il pot estre prime de jor" (l. 609), when they come to the crossroads. Absorbed in thought, Lancelot rides until it is "pres none basse" (l. 739), when he comes to the ford. After his adventure there, he rides on until "bas vespre" (l. 943), when he meets the Hospitable Damsel. After the eventful night of her hospitality, he is up again at daybreak (l. 1293). He rides with her "jusqu'a none" (l. 1848), when they reach the Future Cemetery. Left alone at last, Lancelot rides on until "aprés vespres android conplie" (l. 2026) he meets the First Vavassour. The next day, as soon as he can see light (l. 2202) he sets off for the Stony Gap, which he reaches "a ore de prime tot droit" (l. 2211). Having overcome this obstacle, Lancelot continues on his way with his two companions "Tant qu'il pot estre none basse" (l. 2268). They meet the Treacherous Host "vers none" (l. 2269), escape from his trap and fight on the side of the people of Logres until night parts the combatants (ll. 2449–50). Next day nothing happens, but the passage of time is still marked: they ride from morning to evening without meeting an adventure (ll. 2519–21). Next day they are up early (ll. 2996–97) and at last they reach their goal:

> . . . vienent au pont de l'espee
> Aprés none vers la vespree.                (l. 3019–20)

The passage of time marks the stages of Lancelot's quest, but the quest itself moves us into the future. Lancelot, the knight without a past, is the man who never looks back. His mind is in an eternal present, but his actions are geared to a definite future. The first part of his quest is filled with forebodings. At the very moment that he is hesitating to get into the cart, Chrétien intervenes to warn us of unspecified future ills he will suffer for his hesitation (ll. 366–68). The Damsel of the Crossroads warns Lancelot and Gawain that anyone who undertakes the journey to Gorre will suffer great pain and hardship (ll. 622–24). Lancelot himself fears that if he does not overcome the Knight of the Ford, he will fail in his undertaking, and this fear gives him extra impetus (ll. 874–91). When he reluctantly promises to sleep with the Hospitable Damsel, Chrétien again intervenes to alarm us about the future: Lancelot will suffer great distress on this account and perhaps the damsel will not release him from his promise (ll. 968–74). He gets over this obstacle, only to be faced next day with the obligation of protecting her by the old custom of Logres, and she envisages it as a test for him, whereby she will see if he really will be capable of defending her (ll. 1541–44). The Old Knight of the Meadow picks up the expectations roused by the damsel and stops his son fighting with Lancelot by making him wait until they see what kind of man Lancelot is.

It was a future worth waiting for. In due course they hear of the ultimate confirmation given to Lancelot's heroism. His glory is projected into a future which goes beyond the limits of this romance and all others. In the Future Cemetery, Lancelot reads the inscriptions on the tombstones:

> ". . . Ci girra Gauvains,
> Ci Looys et ci Yvains"                                    (ll. 1877–78)

and many others will lie there too. The end of all physical activity is envisaged, a thought inconceivable in *Erec* or *Cligès*. In this post-physical world, it is naturally Lancelot who will have the highest place: he who will raise the stone from the largest and most beautiful tomb will liberate the captives and eventually lie in that tomb himself. Love is what has brought Lancelot this far and love, if it does not conquer death, at least makes for a glorious end and liberates unhappy people who could not have been freed by the conventional prowess of a Gawain.

From this point on, Lancelot is explicitly and justifiably confident of success. He tells the First Vavassour that he will succeed with the help of God and his own prowess (ll. 2117–22). The Vavassour's sons confidently prophesy to the people of Logres that Lancelot will be their liberator:

> ". . . Seignor, ce est cil
> Qui nos gitera toz d'essil
> Et de la grant maleürté
> Ou nos avons lonc tans esté."                             (ll. 2425–28)

They should honour him for what he has done and for the perils he still has to endure on their account:

> "Si li devons grant enor feire
> Quant por nos fors de prison treire
> A tant perilleus leus passez,
> Et passera ancore assez.
> Mout a a feire et mout a fet."                            (ll. 2429–33)

But there is no longer any doubt of Lancelot's success: no matter what perilous obstacles stand in the way, he is predestined to reach his goal.

The prophetic sequence in the Future Cemetery is what most clearly sets Lancelot apart from other men. Yet, paradoxically, it is also the point at which he is at last given a social dimension. The exact words of the prophecy are, as the Hermit tells Lancelot, written on the tomb itself:

> ". . . letres escrites i a,
> Qui dïent, cil qui levera
> Ceste lame seus par son cors,

> Getera ceus et celes fors,
> Qui sont an la terre an prison.                    (ll. 1911-15)

No mention is made here of the queen. The liberation of the prisoners is a great service to Arthur and the people of Logres, yet Lancelot himself pays no attention to his role as general saviour. He never links his service of Love with the service of the common good: it is left for the other characters to make the connection. The Hospitable Damsel guesses nothing of his love, but correctly divines that he has a mission. The Hermit, who has seen only the knightly strength of Lancelot, nevertheless understands that his principal interest must be the queen, for he tells the knights who are following:

> "Il vet rescorre la reïne,
> Et il la rescorra sanz dote,
> Et avuec li l'autre jant tote."                    (ll. 1984-86)

The First Vavassour is also inexplicably informed of Lancelot's motivation:

> "An cest païs, ce cuit je bien,
> Estes venuz por la reïne."                         (ll. 2144-45)

To which Lancelot categorically replies: "Onques n'i ving por autre chose" (l. 2149). The rescue of the common people is not part of Lancelot's motivation. Chrétien will not permit any impulse to compete with the single driving force that defines Lancelot as an 'amis antiers'. Nor are the people themselves under any illusion about their importance to him. Their attitude is clearly expressed by Guinevere's damsel, who realizes that Lancelot would never have undertaken the battle with Meleagant for her

> Ne por cele autre jant menue
> Qui an la place estoit venue,
> Ne ja anprise ne l'eüst
> Se por la reïne ne fust.                           (ll. 3655-58)

She may not guess the nature of his love for Guinevere, but she accepts that the queen is the most important of all the prisoners of Logres and does not take it amiss that a champion such as Lancelot should give no thought to the common people, the "jant menue."

Lancelot's role is not a social one. Without his love for the queen he would never have undertaken the quest, and it is only because he is so exceptionally highly motivated that he brings it to a successful conclusion. Neither Chrétien nor Godefroi leaves Lancelot in a position of social significance. Erec, Alexander and Cligès all end their career by getting married and ruling a kingdom: Lancelot does neither. Whether in the stone tower where Chrétien leaves him, or acclaimed as Godefroi imagines him, Lancelot remains isolated socially. It cannot be that Chrétien adds the theme of the liberation of the common people to give his hero social weight, as the hero does not assume the role of the liberator. If anything, it adds to his isolation. Lancelot does not participate in the joy of the released prisoners, focussing only on the joy of his anticipated meeting with Guinevere.

Yet the social benefit he confers is a fact, and a considerable one at that. Erec, with the moral support of Enide, liberates one couple who are subsequently drawn into their circle. Lancelot, who has condemned himself to solitude, liberates enormous numbers of people with whom he has nothing in common. Cligès and Fenice imagined that their love improved the whole world; with Lancelot, this illusion becomes a reality. The liberation of the prisoners is a by-product of Lancelot's more spiritual love. Alexander treated the hair of Soredamors with a religious fevour, but this was only a private outburst which ultimately led to their physical and social union in marriage. Lancelot reveres Guinevere's hair, after he has rejected the temptations of the Hospitable Damsel for a love that may never be satisfied and must never be revealed. When at last he is given his reward, he enshrines the event with two spiritual gestures by genuflecting to Guinevere's bed. Lancelot is not aware of his mission as the saviour of an oppressed people, but there are undoubted messianic overtones in the scene in the Future Cemetery, where the written prophecy of a future saviour is fulfilled when the hero proves his predestined role by a marvel, if not precisely by a miracle.[2] Chrétien is not speaking of divine love in human terms, but rather of human love, raised to the pitch of absolute devotion, in quasi–divine terms. Lancelot's love is so absolute that it takes on a superhuman detachment. Whether Guinevere gratifies it or not, Lancelot's love is so disinterested that its effects overflow on the other members of society. His rarefied human devotion saves the people socially as the contemplative devotion of a monk might save them spiritually, and with the same impersonal detachment. It is a love that overcomes all obstacles though it can never have either a social realization or a psychological development.

---

[2]This episode is the focus of Ribard's interpretation of the *Charrette* as a Christian allegory; see his *Chrétien de Troyes*.

# IX. The Adaptation of Roles

The final achievements of Erec and Cligès were marked by their ability being compared with that of another. Erec conquers the mysterious tall knight of the orchard; Cligès equals in tournament the prowess of his uncle Gawain. The public acclaim given to these feats indicates that they are intended to mark the level the hero has reached. Lancelot, once again, is a different case. His exploits as the Red Knight at the tournament of Noauz gain no glory for his own name; he achieves only the most perfect example of an obedience which none of his public understands. In Godefroi's conclusion he ultimately destroys the villainous but powerful Meleagant, but the first two battles are inconclusive because of the intervention of Bademagu and the queen. Lancelot does not need public recognition, as he appears from the first to be fully capable of all he achieves. There is no process of maturing in him as there is in the earlier heroes. Once he has taken the decision to submit to the commandments of Love, there is no further evolution in his character.

Because he is so static and so exceptional, Lancelot needs what none of the earlier heroes needed: a foil. In order to make us appreciate what is achieved by this superhuman hero, Chrétien offers us the contrast of what is achieved by a representative example of chivalrous excellence, Arthur's nephew Gawain.[1] Gawain duplicates Lancelot's role of rescuer, but as he is not the hero, he is doomed to ultimate failure and to having his incidental successes serve only to enhance Lancelot's glory.

In *Erec* and *Cligès*, Gawain's position was unassailable. His sensible objections to the Hunt of the White Deer show him assuming the not unsympathetic role of *raisonneur*. He is a model of discreet courtesy in his method of persuading Erec to rejoin the court at least temporarily. In *Cligès* his relationship to both heroes keeps him on a very high plane throughout, and Cligès is only asked to equal his uncle, not to excel him. His first appearance in the *Charrette* is a return to the role of *raisonneur*. We know that Arthur's behaviour cannot be condoned because Gawain is so categoric about criticizing it (ll. 228-29). It is he who gets the Arthurian court to follow Kay, and when they see Kay's horse return riderless, it is he who hastens on ahead of the others on the quest for the queen. Both literally and figuratively he is ahead of everyone at court, most notably of Arthur himself. It can only be in exceptional circum-

---

[1] For a study of Gawain, which treats him as a character in his own right, see Busby, *Gauvain in Old French Literature*.

stances that anyone will outdo him. He remains a possible hero up to the episode of the cart. He will never know why Lancelot has set aside the claims of reason and got into the infamous charrette. The dwarf tells him to get in too if he hates himself as much as the knight who is already there (ll. 388–91). Gawain, who has no reason to transcend his own interests, thinks the suggestion that he should exchange his horse for the cart is thoroughly irrational, indeed quite mad (ll. 392–96). Ironically, Gawain is outwardly winning at this stage. He has come just as far as Lancelot, he still has a horse in reserve, and he has not degraded himself. Any outside observer would back him to win; only we, who have been given a privileged view of Lancelot's mind, can guess that his exceptional motivation will propel him towards success.

Both Gawain's roles are thankless ones. As a *raisonneur*, his criticisms are ignored. As a foil, he is fated to be outshone. As much as Arthur's weakness is below Gawain's courage and common sense, so Lancelot's superhuman love is above it. For as long as he accompanies Lancelot, Gawain maintains his external superiority. The Damsel of the Tower and her maidens greet him with flattering joy (ll. 439–41). The damsel herself sits beside him at supper (ll. 456–57) and next morning allows herself to be engaged by him in a private conversation from which Lancelot is excluded (ll. 548–52). But Lancelot's real superiority, even on the plane of chivalry, has already been demonstrated to us, though it receives no public acknowledgement. When the damsel tells them about the perilous bed, Gawain is silent and prudently sleeps in the bed he is offered. It is because the bed is especially forbidden to the disgraced Knight of the Cart that Lancelot rises to the challenge and accomplishes the adventure.

Gawain never fails in courtesy. He humanely reproves Lancelot for seeming to wish to commit suicide (ll. 573–78). He does not join in the damsel's reviling of the Knight of the Cart. Yet from first to last he betrays no understanding of Lancelot's motivation. He offers his services to the Damsel of the Crossroads, but they are nothing compared to what Lancelot can offer,

> . . . cil cui amors fet riche
> Et puissant et hardi par tot.                    (ll. 634–35).

Gawain is distressed at having to choose a bridge: it is a Hobson's choice to which he can make no wholly reasonable response: "Del prandre ne puis estre sages," he complains (l. 696), but in the end chooses the slightly less perilous Water Bridge. He then disappears from the narrative, as he must if he is not to distract attention from Lancelot or be completely devalued by comparison with him.

It is only after Lancelot's successful completion of the quest that Gawain reappears. He re–enters at line 5127, having fallen into the river in an attempt to cross the Water Bridge. He bobs up and down in the water and has to be fished out with various improvised implements. He is in a pitiful situation that is dangerously close to being ridiculous. Chrétien cannot bring himself to devalue Gawain completely as this would undercut his role as foil. He compromises by telling us of Gawain's merits while showing us his discomfiture: Gawain is shown floundering in the water, but we are told that he has passed many perils (ll. 5139–41). He is shown, unable to speak and he is treated to a recital of Lancelot's success (ll. 5144–81). The people of Logres tell him that the queen has such a regard for him that she will not leave Gorre till she has news of him (ll. 5182–86), but his proposal to go to the rescue of Lancelot is rejected by the people of Logres who want to leave the rescue to Arthur (ll. 5188–98). Guinevere and Bademagu are pleased to see him again (ll. 5214–27) but, when he is at last about to set out on a quest for Lancelot, a message (a false one) comes to cancel his plans. All he can do is escort Guinevere home and reject the acclaim of the multitude, saying: "Ceste enors me vaut une honte" (l. 5344).

The ambivalence of Gawain's character lies in the fact that everyone praises and respects him, and yet he is never shown doing anything to gain that respect, as the whole definition of his role is to play second fiddle to the hero. The tournament of Noauz poses a problem, for Gawain has no reason not to be "ou toz li biens del mont sera" (l. 5470) and yet what can he be allowed to achieve there? If he defeats Lancelot, it will be an unthinkable degradation of the hero. If he shows himself his equal, as he showed himself the equal of Cligès, he will abolish at a stroke the critical advantage Lancelot is supposed to be given by love. If he is defeated by Lancelot, he will lose face at the Arthurian court and thus lose all value as a foil. Chrétien evidently felt that the safest thing to do was to make him a spectator:

> Gauvains d'armes ne se mesla,
> Qui iert avuec les autres la;
> Qu'a esgarder tant li pleisoit
> Les proesces que cil feisoit.          (ll. 5973–76)

Gawain's expert admiration is what best throws Lancelot's achievements into relief. It is the logical conclusion to the role of foil. In Godefroi's part of the romance, he treats Gawain in the same spirit: Gawain offers help, but when the time comes, his help is not needed. He effects nothing at all in the romance. He can comment on others, but he cannot influence the action.

Gawain, such as he is, is the most substantial of the doubles in the romance, but doubling is frequent in the narrative, or at least the impression of doubling. In the quest section, anonymous damsel follows anonymous damsel with hallucinatory frequency. The Damsel of the Tower, the Damsel of the Crossroads, the Damsel of the Ford, the Hospitable Damsel and the Avenging Damsel all lack a name, a physical description, a personal context and any real rapport with Lancelot. After a while we begin to feel that it is the same anonymous damsel springing up over and over again on the 'droit chemin'. It is the same with the hospitable vavassours: the second is in no way distinguished from the first, and their anonymous households resemble one another very much. They are defined solely by the hospitality they offer. They are exclusively the hero's hosts, so there is an inevitable duplication of their roles. Duplication occurs with other characters in a way that makes it impossible to tell how many characters we are dealing with, as with the two dwarves and Guinevere's two damsels.

The most developed duplication of roles occurs in the two father-and-son relationships, the knights of the Meadow on the one hand and Bademagu and Meleagant on the other. In each case, the father is wise and prudent and capable of appreciating Lancelot's abilities, and the son is evil and violent and overweeningly confident of his own prowess. In each case the father puts a brake on the action. Lancelot's quest is a double one. In the course of pursuing Meleagant he has to convince us both of his exceptional love and his correspondingly exceptional prowess. The quest has serious implications for the Arthurian world, so the combats he engages in must be serious. Yet a trail of dead bodies would raise the pitch of violence too soon. It is only with the defeat of the Arrogant Knight, Lancelot's last adventure before he reaches the Sword Bridge, that the combat becomes mortal, and even then only after much allegorical moralizing on Lancelot's part. His victory over the young Knight of the Meadow was non-violent. The young knight's father obliges him to find out what kind of man Lancelot is before he fights him and, after what they hear at the Future Cemetery, there can be no question of the son taking on a champion of Lancelot's stature. But only someone in authority could have held the young man in check for the necessary length of time, and the most obvious authority is a father. So too with Meleagant. He cannot be destroyed in his first encounter with Lancelot, because the principal developments of the love story are still to follow and his destruction must mark the end of the romance. So his combats with Lancelot are twice interrupted by his father, and it is only outside Bademagu's kingdom that Meleagant is finally destroyed. Only a father had the authority to keep Meleagant's dishonourable designs on the queen in check (ll. 3378–81) and only a father would, as both these fathers do, care enough about his villainous offspring to intervene on his behalf.

Lancelot faces both sons with equal calm. Hate helps him to overcome Meleagant, who is by far the more wicked of the two and the only one he actually confronts in battle, but it is an impersonal kind of hatred, thoroughly subordinated to his obedience as a lover (ll. 3743–47; 3806–30). Lancelot, who opens his mind to no-one, has naturally nothing to communicate to these two enemies. He is so absorbed by his timeless and unchanging thought that all secondary figures are pushed away from him as if by centrifugal force. Most of the minor characters are deprived of a name, but even those who have one, like Bademagu and Meleagant, lose any individuality through the doubling of their roles. Once again, Chrétien makes the narrative express the central issue of the romance: the unchanging reality inside Lancelot's mind withdraws all substance from the outside world, where there is no longer any change or development, only an endless reduplication of roles.

The special atmosphere of Lancelot's quest derives in part from the treatment of Guinevere's abduction in the source, or sources. Chrétien may have taken the story of her abduction from Welsh legend; he may owe something to the story of Persephone; Lancelot's journey to Gorre recalls both the descent of Aeneas into Hades and the descent of Christ into Hell.[2] Nevertheless, for his particular version of the story, Chrétien returns to his old rival, Thomas. Although the abduction of Iseut by a strange king may itself derive from older stories of the abduction of Guinevere, the abduction episode in Thomas's *Tristan* is certainly Chrétien's immediate model. Thomas's version, according to his derivatives,[3] went like this: King Mark grants a rash boon to a stranger who has come to his court, as a reward for his harp-playing. The stranger asks for Queen Iseut, and her husband feels obliged to keep his word and let him take her away. Tristan, who is out in the forest when all this occurs, hears of the queen's fate, hastens after her abductor and rescues her. In the Oxford *Folie Tristan*, it is one of the incidents that Tristan recalls to Iseut's memory:

> "En bois fu si l'oï cunter.
> Une rote pris, vinc aprés
> Sur mun destrer le grant elez."[4]

The threat posed by the outsider in his abduction of the queen, the helplessness of her too honourable husband, the absence of the hero and his success in bringing her back, all these elements are echoed by Chrétien. The attribution of only one role is changed: it is not to a stranger that Arthur promises the rash boon that loses him the queen, but to a member of his household, the seneschal Kay. Chrétien could perfectly well have set up the scene as it is in the *Tristan*, but his fragmentation of the role of the hostile stranger has repercussions in the romance which he clearly intended.

Meleagant has by far the most villainous role that Chrétien creates. By placing an episode that was merely incidental in *Tristan* at the beginning of his romance, Chrétien confers greater weight on the intruder and, by

---

[2]In his *Vita Gildae*, Caradoc of Llancarfan describes how Melvas abducted Guennuvar, wife of Arturus; see Schoepperle, *Tristan and Isolt*, Appendix 4. The abduction of Persephone by the god of the underworld is recounted by Ovid in the *Metamorphoses*, 5: 385–571. Aeneas's journey across mysterious rivers to the land from which no-one returns is described in the sixth book of the *Aeneid*. Christ's Descent into Hell is described in the Gospel of Nicodemus; see *The Apocryphal New Testament*, trans. James, 117–46. For echoes of the Descent in Lancelot, see Owen, *The Vision of Hell*, 200–05.

[3]*Thomas*, ed. Bédier, 1: 168–75; reconstituted passages.

[4]*Folie Tristan d'Oxford*, ed. Hoepffner, ll. 772–74.

removing the 'don' of his excellent harping, Chrétien concentrates his aggression. Arthur is even weaker than Mark, for he has been offered no service which might make it credible that he should give the stranger anything. He sits helplessly by while the declaration of aggression is delivered. He acknowledges his impotence and Meleagant issues his bargain almost as a kind of contemptuous concession (ll. 72–81) before departing, a still nameless and mysterious force for evil. Meleagant's first scene is astoundingly arbitrary: he is the instigator of all the action and is not eliminated until the last lines of the romance, but in his first scene we are given not the slightest reason for his aggression.

Meleagant is a powerful and baffling enemy, but we are not given the chance to ask questions about his mysterious appearance, as Chrétien instantly diverts our attention to another mystery, that of Kay's sudden decision to leave Arthur's service. The whole event of Meleagant's arrival, declaration, bargain and departure is all over within thirty–six lines and is framed by the first two mentions of the seneschal Kay:

> La ou Kes seoit au mangier,
> A tant ez vos un chevalier                                    (ll. 45–46)
> . . .
> La novele an a Kes oïe,
> Qui avuec les serjanz manjoit.                               (ll. 84–85)

Kay is part of Arthur's household before the stranger arrives, and we are re–directed to him the moment the stranger disappears, before we have time to puzzle over the behaviour of either the stranger or Arthur. Kay's impulsive resignation is a mystery too, but it is one that Chrétien is going to solve. The bewilderment of the court, the protests, the offer of the boon and the departure of the queen under Kay's escort, all this takes up nearly seven times as much space as the initial challenge (ll. 84–224). By the time that Gawain is calling on the others to follow Kay, all the thoughts of the court and of the reader are focussed on the danger that threatens the queen through the incompetence of Kay. Meleagant's aggressive irruption into the court is a *fait accompli*; his arbitrary challenge no longer needs to be justified in face of the immediate source of anxiety.

The stranger's villainous abduction of the queen and the failure of the court to protect her are more sharply separated in *Lancelot* than in *Tristan*. The villainy is concentrated in the abductor and the helplessness of the king is accentuated both by the elimination of the motive of reward and by the failure of Kay, the incompetent champion Arthur appoints in spite of himself. Kay's part is to fail, and to fail completely. By comparison, Gawain comes off well and Lancelot, of course, is in another category altogether. It is appropriate that Lancelot, the hero without a past, should triumph over Meleagant, the villain without a past. Their repeated conflicts express the endless clash of opposed forces, lifted out of a social context into the domain of the absolute.

The harper in *Tristan* won Iseut by guile; Meleagant wins Guinevere by a threatening bargain. Guile is developed instead in the character of Kay, enabling him to obtain the rash boon of protecting Guinevere. The harper succeeds in getting just one person into his power; Meleagant has large numbers of Arthur's subjects imprisoned in his kingdom. The hero's rescue of the queen and his defeat of her abductor, which made only an incidental episode in *Tristan*, are expanded to form the whole framework of the *Charrette*. A single adventure, loosely linked to many other comparable ones in the long and eventful career of Tristan, is developed by Chrétien to provide the basis of his more carefully unified narrative.

Before Kay reappears to take on another part of another character's role, Lancelot finds himself playing a carefully selected fragment of the role Thomas gives to his Tristan. In the course of their adventures, Tristan suffers for the sake of his love for Iseut, but Thomas shows him incapable of enduring the demands of constancy once he loses hope of seeing Iseut again. Banished, he hears no news from her for a long time and he can bear this hopeless frustration no more when he finds that another Iseut loves him. After long interior monologues Tristan justifies himself in accepting the sexual satisfaction offered by the second Iseut, rather than remaining constant to the first Iseut from whom he has no longer anything to hope. He marries the second Iseut and so wrongs the first; he then cannot bring himself to consummate the marriage, and so wrongs the second. On the wedding night, his will is painfully divided:

> Tristan se colche, Ysolt l'embrace,
> Baise lui la buche e la face,
> A li l'estraint, de cuer susspire
> E volt iço qu'il ne desire;
> A sun voleir est a contraire
> De laissier sun buen u del faire.          (Thomas, ll. 641–46)

Eventually, the true love he feels for the mistress he may never see again gets the better of the merely physical desire he feels for the woman he has made his wife:

> La grant amor qu'ad vers Ysolt
> Tolt ço que la nature volt.          (Thomas, ll. 655–56)

True love dominates the natural instinct for physical satisfaction. It even takes precedence over honour: Tristan knows that he has a duty to the woman he has publicly acknowledged as his wife (ll. 477–78), whose bed he is in honour bound to share. In the end, love wins. The infidelity to the first Iseut is not consummated, but it has nonetheless been committed in Tristan's mind and ultimately brings about his destruction. Thomas is aware of his hero's weakness and comments on it at length (ll. 285–356). Chrétien, to demonstrate the greater perfection of Lancelot's love, sets up a similar situation, but with a different ending:

Lancelot's constancy never wavers in the face of physical temptation. Hence the rather startling role played by the Hospitable Damsel.

As a condition of her hospitality, the damsel makes Lancelot promise to share her bed. It is certainly not as strong an obligation as the bond of marriage, but it is still a bond of honour which Lancelot will not renege on though he faces its accomplishment with the utmost reluctance, not to say distaste. Unlike Tristan, Lancelot has no difficulty in resisting the attractions of the lady whose bed he shares:

> De tochier a li mout se gueite,
> Ainz s'an esloigne et gist anvers.          (ll. 1228–29)

He will not even speak to her or look at her. His heart will not let him act otherwise, "bele et jante" though the lady is (l. 1237), for he is above the common run of men:

> . . . ne li plest ne atalante
> Quanqu'est bel et jant a chascun.          (ll. 1238–39)

Lancelot is not "everyone." He is one of those rare souls whom Love deigns to dominate exclusively. Correspondingly, the damsel does not behave like Tristan's wife who, when she finds out why Tristan would not consummate their marriage, is filled with the not incomprehensible fury of a woman scorned and Tristan ultimately pays with his life for having slighted her. Lancelot's damsel reacts quite differently. With the amazingly rational acceptance of humiliation we have already met in *Erec*, the damsel accepts defeat gracefully, recognizing, as she says to her guest:

> "Que vos m'avez randu si bien
> Mon covant que nes une rien
> Par droit ne vos puis demander."          (ll. 1269–71)

Chrétien lets Lancelot have it both ways: he has kept his bond of honour to the woman who wanted his love and at the same time remained constant to the absent woman to whom he has given his love. He keeps only the admirable part of Tristan's role of the lover faced with temptation. The damsel is given only a fraction of the role of the second Iseut. She never has the socially binding role of wife and so she can, and does, vanish when she is no longer needed.

To Kay is allotted another fragment of the Tristan role, that of the man accused of adultery with his queen on the evidence of blood in her bed. Thomas's treatment of this episode is difficult to establish,[5] but it survives in the Beroul fragment, treated in a way that contrasts singularly with Chrétien. According to Beroul, Tristan has arranged to join Iseut in the royal bed, when he sees flour on the floor between them. He realizes that a trap has been set, but determines to circumvent

---

[5]*Thomas*, ed. Bédier, 1: 204–05; reconstituted passages.

it. At this point Beroul abruptly informs us that Tristan had been wounded while hunting the previous day. Then we are told that Mark and the dwarf who has set the trap leave the chamber at midnight, and Tristan sets about joining Iseut:

> Tristran se fu sus piez levez.
> Dex! Porqoi fist? Or escoutez!
> Les piez a joinz, esme, si saut,
> El lit le roi chaï de haut.                    (Beroul, ll. 727–30)

Now the narrative significance of the wound becomes clear:

> Sa plaie escrive, forment saine;
> Le sanc qui(en)n ist les dras ensaigne.
> La plaie saigne; ne la sent,
> Qar trop a son delit entent.                   (Beroul, ll. 731–34)

The result is inevitable. Tristan returns to his bed unaware of the damning evidence he has left behind. The dwarf and the hostile barons come in with the outraged husband. Tristan begs in vain to be allowed to defend the queen's innocence and his own in judicial combat, but Mark summarily condemns them to be burnt in public. The news spreads rapidly. Mark in his fury lets Iseut go off to an even worse fate with a band of lepers, but Tristan manages to rescue her and they flee to the forest of Morrois to live the life of outlaws.

Chrétien retains some elements of this sequence: the difficulties the hero must overcome to reach the heroine's bed, his absorption in her which makes him fail to notice the incriminating blood, the dramatic discovery of the blood in the bed, the accusation of adultery by the hero's enemy, and the hero's wish to champion his mistress who is in danger because of him.

Beroul condenses the maximum of drama and pathos into his version. Tristan's wound is of no interest to him until he needs it: the danger it represents is all that matters. He is intent on making us sympathize with his heroes and participate emotionally in their danger and suffering. He never allows us to judge them and constantly presents them as the wrongly persecuted victims of the evil and treacherous barons. As long as we feel with his heroes, Beroul has achieved his purpose.

Chrétien's approach is entirely different. He calculates all his effects in the interests of truth, decency and rational causality. To begin with, the husband is left out. The Arthur we saw at the beginning of the romance has no longer any resemblance to the epic figure of Wace, evoked in Cligès. He is the roi fainéant of Erec, exaggerated to the furthest point Chrétien can go without reminding us of the contemptible Alis of his previous romance. He does not risk letting the husband have any of the sympathy we occasionally extend to the innocent and anguished Mark. Chrétien's solution in the Charrette is the only one that will allow the husband to keep some of his dignity. The adultery takes place long after

Arthur has vanished silently from the scene and in a remote country governed by laws that do not obtain in the kingdom of Logres. The trio of hostile barons in the Tristan story are condensed into the single aggressive figure of Meleagant, and the hostile motivation is strengthened by jealousy: Meleagant's adulterous love for Guinevere is so completely dishonourable that it makes Lancelot's love seem lawful by contrast. The adultery of Tristan is a way of life; that of Lancelot and Guinevere is a single exceptional occasion with no prospect of renewal and as it is never betrayed to the world it causes no shame to the lovers or scandal to the public.

Characteristically, Chrétien seeks to maintain both right and honour in his heroes. Guinevere may have unlawfully loved the supremely worthy Lancelot: she is entirely innocent of the promiscuity Meleagant accuses her of. She can say with genuine indignation:

> ". . . je ne regiet mie an foire
> Mon cors, ne n'an faz livreison."          (ll. 4862–63)

Tristan was willing to fight to defend a lie: Lancelot is both willing and able to defend the truth. Meleagant, seeing blood in Guinevere's bed, looks with evil suspicion at Kay's bed (ll. 4769–71), which is bloody from his unhealed wounds. His unworthy inclinations make him jump to the wrong conclusion and they fully deserve to be crushed by Lancelot's superior love and vastly superior honour. Guinevere, even when faced with a charge of adultery, is spared all indignity by Chrétien. Not for her the ambiguous oaths that Beroul's Iseut is twice obliged to swear. Iseut is twice exposed to public shame: once after the episode of the blood in the bed and again at the Blanche Lande. The first time she escapes through Tristan's cunning in eluding his guards, the second time she escapes through her own cunning in devising an ambiguous oath.

Guinevere suffers no public humiliation. Meleagant tries to bring her to shame but he fails. Guinevere remains in control: she summons Lancelot, who arrives with a company of knights, and tells him the exact nature of the adultery she is accused of. Lancelot can even insist on the swearing of solemn oaths and there is nothing ambiguous about the way he swears that there has been no adultery between Guinevere and Kay. Once again Kay, having been allotted part of someone else's role, is not allowed to carry it through. He can obtain a rash boon, but he cannot play the part of abductor; he can be accused of adultery with the queen, but he cannot be her champion. He is an ineffectual obstacle both to injustice and to justice.

Kay's very helplessness improves the logic of the accusation scene. Meleagant's suspicions, however unworthy, are materially plausible. It was Kay's unsuccessful attempt to rescue the queen that caused the wounds that he still suffers from. As he has already told Lancelot (ll. 4033–65), he would have died but for the courteous ministrations of Bademagu and would have recovered fully but for the treacherous interference of Meleagant. His incriminating wounds have therefore been accounted for by his own rashness, Bademagu's kindness and the villain's villainy and, moreover, all this information was integrated into the narrative well ahead of time.

Lancelot's wound is a brilliantly economic device which draws on elements from two very dissimilar texts. Beroul tells us (ll. 927–45) how Tristan escapes from his captors by persuading them to let him go alone into a little chapel which has only the one door that they are guarding. Once inside, he pulls out the single small window and escapes through it to rescue Iseut and go into exile with her. Lancelot, too, must get through a window to reach Guinevere. He tears out its iron bars, thus displaying at once his love and his strength, but in so doing he wounds himself. In the same way as Tristan, and almost in the same words, he is indifferent to pain in such circumstances:

> . . . des plaies nule ne sant
> Cil qui a autre chose antant.        (ll. 4663–64)

In Chrétien's romance the hero's wound is integrated into the narrative. It is not a casual hunting accident, but a wound received in the interests of love.

Chrétien goes further, and links the incriminating blood with Lancelot's physical being, torn with anguish at parting. Daybreak forces the separation not only of the lovers, but of the heart and body of the hero:

> Li cors s'an vet, li cuers sejorne.
> Droit vers la fenestre s'an torne;
> Mes de son cors tant i remaint
> Que li drap sont tachié et taint
> Del sanc quil li cheï des doiz.        (ll. 4715–19)

The difficulties of the rendezvous, the violence of the situation already inflicted on them, the mortal danger their love will cause them and the intense pain of separation are all actually or potentially present in this one effusion of the hero's blood. Frappier criticized Chrétien's borrowings from the Tristan story as "gauche";[6] on the contrary, they are almost too carefully contrived.

The first scene at the window borrows elements from another literary source much exploited by Chrétien, an Ovidian text, perhaps the most popular legend from the *Metamorphoses*, the story of Pyramus and Thisbe. Chrétien probably read it in the original, along with the tales of Pelops and Philomela which he translated (*Cligès*, ll. 4–7), but he may also have known the lyrical translation made by an anonymous French poet about 1175.[7] His purpose in borrowing from it is the same as his

---

[6]Frappier, *Chrétien de Troyes*, 137.
[7]For a brief survey of Chrétien's use of the Pyramus and Thisbe story, see Lyons, "La Fausse mort"; for the lyrical translation, see the edition of *Piramus et Tisbé* by de Boer.

purpose in borrowing from the Tristan story; to show his superhuman hero surpassing all previous model lovers. So, when Lancelot hears Guinevere grant Bademagu's request that Meleagant be spared, he obeys with the promptness that characterizes the perfect lover:

> Mout est qui aimme obeïssanz
> Et mout fet tost et volantiers,
> La ou il est amis antiers,
> Ce que s'amie doie pleire:
> Donc le dut Lanceloz bien feire,
> Qui plus ama que Piramus,
> S'onques nus hon pot amer plus.          (ll. 3816–22)

Clearly, everything that Pyramus did, Lancelot must do better. Pyramus too is separated from the one he loves by a wall. A crack allows them to speak, but no more. The French poet makes Pyramus bewail his helplessness in the face of this obstacle:

> "Hé, murs,
> Tant par estes espés et durs!
> Mes se je fusse auques seürs,
>      La frete
> Fust a mes mains si ample fete
> Que sans veüe de la guete
> Vous en eüsse par mi trete."          (*Piramus*, ll. 460–66)

Lancelot and Guinevere are in the same position on the night of their rendez-vous. They speak to one another through the bars of a small window and voice their frustration:

> De ce qu'ansanble ne parvienent
> Lor poise tant a desmesure,
> Qu'il an blasment la ferreüre.          (ll. 4612–14)

But unlike Pyramus, Lancelot wastes no time in futile lamentation. All that prevents him from forcing the barrier that divides him from Guinevere is her as yet unexpressed will. "Rien fors vos ne me puet tenir", he tells her (l. 4627) and, receiving her assent, tears out the iron bars with his bare hands and passes through the window to her bed.

The fatal misunderstanding of the Pyramus story is also transformed. Pyramus dies through a tragic accident: seeing a lion with Thisbe's bloodstained scarf, he wrongly imagines that she is dead and runs himself through on his sword; Thisbe, returning alive and well, then kills herself on the same sword to prove her love equal to his and to be united with him in death. Chrétien eliminates all accidents and condenses all the roles of the story into the parts played by his two lovers. They are separated in the first instance not because of an external factor, like the parental enmity of Ovid's lovers, but because of Guinevere's excessive rigour. They each imagine that the other is dead, not because of material evidence in the mouth of a wild beast, but because of rumours put about by an abstract force, 'novele'.[8] In the quest section, news was transmitted as if by telepathy; in the later section, dealing with the reward of love, impersonal 'novele', a quasi–allegorical figure, is both slower and less accurate. Bearers of bad tidings are easily found (ll. 4266–67), but they remain depersonalized. 'Novele' alone, "Novele qui tost vole et cort" (l. 4158), brings the news to the queen that Lancelot is dead.

Guinevere differs principally from Thisbe in having to assume responsibility for the role of separator. Her first reaction on hearing of Lancelot's supposed death is to examine her conscience:

> . . . sovant se prant a la gole;
> Mes ainz se confesse a li sole,
> Si se repant et bat sa coupe,
> Et mout se blasme et mout s'ancoupe
> Del pechié qu'ele fet avoit
> Vers celui don ele savoit
> Qui suens avoit esté toz dis.             (ll. 4199–205)

She has none of the innocent pathos of Thisbe, or for that matter of Enide. She will certainly not fall impulsively on anyone's sword. Her internal debate is highly self–conscious and, as befits Lancelot's lady, deliberate.[9] She acknowledges the quality of Lancelot's love, her own cruelty and her love for him, and she feels that she deserves to die too (ll. 4248–49). She feels indeed that she deserves worse than death: the remorse she suffers is a greater penance:

> "Miauz vuel vivre et sofrir les cos
> Que morir por avoir repos."               (ll. 4261–62)

Lancelot has less on his conscience, so when he hears false news of Guinevere's death, "sa vie an ot an despit" (l. 4275) and he disdains to live another hour (l. 4312). He makes a "brief conplainte" to Death (ll. 4277–301), demonstrating his determination to force reluctant Death to come to him. He proceeds to attempt suicide and is indignant when he is saved in spite of himself. As he is still under the delusion that Guinevere treated him coldly because of his disgrace in the cart, he argues the matter out with himself and justifies his behaviour as that of an "ami verai" (l. 4386), thus consciously and voluntarily renewing his commitment to love. Then, when both lovers have proved their love in the face of death, Chrétien abandons the Pyramus model. 'Novele' is hastily sent out to relieve the minds of all concerned: first Lancelot (ll. 4418–20), then Bademagu (ll. 4425), then the queen (ll. 4432–40), and

---

[8] According to Nitze, 'novele' derives from Virgil's Fama, (Aeneid, 4:173–89); see "Two Virgilian Commonplaces," 442, 445. There is also an Ovidian echo: the indifference of 'novele' to good and bad is reminiscent of the Fama of the Metamorphoses, 9:137–39.

[9] Noble condemns the Guinevere of the Charrette as a "calculating adultress"; see "The Character of Guinevere," 534.

does not rest until it has brought the postscript to the queen that
Lancelot had wanted to die on her account (ll. 4446–53).

The internal monologues of Guinevere and Lancelot take up nearly
all of the three hundred lines which are devoted to the false news of
their deaths. They mark a change from the forward movement of the
quest section to a static, discursive style reminiscent of *Cligès*. Long as
they are, and much though they slow down the pace of the narrative,
the monologues have a significant function in the economy of the
romance because they give both hero and heroine an occasion to take
stock of their true desires and principles.

There is, however, no justification to be found for the two long
discursive interludes in Godefroi de Lagny's conclusion. The first
discourse occurs as an obstacle to be faced by the Avenging Damsel,
Meleagant's sympathetic sister. She is determined to give Lancelot the
'guerredon' she promised him (ll. 2948–51). Like Bademagu, she sus-
pects that Lancelot is in prison when he does not show up as promised
and she makes up her mind to find out the truth (ll. 6382–407). She
searches exhaustively in all directions for over a month (ll. 6408–41) and
finally arrives at the tower which she guesses is his prison. She is not
directed to her goal by the power that drove Lancelot, but simply by
chance, by "Fortune qui l'a tant penee" (l. 6458). She notes the single
tiny window and the suspicious absence of doors and is about to call
out Lancelot's name, when she is prevented by the author:

> Lors le viaut apeler par non:
> Apeler voloit Lancelot,
> Mes ce la retarde qu'ele ot,
> Andemantiers qu'el se teisoit,
> Une voiz . . .                                    (ll. 6476–80)

The damsel is poised for action but she cannot move or even open her
mouth until Godefroi has made Lancelot apostrophize Fortune and
soliloquize for sixty-one lines. Having mentioned Fortune a few lines
earlier, "Godefroiz de Leigni, li clers," as he styles himself (l. 7124),
cannot resist embarking on a thoroughly clerkly digression on one of the
most threadbare medieval commonplaces. He is so carried away by it
that he holds up the damsel and the plot while he makes Lancelot run
through the required clichés. The speech adds nothing to our knowledge of Lancelot's character and detracts from the narrative of his
rescue.

Chrétien never labours platitudes in this way. When, as we saw,
Enide falls from the top to the bottom of the Wheel of Fortune with truly
Boethian abruptness, she passes rapidly from the general to the par-
ticular:

> "Lasse!", fet ele, "a si grant joie
> M'avoit Deus mise et essauciee:
> Or m'a an po d'ore abeissiee

> Fortune, qui m'avoit atreite,
> Tost a a li sa main retreite.
> De ce ne me chaussist il, lasse,
> S'a mon seignor parler osasse."          (*Erec*, ll. 2782–88)

There is scarcely any check to the pace of the narrative and our understanding of Enide's relationship with Erec is heightened.

The second long discourse again demonstrates Godefroi's lack of concern for the overall economy of the narrative. When he shows Meleagant at Arthur's court unexpectedly facing an enemy he thought was in a secure prison, he is not content to make him rage, but gives him a forty-five-line monologue (ll. 6942–86) filled with vain regrets and useless speculations before letting him proceed to the final combat. Chrétien sometimes lets the pace slacken, but he always has a purpose and he never loses sight of it. In his part of the romance every act and speech has its function. The anguished soliloquies of Lancelot and Guinevere are to convince us that they merit the happy outcome of their misapprehensions. As in *Erec* and *Cligès*, Chrétien's fundamental optimism will not let him push a mistaken belief to the tragic conclusion of the Pyramus story. Guinevere may be punished for her excessive rigour by the anguish of remorse, but given that she shows her readiness to suffer by refusing food and drink until she is thought to be dead, Chrétien will not condemn her to die through a chance error of information. In his horror of anything resembling the absurd Chrétien demonstrates his profound rationalism. Just as he could not accept a love brought about by the tragic accident of a potion, so here he refuses to imitate the model of a death brought about by the tragic accident of misinformation. Pyramus and Thisbe were the victims of a cruel fate, but Lancelot and Guinevere are rational creatures in a rational world and, once they have perfected their own wills, no random stroke of the absurd will be allowed to destroy them.

Despite the fantastic elements of the quest section, the *Charrette* is a continuation of the same vein of realism that Chrétien explored in *Cligès*. The difference is that everything in the *Charrette* is more extreme. Fenice feared that no-one would understand her motives and principles: in the *Charrette* even Gawain cannot comprehend Lancelot. Cligès and Fenice needed help from the "marvellous": Lancelot, to his baffled public, is himself perceived as a marvel. Alexander, Soredamors and Fenice had meditated in private on their love: Lancelot, in the sight of others, is lifted out of himself and his surroundings by the transcendent power of his thoughts of love. Cligès and Fenice only believed that the world was improved by their love: Lancelot's love is so exalted that he becomes a messianic figure who liberates Arthur's subjects.

The rational Gawain fails, while the super-rational Lancelot succeeds, achieving astounding feats of chivalry under the impulse of his love. All the roles Chrétien borrows from other romances are adapted with the sole purpose of exalting his hero. Lancelot has a lucid control of his actions that raises him above such tragic lovers as Tristan and Pyramus. Public opinion is contented throughout: Arthur's queen and subjects are saved and all shame and scandal are avoided. Yet the exterior world with all its characters and their concerns are relentlessly driven out of our consciousness by the singleness of Lancelot's preoccupation. Unlike Chrétien's previous heroes, Lancelot is a solitary figure who will never have a place in society. Chrétien explores the theme of the complete lover to its utmost narrative limits. Given his obvious delight in pastures new, it cannot now surprise us to see him turn next to depicting a knight who, in almost all respects, will be the exact opposite of the hero of the *Charrette*.

# YVAIN: LE CHEVALIER AU LION

# X. Externalizing the Narrative

In the *Charrette* Chrétien concentrates on a central figure who thinks; in *Yvain*[1] he shows us a variety of characters who see. In contrast to the Knight of the Cart's world, which is idealized and internalized, the Knight of the Lion's world is externalized and conveyed to us in material terms. Hence the greater naturalism of atmosphere in *Yvain* in spite of a significant increase in Chrétien's use of the "marvellous."

The emphasis on the visual is particularly marked at the beginning of the romance. When Calogrenant is finally prevailed upon to tell his story to the Arthurian court, he insists that he should be listened to with attention:

> "Car ne vuel pas parler de songe,
> Ne de fable ne de mançonge,
> Don maint autre vos ont servi,
> Ainz vos dirai ce que je vi."      (ll. 171–74)

He is the eye-witness of what he is about to report[2] and he tells his audience every detail of what he saw. As he came out of the forest in Broceliande, he saw a battlemented tower (l. 191) and its bailey and ditch (l. 195). Inside the fortress he saw a maiden coming towards him (l. 226); he stared at her (l. 228) and did not care to look at anything else (l. 237). Next morning he rose before one could see daylight (l. 271) and he had not travelled far when he found bulls in a clearing, and saw a churl sitting on a tree stump (l. 292) and saw how grotesque he was (l. 295). The churl got up when he saw Calogrenant approaching (l. 315) and Calogrenant was alarmed when he saw (l. 319) that the churl was doing nothing but stare at him in silence (l. 323). In reply to a request for information about adventures or marvels, the churl directs him to where he will see a fountain (l. 380) of which he, the churl, has never seen the like (l. 392). By pouring water on the stone, Calogrenant will see a tempest rise (l. 397) and see such a thunderstorm (l. 401) that he will be lucky if he escapes unscathed.

We know exactly what Calogrenant expected to see, but he is relentless in giving us every detail of what he actually saw. Having set

---

[1]Citations are from Foerster's text of *Yvain*, in the edition prepared by Reid; see Bibliography.

[2]The great value placed on eye-witness reports in the Middle Ages is based on the authority of Isidore of Seville; see Smalley, *Historians in the Middle Ages*, 22–25. Benoît de Sainte-Maure gives Dares preference over Homer because he supposed him to be an eye-witness of the fall of Troy; see *Troie*, ll. 45–116. Lacy states that perception plays a lesser role in *Yvain* than in *Lancelot*; see *Craft of Chrétien de Troyes*, 25.

off in the direction indicated by the churl, Calogrenant reaches the fountain and all its "marvellous" accessories: he sees the tree and the chapel (l. 412), sees the basin hanging from the tree (l. 419) and wishes to see the marvel of the tempest (l. 432). Having poured the water, he duly sees the storm (l. 440) and after it, when he sees the clear air (l. 455) and then sees birds collecting on the tree (l. 460), he is filled with joy until he sees a knight coming (l. 483), who is wielding a lance bigger than any Calogrenant has ever seen before (l. 537). The knight unhorses Calogrenant with it and rides off without bothering to look at him (l. 543), leaving his discomfited opponent to return to his hosts who see him come back defeated (l. 567) but still treat him courteously.

This preoccupation with the visible is not confined to Calogrenant. The barons jump up when they see Arthur coming to join them (l. 653) and the king's reaction to the story is to swear that he will go and see the fountain for himself (l. 665). No other consideration is mentioned except his desire to gratify his curiosity visually, a desire shared by all the court, who value their king all the more for it (l. 674).

The hero is no different from anyone else. Yvain shares the humiliation of his cousin's defeat and like him, he conceives the event in visual terms. He determines to follow the same path, find the Hospitable Vavassour and his daughter,

> Puis verra les tors an l'essart
> Et le grant vilain qui les garde.
> Li veoirs li demore et tarde
> Del vilain, qui tant par est lez,
> Granz et hideus et contrefez
> Et noirs a guise de ferron.
> Puis verra, s'il puet, le perron
> Et la fontainne et le bacin. (ll. 708–15)

He will not stop until he sees the tree (ll. 773–74). He duly carries out this programme, seeing even greater beauty in the girl than Calogrenant had (ll. 782–84), seeing the bulls and the churl (l. 794) and, when he reaches the fountain, "si vit quanque il vost veoir" (l. 801). The Knight of the Fountain appears when Yvain raises the storm and, as soon as they see one another (l. 815), they engage in combat.

Why are they all so intent on seeing? Why is the visual side of the adventure so heavily stressed? Part of the answer lies with the nature of the things seen. The eyes of all the characters and the attention of Calogrenant's audience and Chrétien's public are all focussed on everything that leads up to the fountain and then on the fountain itself. It will be the scene of four critical encounters for the hero, and its peculiar powers are the pivot on which the plot revolves. It is essential for Chrétien that we accept the phenomenon on which his narrative is based.

The problem is that the Fountain of Broceliande is unequivocally a marvel; this is how the churl understands it (ll. 367–73) and what Calogrenant calls it (l. 432). Arthur too calls it a marvel (l. 667) and Chrétien states in the most factual style that Yvain's wedding celebrations lasted until

> . . . li rois vint a la mervoille
> De la fontainne, . . .                                   (ll. 2172–73)

as if it were as solidly established on the landscape as Laudine's castle. By that stage it is, but a great deal of art has been deployed in order to give it this reality. Far greater art, it may be said at once, than Chrétien has previously shown in his presentation of marvels. His protests about the truth of the magic orchard in *Erec* jar a little in that otherwise unjustified narrative. We may jib at the facility with which the aides of *Cligès* and Fenice produce potions and palaces on request. The marvels Lancelot achieves on his quest have been too much for many modern critics to take, but even the most sceptical susceptibilities are not jarred by the frankly "marvellous" fountain though it features in what is generally regarded as Chrétien's most realistic romance.[3]

It is not a sufficient explanation to say that the fountain does not shock us because it is a piece of well-attested folklore. True, we have Wace's testimony that the rain-making power of the Fountain of Barenton was widely believed in by the Bretons.[4] It is also likely that Chrétien borrowed this marvel from Wace, as he had borrowed Arthurian material from him in *Erec* and *Cligès*.[5] But the point of Wace's description of his visit to the fountain is to mock himself for having been fool enough to expect the marvel to be true. So if Chrétien and his public in Champagne knew of the fountain through Wace, it is as a discredited marvel and Chrétien will have to make a considerable effort to convince us of its reality.

His first step in establishing the credibility of his fountain is to remove it as far as possible from critical scrutiny. Right from the start, Chrétien impresses on us that his story takes place in the remote past. The Arthurian court of the opening scene is not sprung on us abruptly as in *Erec* and *Lancelot*, but carefully introduced as part of a deliberately phrased evocation of a lost golden age. Some of the Arthurian knights are shown talking of Love's law

> Qui lors estoit riches et buens.
> Mes ore i a mout po des suens.                        (ll. 17–18)

"Lors" refers to the distant past, for it was only in the early days of the world that life was better morally; since then, "tut s'an vat declinant" as

---

[3]Frappier, for example, in his *Etude sur "Yvain,"* 273–74, states that "L'observation de la réalité s'est ici approfondie et élargie."

[4]*Roman de Rou*, ed. Holden, ll. 6373–98.

[5]For the anteriority of Wace's description of the Fountain, see Foulon, "Le *Rou* de Wace," 93–102.

the Alexis poet put it.[6] As Arthur is cited as a moral example (ll. 1-3), his court must belong to a remote period. Chrétien transports our expectations away from the observable present back into a golden and unverifiable past. Then, having set his story in the past, he makes an internal narrator take us still further back. Calogrenant places his tale at a fairy-tale remove of seven years from the Arthurian gathering which will be the starting point of the main action. It is remarkable that nothing and no-one within his story are affected by the passage of time: the vavassour and his daughter do not change in their reception of guests, whether hopeful or unsuccessful; the churl and his bulls do not change and everyone at Arthur's court assumes that every item on Calogrenant's itinerary will have remained untouched by time, as indeed it has.[7] The atemporality of Calogrenant's tale is not the least "marvellous" part of it, as we shall see.

Distance in space is even more thoroughly exploited, as distance lends enchantment to the view. Giraldus Cambrensis, dedicating his *Topographia Hibernica* to Henry II, declares that, just as the countries of the remote East have their particular marvels, so Ireland, at the extreme west of the world, is illustrated by its own "naturae miraculis." Nature, he says, is sometimes tired of being serious and so, "remotis in partibus [. . .] Natura ludit." It is worth remembering that among the numerous marvels he reports, Giraldus includes precisely a rain-making fountain in Munster, complete with nearby chapel.[8]

Arthur holds his court at "Carduel en Gales" (l. 7), a place Chrétien envisages as peculiarly and hazily remote, for he represents it as being only a few days' ride from Broceliande in Brittany. When it suits his purpose, as it does in *Cligès*, Chrétien's geography can be as precise as anyone's. When, however, as in *Erec* or *Yvain*, he wishes to transport us to the "Bretagne" of Arthur's traditional haunts, the barrier of the Channel vanishes and insular and continental Britons share a common territory beyond the reaches of geography. In *Erec*, this traditional territory is summarily assumed as a starting point: in *Yvain* it is evoked with conscious deliberation.

Chrétien makes his internal narrator emphasize remoteness in space even more than remoteness in time. Calogrenant insists on the physical obstacles to be overcome in the pursuance of his objective. He finds a path, he says:

> "Parmi une forest espesse,
> Mout i ot voie felenesse,
> De ronces et d'espines plainne;

---

[6]*Vie de Saint Alexis*, ed. Storey, l. 9. This belief originates in St. Augustine's periodization of world history; see Smalley, *Historians in the Middle Ages*, 29-30.

[7]Auerbach, *Mimesis*, 130, notes the fairy-tale quality of Calogrenant's story, but not the deliberateness of Chrétien's use of retrospection.

[8]*Topographia Hibernica*, ed. Dimock, 20-21, 89.

> A quelqu'enui, a quelque painne,
> Ting cele voie et cel santier.                    (ll. 181–85)

The stages of his journey are progressively marked: he goes from a forest to a moor and from there he sees a battlemented tower at a distance which he estimates as a "demie liue galesche" (l. 192). The landscape is not only remote, it is measured in distances which were exotic for the people of Champagne.

Distance in time is briefly evoked by the Hospitable Vavassour who tells Calogrenant that he cannot remember when he last lodged a "chevalier errant" (l. 259). The next stage of the journey takes Calogrenant beyond all contact with familiar courtly manners and values. The spectacle of a herd of wild bulls terrifies him and he devotes twenty-six lines (ll. 288–313) to describing the bestial hideousness of the churl who guards them. It will be this creature, so remote from the experience of Calogrenant and his audience, who directs him to the marvels he seeks. The particular marvel of the fountain is still further away, and the path to it is easily lost (ll. 374–79). It is only at the end of another journey that Calogrenant will at last see the fountain.

Here the importance of sight becomes apparent in establishing the credibility of the fountain. Calogrenant had prefaced his tale with a reminder that his story was not an invention but an eye-witness report. His immediate audience accepts every detail without the slightest incredulity. Chrétien takes care to reinforce the illusion of reality by showing us the fountain through as many eyes as possible. The grotesque churl first tells Calogrenant what he will see (ll. 380–407). Then Calogrenant tells us what he did see (ll. 410–69). The queen tells it all over again to Arthur—and by this time Calogrenant's "conte" (l. 59) has become his "noveles" (l. 658)—and Arthur talks of seeing it himself (ll. 657–72). Yvain anticipates his journey to the fountain by going over every item of what he expects to see, culminating in the storm he will provoke at the fountain (ll. 696–717). The fountain is apparently seen over and over again, in anticipation as well as in retrospect.

An extra illusion of reality is afforded by the slight variants in these visions. Calogrenant's description of the fountain is the most elaborate. Thereafter, perceptions are more fragmentary. Arthur mentions only the fountain and the storm (ll. 665–67). Yvain's curiosity is most stimulated by the churl, and his thoughts just touch on the stone, the fountain itself, the basin, the birds and the tree (ll. 708–17). When he makes the journey, it is again the churl who most engages his interest: when he reaches the fountain, he does not pause to marvel at anything, but gets down to business (ll. 794–804). When Arthur comes, it is just to the marvel of the fountain and the stone (ll. 2172–73); he pours water on the stone, it rains torrentially and the new Knight of the Fountain appears (ll. 2218–27). The vavassour, the churl and the birds have all been eliminated and only the essential part of the marvel is retained.

A significant detail of Calogrenant's description of the fountain is that it does not tally in two respects with the description the churl gave of it. The churl described the tree overhanging the fountain by saying:

> "An toz tans la fuelle li dure,
> Qu'il ne la pert por nul iver"                    (ll. 384–85)

as if it were like the marvellously timeless flora of the orchard in *Erec*. Calogrenant, however, demystifies it by giving it a name and telling us that it is a beautiful pine tree (l. 413). Conversely, the churl says that a "bacins de fer" was hanging from the tree (l. 386) which, to Calogrenant's eyes, becomes a much more "marvellous" object made of purest gold, while the stone, which the churl felt unable to describe, becomes, in Calogrenant's description, a magnificent affair of rubies and emeralds, so amazing that he protests he is not lying about its splendour (ll. 424–31). It is impossible for us to know whether the churl is erring on the side of simplicity or Calogrenant on the side of magnificence.

Chrétien avoids giving us any description of the fountain on his own authority. His way of dealing with its marvels contrasts sharply with his description of the ingenious double portcullis which traps Yvain. In this case he explains in a straightforward, scientific way exactly how the machinery works (ll. 907–31). The portcullis that unexpectedly trapped the hero of the *Charrette* was caused by enchantment (*Lancelot*, ll. 2344–46). The one in *Yvain* is far more ingenious, but is treated in a drily factual style. When the matter can be explained, Chrétien explains it. When it cannot be explained, like the fountain, he leaves it to hearsay. The slight inconsistencies in the different characters' perceptions of it do not provoke our incredulity; on the contrary, they tend to confirm for us the belief that the common core of these reports must be true.

Chrétien makes sure that the fountain will first appear in his narrative in a way that must disarm the most sceptical. Not only is it distanced in time and space, it is distanced within the narrative. We are not shown it at once, but told about it by the churl at several narrative removes. Chrétien tells us of that remote Arthurian court at which Calogrenant told the courtiers how a churl of Broceliande had told him about this marvel. Chrétien takes care not to make the Chinese box effect too obvious and so, although Calogrenant's story is mentioned at the very beginning of the romance (l. 59), we have to wait through a series of lively exchanges between Kay and Calogrenant and the queen, then through Kay's unkind urgings to the queen to get her to make Calogrenant tell his tale, and then the unfortunate knight's pleas to be excused, before his tale is finally begun (l. 175). By that time Chrétien's audience is as curious and impatient to hear what Calogrenant has to say as the Arthurian courtiers are. Even then, the reluctant narrator makes a whole preface out of his unwillingness to tell his story, ending with the protest that nothing he will relate is false.

Calogrenant's description of the fountain is the only one in which its beauty plays an important part. He stresses how beautiful the pine tree is, how dazzling the stone, how joyful the singing of the birds after the storm and how greatly they embellish the already beautiful tree (ll. 414–64). It is a marvel that he makes very attractive visually, and the Arthurian court responds to the attraction. Nevertheless, it is a more sinister marvel socially than the beautiful garden in *Erec*. Far from being an object worthy of admiration, it is, as the first Knight of the Fountain made clear to Calogrenant (ll. 498–514), the single vulnerable point of a fortification, the means whereby one man can cause suffering and distress to a whole domain. It is wonderfully economic as a narrative device for a romance: how better can a domain be challenged—and defended—by a single man?

The strange powers of the fountain are made credible for a reason that has nothing to do with time or space or narrative distance. Its marvels are made acceptable by remoteness, but its reality is brought home to us by being integrated into the hierarchy of creation. The churl declares that the tree is the most beautiful that Nature could make (l. 382), and Calogrenant reminds us that God remains in control: he was terrified when the storm broke,

> "Mes Des tant me rasseüra,
> Que li tans gueires ne dura
> Et tuit li vant se reposerent:
> Quant De ne plot, vanter n'oserent." (ll. 451–54)

Chrétien reasserts this point in his own name when Yvain comes to the fountain. The storm duly rises at Yvain's provocation, but then,

> . . . quant Des redona le bel,
> Sor le pin vindrent li oisel. (ll. 807–08)

The fountain may be "marvellous," but it is not absurd. Presented as part of the universal order, constantly under divine supervision, it becomes the most solidly established fact of the narrative data. When Calogrenant returns from Broceliande, he says that he thought himself a fool: "por fol me ting" (l. 578), exactly the words Wace uses of himself (*Le Roman de Rou*, l. 6398). Calogrenant is not without folly, as we shall see, but it is not the same folly as Wace's. Whatever else he may have to reproach himself with, it is not the folly of having gone to see something that did not exist.

It is characteristic of *Yvain* that the focus of the narrative should be an external object, available to everyone's sight and not, as in the *Charrette*, a state of mind comprehensible only to the hero. Throughout *Yvain*, the observation of externals is stressed to a degree that makes it fair to describe it as a materialistic romance by comparison with its predecessors. Erec's problem was entirely a problem of the will: on every occasion, when he knows what he wants, whether it be revenge, love, or rehabilitation, he goes as straight to the point as possible and, preoccupied with the essence, pays little attention to the accidents of life. Alexander, concentrating on his development as hero and lover, thinks of nothing but the ideally heroic and the ideally amorous. Cligès and Fenice delegate their material problems to subordinates. Lancelot, absorbed in quasi-spiritual contemplation, has eyes for nothing more material than the golden hairs in Guinevere's comb.

With *Yvain*, we move into a new fictional world. It is the first romance by Chrétien—or indeed by anyone—to use the kind of material realism that has been such a familiar part of narrative fiction since the early nineteenth century. The most striking example of this realism in *Yvain* must, for any modern reader, be the complaint voiced by one of the women weavers about their hard lot in the Castle of Pesme Avanture (ll. 5306–17). They only receive, she says, four *deniers* for every *livre*'s worth of work they do, and though most of them do twenty *sous*' worth of work or more every week, what they get from it is not enough to keep themselves fed and clothed. It is an evocation of sordid misery and exploitation worthy of Zola.

We must note, however, that there is no evidence Chrétien was drawing on real-life working conditions.[9] He would probably be amazed at the powerful impression of reality his references to money make on readers in an industrial age. Workers complaining about pay and conditions strike a much readier chord of response in us than, for example, a chivalrous hero debating within himself whether to come to the rescue of a lion or a serpent. But we have no reason to suppose that Chrétien shared our point of view. The evidence, indeed, leads us to suppose that he did not. Yvain's rescue of the lion is highlighted as the turning point in the hero's career, whereas his response to the weavers persecuted by a hard master (ll. 5338–44) is less emotional than his response to the rich family persecuted by the giant Harpin (ll. 3898–4090). It is only his 'pesme avanture' because the two diabolical creatures he has to fight are more difficult to overcome than Harpin or any of his other earlier opponents. In the overall economy of the narrative, the external reality of the weavers' sufferings is less important than the internal reality of Yvain's decision to defend nobility against baseness.

The women's sufferings do have a genuine though paradoxical significance in the romance. In a philosophical sense, *Yvain* is the least realistic of Chrétien's romances precisely because it is the one that is expressed in the most material terms. In the earlier romances, Chrétien has a vision, however partial, of a more perfect reality. The essence of each situation is more difficult to perceive in *Yvain*, for everything is clouded with the accidentals of everyday living. The characters have

---

[9]The question has been examined by Hall, "The Silk Factory in Chrestien de Troyes' *Yvain*," 418–22, by Jonin, "Aspects de la vie sociale," 51–54, by Frappier in his *Etude sur "Yvain"*, 125–27, by Gallais in "Littérature et médiatisation," 57–73 and by Carasso-Bulow, *The Merveilleux in Chrétien de Troyes' Romances*, 90–91.

eyes, but do not always see the same thing; they have ears, but, as Calogrenant says, they do not always hear the real sense of what is being said (ll. 149–70).[10]

However deceptive the external world may be, it does not melt away before the powerful motivation of a Lancelot. On the contrary, the characters in *Yvain* never escape from the material side of life. There is far greater emphasis in *Yvain* on food and clothes than in any other romance. Chrétien has never paused over food before. He never gave us a line of description of any nourishment that passed Lancelot's lips, but we are shown Yvain responding gratefully to Lunete's offer of sustenance; when she produces a roast capon, fine bread and a flagon of wine,

> . . . cil cui il estoit mestiers
> Manja et but mout volantiers.          (ll. 1053–54)

To mention physical needs is to make us conscious of physical limitations. Insofar as he is shown feeling these needs, Yvain is seen as being only a man like any other. When, in his period of madness, he eagerly bites into the bread the hermit leaves for him, Chrétien gives us eight lines of description of how poor and bitter this bread was (ll. 2845–51). Yvain's mental degradation is measured in material terms.

Chrétien's new preoccupation with material things is not a new perception of reality, but of the difficulty of perceiving reality. What his characters see, they see through a glass darkly. Chrétien's emphasis on material reality is linked to a greater awareness of evil and misfortune than he had earlier shown. Thus Calogrenant makes his difficult way along a path choked with thorns and briars to become the first sympathetic character in Chrétien to suffer defeat in battle. In *Erec*, Chrétien had thought only splendid things worth describing. In *Yvain*, he describes the grotesque churl and the wretched weavers. Even the physical pain of battle is more closely noted. Yvain comes so close to catching up with the defeated Knight of the Fountain that he can hear him groan with pain (ll. 888–89).

Chrétien's depiction of a fictional world in which the physical realities are always present is best illustrated by a passage which could not possibly have figured in one of his earlier romances: the problems of the disinherited sister of Noire Espine. The episode opens in the neatly contrived manner we expect from Chrétien: the girl arrives at Arthur's court to seek help, but her elder sister who wronged her has also forestalled her and secured the services of Gawain (ll. 4703–71). Meanwhile, the family rescued from Harpin come, as they had promised, to report to Arthur their deliverance from persecution through the prowess

---

[10]Calogrenant's appeal for serious attention is seen by Gallais as Chrétien's own exordium, displaced from its normal position in the prologue; see "Recherches sur la mentalité des romanciers," 491.

of the Knight of the Lion. When the girl hears of this, it is reasonable, indeed inevitable, that she should think of engaging the services of this knight

> Qui met sa painne a conseillier
> Celes qui d'aïe ont mestier.　　　　　　　　　(ll. 4819–20)

So far, so good. She sets to find him, but her quest is a failure. This is a new note for Chrétien. The girl covers a good deal of ground without succeeding in getting any news of the champion she seeks for a just cause. Yvain is not a hero like Lancelot, who can project news of himself as if by telepathy. The convenient 'novele' of the earlier romances has been eliminated. Here the unfortunate girl falls ill with discouragement and is unable to continue her quest (ll. 4821–29). Her place is taken by a friend, another girl who eventually succeeds, though with the greatest difficulty, in tracking down the Knight of the Lion.

Why does Chrétien substitute one damsel for another, in all respects identical? What can the narrative gain from the introduction of an anonymous damsel, functionally indistinguishable from the one she replaces? She has nothing in common with the nameless ladies who test Lancelot's heroism. All she will ask, when she finally catches up with Yvain, is that he should do again what he has done before and come to the aid of a damsel in distress—in short, exactly what her friend would have asked.

Her significance lies entirely in the way she rounds out the background of Yvain's activities. In *Lancelot*, the direction of interest was centripetal, everything being focussed on the hero's mind. In the much more physical world of *Yvain*, our interest is continually directed centrifugally. Instead of making the minor characters subordinate to the hero as in *Lancelot*, Chrétien here pursues the opposite aim. His "materialized" hero moves through a densely populated world of people taken up with their own affairs, whose lives he impinges on for a variety of reasons, none of which is ever his own unprompted decision. Yvain's world is both more physical and more insecure than Lancelot's and its uncertainties are nowhere better underlined than here. Chrétien first shows us how right it is that the heiress of Noire Espine should be championed by Yvain, and then shows her threatened by discouragement and illness. When we meet her again, Chrétien reminds us that her illness still marks her (ll. 5827–30). Physical weakness and physical distance come close to undermining the course of justice.

The obstacles the friend encounters are not the dramatic and romantic problems that confronted Enide, but physical problems we have not encountered before. The Arthurian forest is no longer a place of adventures and marvels. It is a cold and hostile environment. Pitch darkness falls and the girl has no lodging. No hospitable vavassour has made his usual timely appearance. Moreover, it is no longer midsummer: even worse than the dark is the rain and the mud that her mount sinks into (ll. 4836–54). When her desperate prayer is answered, she still has a long way to go before she finds shelter and an even longer way to go before she catches up with Yvain. Then, when her mission is accomplished, she disappears from the narrative, leaving behind her the impression that Yvain's world is more populous and more variously threatened than we would otherwise have known it to be.

The hero really belongs to his world, unlike the hero of the *Charrette*, who remains detached from both Logres and Gorre. Chrétien introduces Yvain to us as a man firmly entrenched in his milieu. Instead of a formal and eulogistic presentation such as he gave of Erec, Alexander and Cligès, or a deliberately low-key introduction as in *Lancelot*, Chrétien first shows us Yvain as part of a typical group of Arthurian knights:

> A l'uis de la chanbre defors
> Fu Dodiniaus et Sagremors
> Et Kes et mes sire Gauvains,
> Et si i fu mes sire Yvains,
> Et avuec aus Calogrenanz,
> Uns chevaliers mout avenanz.               (ll. 53–58)

He is part of the Arthurian décor. He does not even merit any particular epithet like his cousin. Even when he marks himself out from the others by offering to go and avenge his kinsman's shame, Kay does everything he can to belittle his aspirations (ll. 590–611). Yvain sets out alone for the fountain in the typical manner of a romance hero, but Calogrenant had been alone too. All the members of the court are curious to see the fountain, and Yvain is no different from them. The differences between his journey and Calogrenant's are of degree, not of kind. Yvain sees even more beauty in the damsel, even greater hospitality in her father (ll. 779–84). If he succeeds where Calogrenant failed, it is only because he is rather better at exactly the same kind of exercise. There is no indication that the difference between the successful hero and his unsuccessful companion is a radical difference of motivation of the kind we were shown between Lancelot and Gawain. No–one marvels at Yvain any more than they had at Calogrenant. It is Yvain who is anxious to marvel at the fountain. Like everyone else, he is impatient to gratify a visual curiosity.

Yvain's preoccupation with externals marks his first acquaintance with the heroine. Again there is a direct contrast with Lancelot, lost in thoughts of a lady he does not even speak to until the principal action of the romance is over and who is never described to us. The absence of physical description is a measure of the quasi-spiritual quality of Lancelot's love. Yvain, on the other hand, starts with a purely visual appreciation of Laudine. By a conveniently "marvellous" contrivance, he is able to see her without being seen. While the people of the castle seek in vain for the one who killed their lord, his widow appears:

> . . . une des plus beles dames,
> Qu'onques veïst riens terriienne.              (ll. 1146–47)

Having seen her, Yvain tells Lunete that he would like to see the funeral procession, when what he really wants is a chance to see the lady again, and he gets his chance when Lunete places him at a little window (ll. 1271–87). This is quite unlike any other occasion when the hero sees the heroine for the first time. The closest parallel is when Lancelot sees Guinevere from a window. The contrast of attitudes is all the more striking. Lancelot appears to be unaware of material barriers until Gawain restrains him from falling. Yvain too is filled with an impulse to hasten to his lady, but he accepts the common–sense advice of Lunete to stay where he is (ll. 1305–32). He resists the temptation to run and hold her hands and eventually the other mourners retire, though Laudine goes on lamenting and Yvain goes on watching. Her grief is spectacular: she manages to wring her hands and read a magnificent psalter simultaneously (ll. 1411–15).

There is no reason why Laudine should not externalize her sorrow, but we are reminded by contrast of Enide's heartfelt and silent grief (*Erec*, ll. 5827–32). Yvain is more impressed by the lady's beauty than by her protestations of grief, or indeed any of her feelings. When Love wounds his heart through his eyes (l. 1368), he knows that she must hate him now, because he killed her husband, but he is equally confident that her feelings cannot remain constant because she is a woman:

> "D' 'ore androit' ai je dit que sages;
> Que fame a plus de mil corages.
> Celui corage, qu'ele a ore,
> Espoir changera ele ancore, –
> Ainz le changera sanz 'espoir',
> Si sui mout fos, qui m'an despoir."              (ll. 1435–40)

Nothing is more commonplace in medieval literature than attacks on female constancy,[11] but this is the first time that Chrétien has generalized about women. Just as Chrétien's new hero is a less idealized and more representative figure than his predecessors, so the new heroine is characterized as belonging to the common run of women. The most disturbing part of the comment is that it is made by the hero. Yvain is not overpowered by the lady's worth; there will be no–one to lecture him on her admirable 'sagesse'. All we know about Laudine in the first instance is that her beauty inspires love and that the spectacular display of her grief does not convince even the man who loves her of its constancy.

Our introduction to Laudine demonstrates the increased economy

---

[11]The sentiment echoes Virgil, but the particular expression Chrétien gives it is borrowed from Ovid. See Nitze, "Two Virgilian Commonplaces," 439–41.

and complexity of Chrétien's narrative techniques. Previous portraits of heroines had been static, detachable pieces of rhetoric. Here he achieves a complete fusion of simultaneous action and description. Both Yvain and Laudine are caught up in the development of the plot as he watches and she is watched. Laudine grieves for Esclados, whom Yvain aims to replace, and he continues to run risks by remaining in her castle, not only in order to go on seeing her but also to obtain some proof of his exploit for the doubting Kay (ll. 1339–59). He does not see an ideal beauty in ideal circumstances, but obtains glimpses of a relatively typical woman who is as yet unaware of his existence, and who is occupied in regretting a past that lies outside Yvain's experience.

As regards the physical details, Laudine has of course the beautiful golden hair which is *de rigueur* for all heroines, but it is not a subject for reverential and isolated contemplation like the golden hair of Soredamors and Guinevere. We see it through Yvain's eyes as she tears it with grief and he watches her with distress. He only sees her eyes in the act of weeping (ll. 1462–71). Her beauty, her grief, Yvain's admiration and his distress are repeatedly conveyed to us in terms of what the hero sees and how he reacts to what he sees (ll. 1473–79). Neither we nor Yvain see Laudine's beauty directly, but only obscurely, through the effects of her grief. We can only speculate on what she would look like in ideal circumstances, as Yvain does:[12]

> "Don ne fust ce mervoille fine
> A esgarder, s'ele fust liee,
> Quant ele est or si bele iriee?"          (ll. 1488–90)

He then speculates on the respective parts God and Nature must have played in making her, but his point of departure remains this specific vision, blurred by the physical effects of life as it is being lived. He does not progress to a more spiritual or abstract level, but continues to watch her until she goes away (l. 1517). When at last he meets her, he admits that it is his eyes that are responsible for his love for her (ll. 2019–20).

Yvain too is seen, and judged on sight. When Laudine brings him before her own men, their reaction to the person they guess will be their new lord gives us our first view of Yvain:

> . . . mes sire Yvains fu si janz
> Qu'a mervoilles tuit l'esgarderent.          (ll. 2056–57)

To them, Yvain "a mervoilles sanble prodome" (l. 2063). Once again, it is not a detached rhetorical description, but an observation within the

---

[12]Lines 1488–90 are a reminiscence of Ovid to be added to those listed by Guyer in his article "The Influence of Ovid on Crestien de Troyes." Compare *Metamorphoses* 7: 730–33, where the grief of Procris for her husband is described:
> Tristis erat (sed nulla tamen formosior illa
> esse potest tristi) desiderioque dolebat
> coniugis abrepti. tu conlige, qualis in illa,
> phoce, decor fuerit, quam sic dolor ipse decebat.

narrative. Yvain's prospective subjects have the greatest interest in deducing what they can from his appearance. Yet their judgment has no authority, for they have already been contemptuously dismissed by Lunete as hopeless fighters (ll. 1628–30). How are they competent to judge a 'prodome' by his appearance? The damsel who takes back Laudine's ring from Yvain will comment bitterly on the deceptiveness of those "larron, qui prodome ressanblent" (l. 2736).

Yvain always puts up an excellent appearance as a fighter, and those who watch him are impressed. When he starts his chivalrous life afresh at Norison by leading the assault on Count Alier, those who remain in the castle watch him (l. 3198) and continually press each other to witness each visible sign of his heroic prowess:

> "Veez or, comant cil se prueve,
> Veez, come il se tient an ranc,
> Veez, come il portait de sanc
> Et sa lance et s'espee nue,
> Veez, comant il les remue,
> Veez, comant il les antasse."                (ll. 3212–17)

And so on for seventeen more lines. All of them, "por la proesce qu'an lui voient" (l. 3252), wish that he would take their lady and rule their land. Yvain had recently proved himself unworthy of another lady and another land, yet it would hardly be just to say that the opinion of the people of Norison is mistaken. It is correct as far as it goes, which is only as far as they can see.

Conversely, Yvain is greatly underestimated by the strangers who greet him at the Castle of Pesme Avanture. They do everything they can to repulse him because they are so confident that he will fail. The wise elderly lady who explains their conduct (ll. 5143–62) says that it would give her great joy if he were to return safely, but this is impossible (ll. 5171–74). Despite her wisdom she cannot divine any special quality from Yvain's outward appearance, unlike the ordinary people who were able to divine Lancelot's mission. The visible part of Yvain never gives the whole clue to his identity, though this is all that the other characters have to work on.

The perceptions of characters who know Yvain are more complex. The first real information we are given about him does not come from any intuition of his status as hero, but from the previous experience of another character. In the castle of Esclados, Yvain is rescued by Lunete, who is acquainted with his public, social identity:

> "Bien sai, comant vos avez non,
> Et reconeü vos ai bien:
> Fiz estes au roi Uriien
> Et avez non mes sire Yvains."                (ll. 1016–19)

The significant point of her recognition is the moral recognition which preceded it. She knows him as the only knight who treated her courteously at Arthur's court (ll. 1001–15). She does not expect him to remember her; his courteous behaviour was evidently disinterested, almost impersonal, but it is this timely remembrance of the spontaneous action of a noble nature that at last indicates to us that Yvain is the stuff of which heroes can be made.

Memories, however, are various and selective. The damsel who comes across him in the wood in his madness has to examine him for a long time before she realizes who he is: paradoxically, he is unrecognizable because he is naked (ll. 2894–900). At last she finds a sign that makes it possible for her to identify him: Yvain has a scar on his face. When all was going well for him, all that people saw was that his beauty was that of a 'prodome'. In his shame and disgrace, the scar singles him out. The visible remains of a physical wound are brought to our notice just as Yvain is suffering his greatest mental wound, the madness he suffers as a result of his guilt.

The lady of Norison's damsel would have recognized Yvain easily if he had been wearing the rich clothes of their common courtly milieu (ll. 2897–900). Throughout the romance, the other characters' perceptions of Yvain are so partial that they only recognize him in terms of their relationship with him. When Arthur raises the storm at the fountain, he converses with its victorious defender, but admits that he cannot identify him unless he hears him named or sees him disarmed (ll. 2275–78). Gawain, who is closer to Yvain, could have recognized Yvain's voice had it not been "roe et foible et quasse" (l. 6234) but he is not morally equipped to identify the Knight of the Lion.

Yvain's wife does not recognize him in the course of the dialogue they carry on after he has defended Lunete. His recognition of her is so eager that it is achieved almost by anticipation:

> . . . lui est mout tart que il voie
> Des iauz celi que del cuer voit,
> An quel leu que ele onques soit;
> As iauz la quiert tant qu'il la trueve.          (ll. 4344–47)

Chrétien shows us Yvain suppressing his anguish at the sight of Laudine and at the same time looking with pity at the poor women who are lamenting Lunete (l. 4352). We see that this is a different man from the one who carelessly forgot his lady, but all that Laudine can see is the excellent knightly performance of a stranger. Yvain returning in disguise to his lady cannot, like Tristan in such circumstances, prove his identity as her lover by producing the ring she gave him. When he forfeited that symbol of true love, he forfeited his identity as the man she loves. All that he can reveal to Laudine are the unhappy circumstances surrounding the life of the Knight of the Lion.

By the end of the romance, the situation has changed. Yvain now believes that he has suffered enough for his folly, and can hope for forgiveness (ll. 6780–82). Any dialogue would betray him. Lunete therefore contrives to reveal his identity before he can be called upon to speak. Even here, Laudine has no inkling of his identity. No intuition enlightens her and no lingering sentiment attaches her to the past. Her husband's offence is not glossed over: it is eliminated from her memory when she agrees to honour her word to the Knight of the Lion. Laudine, unaware to the end of all that has happened to Yvain since they parted, agrees to reassume her part in his life without ever obtaining a complete view of his personality.

The best view of Yvain does not depend on direct sight. When the family he rescued from Harpin duly come to spread his fame at Arthur's court, they confer a moral identity on him independent of his physical appearance. The disinherited sister of Noire Espine understands that this exploit is not an isolated act and that the defining behaviour of the Knight of the Lion is to come to the aid of damsels in distress (ll. 4819–20). Her friend who takes over her quest is even further removed from the physical identity of Yvain. As she tells her host, she is seeking someone she has never laid eyes on (l. 4902). The only visual clue she has is that he is accompanied by a lion, the external symbol of his commitment to championing the just cause. It is enough for her host, who is none other than the lord whom Yvain rescued from Harpin and, as he tells her:

> ". . . tot veant mes iauz l'ocist.
> A cele porte la defors
> Demain porroiz veoir le cors
> D'un grant jaiant, que il tua."   (ll. 4914–17)

The visible signs of Yvain's service to others point the damsel on her way, rather than a description of the man or his armour. Even when she finally catches up with him, she knows that everything depends on his living up to his reputation (ll. 5045–49). If he will not help her distressed friend, she says, "Donc l'a vostre renons traïe" (l. 5075). Yvain has acquired an identity that no longer depends on anything external; it is based on his continually renewed commitment to the defence of right.

The physical limitations of Yvain's world are most strikingly illustrated by the difficulties damsels experience in tracking him down. Lancelot's powerful mental impulse propelled him irresistibly along his 'droit chemin'. In *Yvain*, the characters pick their way laboriously towards their goals. The heiress knows who she is looking for, but cannot find him. She traverses "mainte contree" (l. 4822) without being able to get any news of him. The damsel who takes over her mission labours under even greater difficulties. Her first and very indirect clue is the sound of a horn indicating possible shelter (ll. 4861–64). Her hosts can only point her one stage further, to Laudine's castle (ll. 4937–40). Once there, she is directed a little further, to the scene of Lunete's defence, then to the church where Lunete has gone to pray. Lunete can do no more than show her the last place where she saw Yvain and recommend her to follow the direction he rode off in (ll. 4991–5005). The damsel goes on alone until she reaches the house where Yvain was nursed. There she is put on the track and hastens onwards until at last she can exclaim: "Or voi ce que tant ai chacié" (l. 5043). By patient, limited stages, rather than by any internal impetus, she finally reaches her goal.

Yvain heads for his various goals just as short-sightedly. After he hears how Calogrenant rode out, "querant avantures" (l. 177), found a "chemin a destre" (l. 180) which led him, through difficult and uncertain country, to the hospitable vavassour and thence to the churl who pointed out the "droite voie" (l. 376) to the fountain, Yvain has a specific destination to make for, and understands that it can only be reached by omitting no stage of his cousin's journey. There can be no short cuts: the same perils must be overcome, the same hospitality accepted before he can at last be put on the right road to the fountain.

Even in his new life that begins after he has been cured of his madness, Yvain never has a mental sense of direction comparable to Lancelot's. When he defends the lady of Norison from Count Alier, he appears to be setting out on a new path. Yet when he leaves her, he "se mist a la voie arriere" (l. 3324) without any conscious new purpose. Even after he decides to rescue the noble lion, he still does not choose a path. The two wander aimlessly for a fortnight until chance brings them to the fountain:

> Tant qu'avanture a la fontainne
> Dessoz le pin les amena.                    (ll. 3490–91)

Yvain had no conscious plan to return to the fountain: the sight of it causes him almost unendurable self-reproach. Yet having once committed himself to fight for the true nobility represented by the lion, the chance that directs his steps is not without a certain providential element. All he can see is evidence of his fault, but through the crack in the chapel wall Lunete can see him—a partial vision as always, but enough to save Yvain from the fate of Pyramus and to put him on the road to repairing an injustice that was indirectly of his making.

The lord whom he rescues from Harpin sees him in the role of providential liberator, as he later tells the substitute damsel:

> ". . . a un mien mout grant besoing
> Le m'anvea Des avant ier.
> Beneoit soient li santier
> Par ou il vint a mon ostel!"                    (ll. 4908–11)

Yvain has no sense of the paths he follows. He never sees beyond the next stage of the undertaking in hand. Having promised to defend Lunete the following day, he turns his attention to the immediate problem of getting shelter. With his lion, Yvain travels until they see a castle, whereupon they make for it at once (ll. 3784–85). He is just as

direct about the next stage, covering the same ground back to the chapel
next day (ll. 4315-17). The intervening combat with the giant Harpin,
which seems like the workings of providence to the afflicted lord, is
perceived by the hero only as a source of anguish. He is the only person
who can fight off the danger threatened by Harpin and the danger
threatened to Lunete, and he dare not delay over the first of these tasks
for fear of failing in his commitment to the second. Even though he
succeeds in killing the giant in time to rescue Lunete, he cannot see
ahead into his future, and he tells the grateful family who press him to
return

> . . . qu'il ne les ose
> Asseürer de nule chose;
> Qu'il ne set mie deviner,
> S'il li doit bien ou mal finer.                    (ll. 4269-72)

At his incognito interview with Laudine, he says that he dare not stay
until he is sure that his lady has forgiven him (ll. 4621-26). He has no
hope of forgiveness at this stage and so he rides on, apparently at
random, till he reaches the next point of shelter (ll. 4662-63). He
gratefully accepts the hospitality offered, acknowledging his need of it.
He is also given medical treatment, which lasts until whatever time he
and his lion are cured "et que raler s'an durent" (l. 4702). But where are
they going to? Yvain may have a goal, but he does not have a
destination. When we meet him again, he is being asked to champion
the heiress of Noire Espine. Far from pursuing a path of his own, Yvain
is repeatedly drawn into the paths of others.

Like any other hero, Yvain suffers and needs medical help. Erec was
treated with an ointment made by Arthur's sister Morgan, and Lancelot
was treated with the Three Marys' ointment. In apparently the same
vein, the lady of Norison proposes to treat Yvain with an ointment "que
me dona Morgue, la sage" (l. 2953). There is an obvious similarity
between Yvain's situation and Erec's, for they have each precipitated a
crisis in their lives by neglecting one side of their commitments. Erec,
however, by the time he receives help from Morgan's ointment, is well
on the way to rehabilitation, and he has always been in control of his
actions, even his remorse. Yvain, on the other hand, once he is made
conscious of his fault, is unable to sustain the burden of his guilt and his
mind gives way. The contrast with Lancelot is even more complete: the
constant mind of the hero of the *Charrette* knows no weakness; even his
suicidal despair is heroic and his single momentary lapse is the result of
weighing two incompatible forms of good.

Yvain's fault is by far the most serious as it involves breaking a solemn
promise. The wound to be healed is much more serious than the
physical injuries received by his predecessors: Yvain's whole rational
being is undermined. Social existence becomes impossible for him and
he flees to the forest to a savage and insane solitude, relieved only by the

charity of a hermit. The knight crossed in love and forced to leave the court where he was honoured for a savage life in a forest, hunting to survive and helped only by a hermit, is a figure that inevitably conjures up the memory of the Tristan story. *Yvain* is the last romance in which Chrétien evokes this great influence on his work, and the only one where he evokes it not to exalt his hero by comparison, but to underline his weakness. Tristan goes into exile in the forest of Morrois because he has been so intent on his love that the evil barons would not tolerate it. His misfortune comes from without: Yvain's comes from within. Tristan feigns madness in order to return to Iseut: Yvain's real madness is a result of his failure to return to Laudine.

Yvain's condition is serious, but no king intervenes to cure him. He is healed by a chance act of charity. He is discovered by one of the damsels of the lady of Norison who, as we have seen, has great difficulty in recognizing him. She is shocked and grieved at his condition, but not unduly surprised. His visible symptoms enable her to guess that he has gone mad with sorrow, and she explains this to her lady as if it were one of the better known facts of life (ll. 2926–28). Both the damsel and her mistress piously wish that God may give him back his wits. Divine support is essential: the instrument of it is the ointment that the lady happens to remember that she happens to have (ll. 2948–53). And she only has a limited amount of it. She instructs her damsel to use it only on Yvain's head, the afflicted part. But the damsel gets carried away and uses it all and the lady is left regretting her irreparable loss (ll. 3124–25). In the limited world of Yvain, even Morgan's ointments are finite.

After his madness, Yvain never again displays spontaneous eagerness for fighting. Nor are his recoveries ever marvellously rapid or he himself ever heroically impatient to be up and doing. He does not protest when the damsel tells him he needs at least a fortnight's rest (ll. 3082–83). By the time he fights count Alier, he is fully restored (ll. 3153–54). After his defence of Lunete, he gratefully accepts medical help from the nearest house and stays there for as long as it takes to recover completely (ll. 4661–702). Even after his final combat with Gawain, Yvain displays no impatience to return to Laudine until after he is healed (ll. 6498–510). Unlike Erec and Lancelot, Yvain, the most vulnerable of Chrétien's heroes, never transcends his physical limitations.

The healing ointment, it has been suggested, derives from the magic resources of Benoît de Sainte-Maure's Medea, like the two magic rings Yvain is given.[13] The ring Lunete gives him enables him to see without being seen. It is an outrageously artificial device, but not unacceptable in a romance where so much emphasis is placed on the visible. If the use of such a "marvellous" prop compromises to some degree the hero's independence of action and enables him to get a slightly unfair view of

---

[13]See Reid's notes to lines 1023, 2600 and 2952. For the possible influence of St. Bernard, see Cook, "The Ointment in Chrétien's *Yvain*."

the heroine, this is not inappropriate in a romance where, for the first time, the central characters are not idealized.

Laudine's ring has more subtle powers, capable of purely symbolic interpretation. When Yvain warns her that he may be prevented from returning within the appointed time, she is ready to counteract his rather Freudian anticipation of failure. She assures him that no obstacle barring death will prevent him returning "tant con vos sovandra de moi" (l. 2599) and gives him a ring:

> "Prison ne tient ne sanc ne pert
> Nus amanz verais et leaus,
> Ne avenir ne li puet maus,
> Mes qu'il le port and chier le taingne
> Et de s'amie li sovaingne
> Einçois devient plus durs que fers."     (ll. 2604–09)

Unlike Medea's ring, Laudine's has no intrinsic power. All depends on the wearer being a true lover and being mindful of his lady. Once he fails, its protection fails. The giving and taking of this ring are only the material sign of the contract of trust between them.

Yvain fails to be mindful of Laudine and is duly stripped of the symbolic ring. There is a painful implied contrast with Lancelot, who thinks constantly of Guinevere without any prospect of really winning her. Yvain begins by winning Laudine and never thinks of her until it is too late. Long after the appointed time, he suddenly remembers his promise to return and when he thinks of what he has done his intense guilt produces an unexpected effect:

> Tant pansa que il vit venir
> Une dameisele a droiture.     (ll. 2704–05)

Who is she? The constant and intense thought of Lancelot seemed to destroy physical obstacles. Yvain's first guilty thought seems to conjure up a personification of his self-reproach.[14] This anonymous damsel is not like the others in *Yvain*. She has no other function in the narrative except to express reproach. She salutes the king and court as she comes and goes, but her harangue is exclusively addressed to Yvain. No-one else speaks to her or even appears to see her. Yvain then goes mad and Chrétien moves from showing us his personified thought to showing him entirely from the outside, through the eyes of the frightened hermit.

Yvain's world has none of the internalized unity of Lancelot's. The Knight of the Lion does not live in an idealized environment. Everything in it is apprehended in external, visual terms, even the "marvellous"

---

[14]As Topsfield puts it in *Chrétien de Troyes*, 184: "The damsel may be a real person, may be a supernatural being, and may as well be the creation of Yvain's distressed mind which is now at breaking point." In any event, she is not to be confused with Lunete, as Geschiere makes clear in "Deux vers d'*Yvain*."

fountain. The hero's own character is built up for us from the fragmentary and sometimes mistaken perceptions of others. Unlike Erec, Yvain has no personally chosen 'voie' from which he refuses to be deflected. Unlike Lancelot, he is not sustained by an interior vision. Between Yvain's first and last visits to the fountain, Chrétien never gives him a quest of his own. Nor does Yvain ever transcend his environment like Lancelot. He makes his uncertain way through a material world in which external pressures never cease to be felt.

# XI. The Delicate Balance

The harmonious symmetry of the narrative structure of *Yvain*, particularly of the section dealing with the hero's rehabilitation, suggests an ordered and optimistic view of the world. The fine example of a 'bele conjointure', whereby Chrétien encapsulates Yvain's second and fourth adventures within, respectively, his first and third, promises a more mature version of the confident world portrayed in *Erec*. It is not what we are given. Right triumphs in the end, but Yvain's whole world is permeated with various kinds of wrong and throughout the romance every instance of good is shown to exist in tension with some degree of evil.

The *Charrette* had a thorough-going villain to match its superhuman hero. In *Yvain*, evil is less concentrated and more unexpectedly diffuse. A hint of this new complexity occurs in the prologue and the opening scene of the romance. The exemplary prowess and obedience to love that characterized Arthur and his court in the distant past is evoked in order to revile by comparison the degraded present. The remoteness in time of this Arthurian excellence helps to put us in the right frame of mind to accept the fountain, but it is the moral aspect of this lost golden age that Chrétien explicitly insists on, concluding:

> Mes por parler de çaus qui furent
> Leissons çaus qui an vie durent!
> Qu'ancor vaut miauz, ce m'est avis,
> Uns cortois mors qu'uns vilains vis. (ll. 29–32)

Yet from the first line of his story, Chrétien portrays Arthur's world as morally ambivalent: at the ritual court held during a Christian feast in springtime, Arthur abandons his men and they criticize him for it.[1] He can even be considered a threat by innocent people. After he rejoins his men, he swears to lead an expedition to the fountain, a simple act of curiosity which his men approve of, but which the inhabitants of the domain interpret as an aggressive act of intended domination (ll. 1613–37). In the meantime, the rest of the court has fallen short of the ideal: Calogrenant has been forced to tell the story of his shame, Kay has been venomous, Yvain hasty and even the queen has been discourteously

---

[1]The discrepancy between the Arthur of the prologue and the Arthur of the opening scene of the romance has been widely noted. See Diverres, "Chivalry and *fin'amor*," 96; Newstead; "Narrative Technique," 433; Lonigan, Chrétien's "*Yvain*," 9; Uitti, "Narrative and Commentary," 163–64. Contradictions throughout the romance are studied by Hunt in *Chrétien de Troyes: "Yvain."*

pressing. The courtly past has been contaminated by the uncourtly present.

Chrétien's presentation of Kay tells us much about the new function of evil in the narrative. The seneschal is no longer merely unsubtle and overconfident, as he was in *Lancelot*. He is now categorically malicious. Calogrenant cannot make a civil gesture to the queen but Kay,

> . . . qui mout fu ranposneus,
> Fel et poignanz et afiteus,　　　　　　　　　　(ll. 69-70)

pours out the sneering scorn he cannot hold back. The most curious effect of Kay's malice is the philosophical reaction of its victims. Calogrenant dismisses the abuse, saying that Kay has often insulted better men than he and generalizes on this kind of inherent malice:

> "Toz jorz doit puïr li fumiers
> Et taons poindre et maloz bruire,
> Enuieus enuiier et nuire."　　　　　　　　　　(ll. 116-18)

There is no thought of revenge, or even of correction. Kay is part of a world in which some creatures are harmful by nature and it would be as pointless to reproach Kay for insulting you as to reproach a gadfly for stinging you. The queen agrees that Kay is incorrigible:

> "Costumiers est de dire mal
> Si qu'an ne l'an puet chastiier."　　　　　　　　(ll. 134-35)

Yvain too endures Kay's gibes philosophically, if with rather heavy irony (ll. 630-37).

Yet Kay's malice is not to be taken lightly, for it sets in motion a chain of harmful events. In the *Charrette*, Chrétien had emphasized his long service and the value Arthur put on it (*Lancelot*, ll. 89-129). In *Yvain* Kay is given no positive side at all, yet he is still so favoured by Arthur that no-one else can hope to be given the right of combat at the fountain. Yvain is forced to anticipate Arthur in secret. Worse, in order to prove that he really has achieved the revenge he promised, Yvain knows that his word will not be enough and that his own honour will be impugned unless he can bring back visual proof of his victory. So he pursues the defeated Esclados,

> Que des ranposnes li sovient
> Que mes sire Kes li ot dites.
> N'iert pas de la promesse quites
> Que son cosin avoit promise,
> Ne creüz n'iert an nule guise,
> S'ansaingnes veraies n'an porte.　　　　　　　　(ll. 894-99)

In *Yvain*, a "marvellous" fountain provokes no incredulity, but a claim of victory, though made by one of Arthur's own knights, will not be accepted without proof by the evil-minded Kay.

Kay and the fountain have one thing in common: each is a permanent

part of Yvain's world, and their potential for harm is never eliminated.
It is a world well stocked with characters presented as exclusively evil
or harmful: the giant Harpin de la Montagne and the diabolic 'netuns'
of the Chateau de Pesme Avanture are wholly evil; Count Alier,
Laudine's seneschal and the elder sister of Noire Espine exist only as
incarnations of injustice or aggression.

Evil is a permanent part of this world and almost all the characters
participate in it to some degree. Its most characteristic manifestation is
as an inadequacy or excess. Even the sympathetic characters alternate
between failing to reach the mark and overstepping it, and their
impulses towards good are counterbalanced by the evil within them and
without. The difficulties of achieving a balanced and moderate way of
life are fully explored. Good and evil are held in delicate balance, with
evil being more in evidence and good sometimes only potential.[2] In
*Yvain* there is neither the confident, forward-looking optimism of *Erec*,
nor the pervading gloom of Thomas's *Tristan:* it has a more varied moral
landscape than either.

The problem of a balance to be redressed existed in *Erec*, where the
hero erred through an excessive indulgence in the pleasures of love. Yet
the instant Erec is made aware of his fault he puts himself on the road
to rehabilitation. The imbalance in Yvain's life is more difficult to put
right because it is an inextricable part of the world he lives in. Yvain's
adventures are sparked off by his cousin's tale, and Calogrenant, as he
repeatedly tells us, is relating the story of his shame. He concludes with
the bitter observation:

> "Einsi alai, einsi reving,
> Au revenir por fol me ting."                      (ll. 577–78)

What exactly do his shame and folly consist of? He did not think that his
original mission was foolish. Unlike Wace, he does not say: "Fol i alai"
(*Roman de Rou*, ll. 6396, 6397). No-one, not even Kay, thinks of criticizing a knight at arms for wanting to keep himself in practice and even
in retrospect Calogrenant has no reservations about the spirit in which
he set out (ll. 176–79). What he reproaches himself for is not any
inherent wrongness in his quest for adventures, but for having, so to
speak, bitten off more than he could chew.

He wanted to see the storm, so he poured the water on the stone, but
he went too far: "mes trop an i versai, ce dot" (l. 439). He would have
undone his foolishly excessive act if he could, for the ensuing storm
terrifies him. Yet no sooner is it succeeded by calm and birdsong than he
makes a similar error. By delaying too long to indulge the pleasure of

---

[2]Diverres suggests that Yvain's career may be modelled on Chrétien's reminiscences of
the battle between the Vices and the Virtues in the *Psychomachia* of Prudentius; see
"Yvain's Quest for Chivalric Perfection," 214–28.

listening, he has to face the Knight of the Fountain who is taller and better equipped than he is and he cannot measure up to the challenge.

Calogrenant's foolish excess is the first that upsets the precarious balance of a world already contaminated by evil inclinations. Yvain's first act is to attempt to redress the balance of honour on behalf of his cousin and himself. As far as fighting goes, he succeeds. He pours a whole basin of water on the stone and is well able to cope with the effects. Though he is no superman, Yvain cannot be reproached with over-estimating his chivalrous capacities. His folly lies in another direction and only comes to light after his victory at the fountain.

Arthur's case is more ambiguous. He too pours a full basin of water on the stone. He is unable to back up the challenge this constitutes because, as Yvain foresaw, he grants the incompetent Kay the honour of the battle. No harm comes to the court because the new Knight of the Fountain is Yvain, and as Arthur's loyal subject he will take nothing away from his king, not even the lawful prize of Kay's horse. Arthur as an individual acts with the foolish excess of Calogrenant. It is only his position as king that saves him from being publicly shamed.

Arthur's actions are repeatedly criticized. His absence causes dissatisfaction among his men (ll. 42–49), though his decision to go and see the fountain was unthinkingly endorsed by all (ll. 673–76). Gawain, who offered rational reproaches in *Erec* and *Lancelot*, is silent here. The episode at the beginning of the *Charrette* has not been forgotten. Arthur's poor response to Meleagant's challenge, confined to the privileged reproaches of his nephew in the *Charrette*, is criticized by ordinary people in *Yvain*. Lunete, who is prepared to make allowances for unchivalrous behaviour towards herself (ll. 1004–11) is unequivocal in her condemnation of Arthur's conduct in respect of his wife: "Li rois fist que fors del san" (l. 3708), in letting her be taken off by the strange knight. The lord who is persecuted by Harpin repeats the story with even more scathing comment:

> "Neporquant ja ne l'an eüst
> Menee por rien qu'il seüst,
> Ne fust Kes, qui anbricona
> Le roi tant, que il li bailla
> La reïne et mist an sa garde.
> Cil fu fos et cele musarde,
> Qui an son conduit se fia."                    (ll. 3921–27)

The opening scene of the *Charrette* is no longer treated as a necessarily arbitrary *mise en scène*. From the viewpoint of *Yvain*, Arthur's failure to make an adequate response to Meleagant has far-reaching effects. Gawain felt obliged to attempt to repair his uncle's folly, so it is Arthur's fault that Gawain is not available at home, where help is constantly needed. Arthur's inadequacy, which appeared in the *Charrette* only as a means of disposing us in Lancelot's favour, is shown in *Yvain* to affect even those less important people with whom the king does not come into contact.

If the king is weak, it is not surprising that his entourage is less than perfect, even the hero. Modern commentators have criticized Yvain severely,[3] yet all his actions up to the moment he sees Laudine are defensible in their context. He wants to avenge his kinsman's honour. Even Kay does not criticize Yvain's intention, but only his ability to carry it out. Yvain, though confident of his own prowess, knows that Arthur will give the battle to the unworthy Kay; so the only way he can keep his word to his cousin is by stealing a march on the king. He pursues his defeated opponent only because Kay's evil tongue forces him to. His courage when trapped in the enemy's stronghold impresses Lunete with his worth (ll. 998–1000) and even Laudine ends by admitting that Yvain did no wrong to her husband, who would have killed Yvain if he had been able to.

Erec and Lancelot are set apart from Arthur from the moment they are introduced to us. Yvain cannot escape so easily. Chrétien's fourth romance has a more developed social dimension than any earlier work and its hero is an integrated member of the Arthurian court, forced to participate in its imperfections. It is not Yvain's fault if his cousin is incompetent, his king inadequate and the king's seneschal incurably evil-spoken. In this tainted environment, Yvain acts as honourably as he can.

The balance is upset when Yvain sees Laudine. He is so carried away by the sight of her that Lunete has to warn him "qu'il se gart de folie feire" (l. 1308). From exclaiming on the folly of loving a woman who must hate him, Yvain changes to exclaiming on the folly of being unconfident: "Si sui mout fos, qui m'an despoir," he says complacently (l. 1440). It is folly to despair of winning any woman, he says, since the very nature of woman is to be fickle. His excess of love is already matched by an excess of confidence.

The object of his love is no less extravagant. Laudine is "si fole" (l. 1150) that she tears her hair "come fame desvee" (l. 1156). Lunete criticizes her for indulging her grief "folemant" (l. 1599) and Laudine, while recognizing the soundness of Lunete's advice, perversely rejects her suggestions. As a heroine, Laudine has none of the exceptional qualities of her predecessors. She has neither the 'sagesse' of Enide, nor the courage of Fenice nor the imperious dignity of Guinevere. Chrétien tells us that she shares the common folly of the common run of women:

> . . . une folor a an soi,
> Que les autres fames i ont,
> Et a bien pres totes le font,

---

[3]See Frappier, *Etude sur "Yvain,"* 199–200; Diverres, "Chivalry and *fin'amor*," 93–95. Hunt goes as far as to call him a 'vilains vis'; see "The Dialectic of *Yvain*," 287.

Qui de lor folies s'escusent
Et ce qu'eles vuelent, refusent.                    (ll. 1640–44)

She indulges her foolish perversity to the full, but has scarcely dismissed Lunete with the words "trop m'enuies" (l. 1648) when she realizes how wrong she was and swings to the opposite extreme of impatient eagerness to replace the husband she has been so extravagantly lamenting. She acknowledges that she spoke to Lunete "come fole" (l. 1797) and complains now that she cannot wait even the minimum time necessary to bring her new suitor from Arthur's court (l. 1832).

The theme of the hastily consoled widow is an old one and Laudine certainly owes something to the Widow of Ephesus, a story revived in 1159 by John of Salisbury.[4] John recounts how the widow first gives herself up to extravagant grief at the loss of her husband and is reproached by her confidante for her typically feminine obstinacy (as Laudine is reproached by Lunete at lines 1652–53). She goes rapidly from one extravagance to another by consoling herself with the first man she meets. John admits that generalities on the weaknesses of what he likes to call the inferior sex are a source of amusement much exploited by writers and he will not vouch for the truth of this story, though he recounts it with evident relish.

Chrétien was inevitably familiar with the fertile vein of anti-feminist literature current in his period,[5] but he rises above commonplaces in his treatment of the story. Laudine is not an idealized woman, but her rapid consolation is at least given rational support. As Chrétien tells it, the confidante quietens the widow's extravagant grief by pointing out the urgent necessity of remarrying in order to protect her domain (ll. 1614–17). Laudine's grief for Esclados is in any case impersonal: she bewails his loss as an excellent knight rather than as an irreplaceable individual (ll. 1288–99). When Lunete convinces her that it is possible to replace him with an even better knight (ll. 1674–772), her hasty remarriage becomes rationally acceptable.

On his side, Yvain has no sooner won her than, pressured by Gawain, he determines to take leave of her. Laudine does not oppose his departure: she accepts that he must avoid being called "recreant" (l. 2561). It is Yvain who swings from being grief-stricken at the thought of leaving her to being uncertain that he can return to her. His strongest desire is to go, "ou face folie ou savoir" (l. 2544). It is not his desire to avoid 'recreantise' that is wrong, but his excessive indulgence in the life

---

[4]*Policraticon*, ed. Webb, 2: 301–04.
[5]A typical example occurs in the *Expugnatio Hibernica*, ed. and trans. Scott and Martin, 24. One the most notorious anti-feminist texts of twelfth century is Walter Map's *Dissuasio Valerii*, in *De Nugis Curialium*, ed. James, 143–59. One of the most virulent is the last book of Andreas Capellanus's *De Amore*. The oriental anti-feminist tradition is represented by the stories in the *Disciplina Clericalis*. Notable anti-feminist passages in romance include *Troie*, ll. 13441–56 and Thomas's *Tristan*, ll. 2595–605.

of "tantes" "paveillons" (l. 2803). This folly leads to his real and devastating 'folie,' which is eventually cured, but at a cost: one excess leads to another. The damsel of Norison forgets the limits her lady set her and foolishly applies the precious ointment not only to Yvain's affected part, his head, but all over his body (ll. 2996–3006). This foolish excess causes the serious loss of the remaining ointment. Like Yvain, the damsel was engaged in a pursuit that was good in itself, but harmful when indulged beyond the reasonable limits set out in advance.

The damsel's lady suffers from the dangerous excesses of a neighbour, Count Alier, who is unjustly encroaching on her territory. These pretensions are duly repressed by Yvain, but the very excellence of his support only leaves the lady of Norison with a corresponding sense of deprivation when Yvain insists on leaving her (ll. 3325–29). Because she helped him, he helped her. Yet he refuses to stay with her and forget Laudine. His grateful defence of the Lady of Norison has given him a new start in life, not yet consciously formulated. Chrétien proceeds to place Yvain in a situation devoid of personal and social context, where he can make his moral choice with the greatest possible freedom.

Yvain departs, aimless and alone. He comes upon a lion being attacked by a fire-breathing serpent. This is indeed a marvel, but Yvain now wastes no time in gratifying a sense of visual wonder:

> N'ala pas longues regardant
> Mes sire Yvains cele mervoille.                    (ll. 3352–53)

Here there is a moral choice to be made, and Yvain pauses only long enough to weigh the merits of either side and be sure that his help is given to the right side:

> A lui meïsme se consoille,
> Au quel des deus il eidera.
> Lors dit qu'au lion secorra;
> Qu'a venimeus et a felon
> Ne doit an feire se mal non.
> Et li serpanz est venimeus.                        (ll. 3354–59)

From that moment to the end, Yvain never fights against any side that is not clearly 'felon,' unlike, it must be said, his friend Gawain. He rescues the "beste jantil et franche" (l. 3375) and the lion remains with him as a constant reminder of his decision to uphold right.[6]

The narrative technique of the encounter is unlike anything else we find in *Yvain* and this is no doubt deliberate, for the significance of its place in the hero's life is without parallel. It is a marvel, as Chrétien says, but not like the marvel of the fountain. Here, instead of having to persuade us of the reality of the marvel, Chrétien points out with a

---

[6]Harris claims that Yvain "merely makes a sort of sporting decision." See "The Rôle of the Lion," 1148. Haidu argues that the lion could also be seen as a symbol of evil; see *Lion-queue-coupée*. It is difficult to reconcile either of these views with the text.

confident absence of justification the essentially opposed natures of the lion and the serpent.

Peter Damian had told the story of how some merchants came to the rescue of a lion attacked by a fierce "draco" and how the "nobilissimus bestiarum," instead of going away as soon as it was freed, stayed and hunted for them out of gratitude.[7] The merchants, however, did not deliberate on the choice of animal to rescue, an essential point for Chrétien. In the *Disciplina Clericalis*, Petrus Alfonsi warned against rescuing serpents: he tells the story of a man who rescued a serpent which then tried to strangle him. When asked why it returned evil for good, it replied that it was only doing what its nature ordered.[8]

Yvain's decision is the only moment of moral absolute in his career. Up to this moment, he was only moved by external stimuli to pursue vengeance, love and gratitude. Here he makes a wholly disinterested moral decision. He rescues the nobler animal but expects no thanks for it. On the contrary, he is prepared for the lion to turn on him and is surprised when it expresses gratitude (ll. 3388–401). With the lion, which confers a new identity on him, Yvain sets out on his new life.

Yvain becomes the Knight of the Lion in a way that is strikingly similar to the way Lancelot becomes the Knight of the Cart. Yvain too is faced with a decision requiring immediate action and the choice he makes gives him a new title. Like Lancelot, he is already launched on a particular way of life. The decision to defend the lion, like the decision to enter the cart, is the logical outcome of a commitment already made. There is certainly a difference: Lancelot chooses between two forms of good and is wholly master of the consequences, whereas Yvain chooses between good and evil and cannot entirely save the good side from the effects of evil. He is obliged to cut off part of the lion's tail in order to save him from the serpent. In the imperfect world Yvain inhabits, the creatures he rescues continue to suffer: the lady of Norison loses her ointment and her defender; the heiress of Noire Espine shows the effects of her illness; and two of Gawain's nephews die before Yvain kills Harpin. We are no longer in the entirely optimistic world of *Erec*.

After his single moment of absolute moral experience Yvain returns forever to a world in which good and evil are in constant and precarious balance. Although he has achieved a greater moral consciousness, the effects of his past excesses continue to dog him. The first person he meets when he sets out with the lion is Lunete, who is in peril of her life because of his folly in failing to return to Laudine. When he exceeded the time limit, Laudine blamed Lunete, and the evil seneschal denounced her. Yvain's single act of excess has had social reverberations beyond what he could possibly have foreseen: his fault provoked

---

[7]Peter tells the story in the context of a letter to the monks of Cluny. The text is printed in the *Patrologia Latina*, 144: 385. It is discussed by Brodeur in "The Grateful Lion: a Study in the Development of Mediaeval Narrative," 492, 499–502.

[8]*Disciplina Clericalis*, ed. Hilka and Söderhjelm, 12.

Laudine's anger, giving an opening to the seneschal's treachery against Lunete on whom so many poor women depend (ll. 3661-87; 4357-84).

Yvain's obligation to Lunete is very great. He readily agrees to champion her, but Chrétien does not make things so simple for him. Chrétien now confronts him with the immediate need and anguish of the family persecuted by Harpin, and Yvain has to weigh his pain at refusing people he wants to help against his duty to Lunete. He will not now make the mistake of putting present concerns above previous commitments. He would be glad to help, he tells his host "Se trop n'eüsse grant besoin" (l. 4041). His mind is made up. But the heart--breaking effort of abandoning them in their need paralyses him until the giant actually appears.

When he returns in the nick of time and saves Lunete, Laudine, who does not recognize him, nevertheless appreciates objectively the prowess of the Knight of the Lion and is surprised to hear him say that his lady has cause for resentment against him:

> "Certes", fet ele, "ce me poise.
> Ne taing mie por tres cortoise
> La dame, qui mal cuer vos porte.
> Ne deüst pas veer sa porte
> A chevalier de vostre pris."          (ll. 4593-97)

If she had stopped there, it would simply be a case of dramatic irony exploited at Laudine's expense. From our privileged knowledge of the new Yvain we can feel how much, at least potentially, he deserves forgiveness. But there is no facile, sentimental reconciliation. Laudine, considering the matter with detachment, realizes that the unknown lady may have justice on her side: she would be wrong to reject him, she says, "Se trop n'eüst vers li mespris" (l. 4598). Yvain, painfully aware of the exceedingly great wrong he has done her, does not dare reveal his identity.

Yvain cannot directly redress the balance of his life, because the only means of expression available to him is knightly prowess. At most, he can show that his motivations have been modified. His commitment to chivalrous honour remains unchanged. He is not eager to fight Harpin, but when he succeeds in killing him, he asks that the exploit be recounted to Gawain:

> "Car por neant fet la bonté
> Qui ne viaut qu'ele soit seüe."          (ll. 4280-81)

The friend of the heiress of Noire Espine appeals effectively to his sense of knightly honour. She wants to know

> "Se vos venir i oseroiz
> Ou se vos án reposeroiz."          (ll. 5093-94)

To which he has an instant reply:

> "Nenil", fet il; "de reposer
> Ne se puet nus hon aloser,
> Ne je ne reposerai mie."                    (ll. 5095–97)

Yvain lost Laudine through an excessive concern with knightly reputation, but he never imagines that he can win her back by the contrary excess of neglecting it.

He accepts the challenge and sets out with the damsel for Arthur's court. As night falls, they reach a castle where the inhabitants shout dire warnings about the fate that awaits Yvain in the fortress (ll. 5106–18). It is reminiscent of the Joie de la Cort episode in *Erec:* in each case, the hero is on his way to Arthur's court when he accidentally comes across a castle with a mysterious adventure attached to it which everyone tries to dissuade him from attempting. Yvain, like Erec, will go his own way and succeed, but the adventure is very different.

There is no promise of general joy to entice Yvain. Chrétien gives the castle its name: it is the Chastel de Pesme Avanture. The inhabitants are castigated by Yvain as "janz fole et vilainne" (l. 5119), but their hostility is dictated by fear, as a courteous elderly lady explains (ll. 5142–62). No-one actually forbids him to go up to the fortress, but she advises him to go away. Yvain replies that he is sure that to follow her advice would be to his profit and honour, but that he can find no other shelter for that night (ll. 5163–67). This is entirely unlike the dialogue between Erec and Evrain. Instead of the hope of a general courtly joy, there is the spectacle of a general popular fear. Unlike Erec, who ignores advice that is sensible rather than heroic, Yvain would accept the sensible advice if he could. When he decides to go ahead, the lady then says that it would give her great joy to see him return, but that his return is impossible (ll. 5168–74). Yvain courteously wishes that this joy may be granted to her, and goes forward with the cryptic remark:

> "Mes mes fos cuers leanz me tire,
> Si ferai ce que mes cuers viaut."                    (ll. 5176–77)

The Guiot manuscript has the more conventional reading "fins cuers," but "fos cuers," the *lectio difficilior* of manuscripts G, S, V and A, is surely correct. Yvain is rationally aware that to proceed is folly. Given that he is already committed to championing the heiress of Noire Espine in the very near future at Arthur's court, Yvain is taking a risk. Erec had leisure for his final, crowning adventure. Yvain has taken on responsibility for a just and urgent cause, and any diversion places him in the same painful dilemma he faced over Harpin. It is folly indeed to obey his heart, but at the same time it is the only action capable of bringing joy to anyone at Pesme Avanture.

As soon as he enters the fortress he sees three hundred damsels slaving miserably over the rich cloths they are working on, and he discovers that they are the victims of the thoughtless folly of their king who "aloit por aprandre noveles [. . .] come fos naïs" (ll. 5258–60). In his aimless quest for news, this weak, fearful young king came up against a peril he was unequal to, only saving his life by sacrificing the liberty of his subjects: he sends an annual tribute of thirty maidens to this castle which is inhabited by two sons of the devil (l. 5271). The theme of an annual tribute of young people to some monstrous creature was familiar to Chrétien's audience from the story of Tristan and the Morholt, if not from that of Theseus and the Minotaur. At Pesme Avanture, Chrétien stresses the inadequacy and irresponsibility of the young king and how his weakness exposes the defenceless damsels to the omnipresent evils that are always ready to strike the helpless. The servitude of the maidens will last for as long as the monstrous creatures live: they have no hope of help, least of all from their own lord.

We are introduced to the monsters with sinister indirectness. Yvain goes through the castle until he comes to an orchard where a 'prodome' and his wife are listening to a romance being read to them by their beautiful daughter. All three hasten forward to greet him. This is a disconcerting change of scene. Surely it is impossible to connect such a sympathetically presented family with the horrors Yvain has just heard and witnessed in the weavers' workroom? Chrétien hints that the hosts may be deceiving their guest. He broadens the hint when he notes the excessive lavishness of their hospitality (ll. 5438–39). The hero, on the contrary, takes care to do everything in an orderly way. Next morning, as soon as possible for one who "tot fet par devisement" (l. 5451), Yvain hears mass, and is about to depart when the blow falls. Although he was warned in the workroom that he would be forced to fight (ll. 5332–37), he was disarmed by the effusive welcome of his host and it comes as a "novele felenesse" (l. 5458) to him to realize that the man he saw as a 'prodome' will not let him depart until he has fought with the two half–devils. With great reluctance Yvain resigns himself to a combat he would much rather have avoided (ll. 5506–11).

Though the physical challenge comes from the hideous monsters, the moral responsibility for it lies with the lord of the castle. It is a horrific amplification of the link once sketched between Yder and his evil dwarf in the much more innocent world of *Erec*. Yder at least paid with his own person for the aggression of his dwarf; he acknowledged, not ignobly, that he had been fairly defeated by Erec and, minus the dwarf that incorporated his evil impulses, he is ready to become an acceptable Arthurian knight. The lord of Pesme Avanture is a different case. He is the man who, as the weaver told Yvain, was "riches de nostre desserte" (l. 5318). He forces his guest into mortally dangerous combat. Yet he refuses to take responsibility for his actions. He represents himself as the powerless instrument of an immutable custom that he is obliged to uphold, be it right or wrong (ll. 5467–73). Should Yvain vanquish the monsters, he will be given the lord's daughter in marriage. Though the lord benefits from the tribute of maidens, he seems even more anxious to benefit from the acquisition of a valiant son-in-law. He claims it is in his interest to have the custom abolished so that his daughter can be married (ll. 5502-05). The custom has indeed had a "trop longue duree" (l. 5503) in that it exploits three hundred maidens. The more he dissociates himself from responsibility for what goes on in his castle, the more he incriminates himself. Having forced Yvain to fight, he cannot believe that the victorious hero will refuse his daughter. Unlike Yder, the moral scales never fall from his eyes. Worse, we are given no reason to suppose that he will not continue to flourish like the green bay tree, despite the loss of his tribute. Yvain does not succeed in eradicating the evil of the castle: one of the monsters lives on.

Yvain's liberation of the oppressed maidens is a characteristic example of the help which is such a substantial theme in the romance. Yvain rescues them, but their rescue does not have the joyful and unambiguous finality of Erec's rescue of Cadoc. The grotesque adversaries are not wholly destroyed, and the innocent victims must return to the doubtful protection of their inadequate king.

In *Yvain*, much help is given, but even more help is needed. Lunete can help Yvain, but she cannot help herself against the seneschal. She is promised help by Gawain but it is not forthcoming when she needs it. Yvain is the hero of the romance because he is the only character who is always able and willing to offer support. Over and over again he labours to redress the balance of good against evil. Help is only required against misfortune and the misfortunes in *Yvain*, as in all Chrétien's romances, are not random strokes of fate, but produced by some person's culpable excesses or inadequacies.

The only unprompted act of service within the narrative is performed by the frightened hermit, who gives Yvain some of his bread "par charité" (l. 2839), but prays that this naked madman will go away and leave him alone. Yvain, however, returns with venison and establishes a primitive co-operative relationship with the hermit and so survives. Nevertheless, Yvain in his right mind does not count on such help. When he regains his wits and sees that he is naked, he is horrified to realize that he could easily have been killed (ll. 3028-32). He wakes up into a world where help is endlessly needed against multiple and sometimes simultaneous evils, and where his own strength and good-will are not always enough. When he comes to defend Lunete, on whom so many poor women depend for "consoil et aïe" (l. 4364), he recognizes that in the unequal combat against her trio of accusers he needs the extra help God gives him for fighting on the right side (ll. 4425-48). He receives spiritual support from the prayers of the women "qu'autres bastons n'ont" (l. 4520) and physical support from his lion (ll. 4538-58). At Pesme Avanture, his diabolical adversaries try to deprive him of the indispensable help of his lion and almost succeed. In the final combat with Gawain, the disinherited sister prays that Yvain may receive the help due to a just cause (ll. 5983-90), a help that he urgently needs. It is

only that added help and the corresponding weakness Gawain suffers
for supporting the wrong side (ll. 6345–47) that prevent Yvain from
being defeated. It is typical of this romance that the hero has no final
glorious triumph like that of Erec over Mabonagrain or Lancelot over
Meleagant. Evil maintains its full weight to the end and remains a
strong counterbalance to the best impulses, to the most disinterested
offers of help.

As in *Erec*, actions provoke reciprocal actions, but the characteristic
'guerredon' of Yvain is not, as we might expect, a reward for services
rendered, but revenge. True, the first mention of a 'guerredon' is when
the courteous vavassour asks as recompense from Calogrenant that he
should lodge with him again on his return (l. 264). For a moment we
are lulled into thinking that in this wilderness a perfect balance of
courteous services is normal. But by the time Calogrenant returns,
everything has changed. He has been unable to sustain the challenge
he issued at the fountain, and the main action of the romance will be set
in motion by his cousin's promise to avenge his shame.

Yvain, though he opposes retaliation, especially against a companion
(ll. 641–45), nevertheless believes that revenge is due to his kinsman. He
wounds Esclados mortally, thus exciting a desire for revenge among the
dead man's followers. The victim's widow, however, acknowledges that
her husband would have killed Yvain if he could: either conclusion to
the combat must inevitably provoke revenge. She unconsciously
avenges her husband when the man who killed him falls in love with
her (ll. 1362–63): a poor revenge, as it turns out, when Yvain fails to
replace her first husband adequately. When he goes mad, he longs to be
avenged on himself for his own folly (ll. 2793–95). The giant Harpin
sneers at him, saying that whoever sent Yvain out to fight against
Harpin could not have better avenged himself, no matter what wrong
Yvain had done him (ll. 4184–89). He speaks too soon: the lord of the
castle will be able to tell the damsel seeking Yvain how the Knight of the
Lion avenged him on his mortal enemy (ll. 4912–13). In the course of the
combat, Yvain is spurred on to fight the harder in order to avenge the
wounds inflicted on his lion (ll. 4549–52). The weaver at Pesme
Avanture bewails the oppression that she and her companions suffer
undeservedly (ll. 5262–65); their king's weakness has in effect been
avenged on them. Twice the burden to be discharged is appropriately
imagined as a debt. Yvain, unrecognizable as the Knight of the Lion,
confesses to Laudine that he is labouring under a debt he cannot clear
(l. 4610). In the final combat, Gawain recognizes that Yvain has paid
back with interest every blow he has dealt him (ll. 6258–62).

Only Lunete offers an effective 'guerredon' for services rendered, but
the further help she gives Yvain in arranging his marriage nearly costs
her her life. Yvain is at fault, but so are others. Unlike *Erec*, where
services are always duly rendered, and unlike the *Charrette*, where
services are sometimes superfluously offered to or by characters who

never reappear, services in *Yvain* are offered, and needed, and are then unavailable. As we have seen, help is never available from Arthur's court as it ought to be, and when Lunete is in urgent need of the services Gawain promised her, he is not available to keep his word.

Lunete's first service to Yvain has an added significance in the narrative. She is glad to have the chance of helping him in return for what he once did for her, and her recollection of his courteous past action gives us new information about both the hero and his environment. This back-and-forth movement in time is something new in Chrétien. In *Erec*, nothing of the hero's pre-plot life affects anything that happens in the story: his looks, rank and personal achievements are set out at the beginning of the romance and he carries on from there in a straight line. Lancelot is not even introduced to us, and he certainly never looks back. It is typical of *Yvain*, however, that an action the hero has evidently forgotten resurfaces to affect his present and his future. We lose the confident, forward movement of Erec and Lancelot, but gain a greater range of possible influences on the hero's career. After Yvain recovers from his madness, he lives in a permanent state of tension between his present state and his past memories which, on the first occasion they are evoked, are too powerful for him to bear.

Erec and Lancelot forge their way ahead. They look to the future while Yvain thinks back over the past. Lancelot concentrates so intently on his thoughts that all the figures he encounters seem shadowy and insubstantial. The less than superhuman Yvain lets thoughts of chivalry distract him from thoughts of love: he never transcends his material environment and is constantly surrounded by other characters, all with their own preoccupations which they succeed in making his.

Over and over again, Chrétien shows us that actions involving Yvain are simultaneous with other actions which may not concern him directly. In the very first scene, he begins by giving us juxtaposed glimpses of Arthur retiring to join the queen and Calogrenant telling his tale to Yvain and the others. Then the two areas of action converge:

> Que que il son conte contoit,
> Et la reïne l'escoutoit,
> Si s'est de lez le roi levee
> Et vint sor aus si a anblee.　　　　　　　　　(ll. 61–64)

After she joins them, our attention is divided again:

> Que que il parloient einsi,
> Li rois fors de la chanbre issi.　　　　　　　　(ll. 649–50)

Action can occur, or be ready to occur, in places other than the spot where the hero happens to be.

It is typical of this romance that one action is taking place "while" (que que) another is taking place elsewhere. Frappier notes Chrétien's fondness for this temporal conjunction and points out its superiority, in the short octosyllabic line, over more cumbrous locutions such as 'endementres que'.[9] It is not quite true, however, as Frappier claims, that Chrétien is the first to use 'que que' in this sense. There are at least two instances of it in the *Roman de Thèbes* (ll. 10235, 10271). The real significance of Chrétien's use is where he employs it. In *Erec*, 'que que' occurs only once (l. 6327) and never in the course of the hero's adventures. In Yvain, on the other hand, the hero's adventures are just one current in a wider stream, so the expression is appropriate and frequent.

When Yvain pursues Esclados to his castle, his preoccupations run parallel with the varied reactions of his victim's entourage. As he takes in the gravity of his situation, trapped between the two portcullises,

> D'une chanbrete iluec delez
> Oï ovrir un huis estroit,
> Que que il iere an cel destroit;
> S'an issi une dameisele.                    (ll. 970–73)

Lunete, who chances upon Yvain (ll. 976–77), makes us first side–step into her life, then move back in time to her recollection of Yvain and Arthur's court and then move forward again to the present, now enriched with past experience. Even the present is subdivided: thanks to Lunete's help, Yvain can concentrate on watching Laudine 'que que' the inhabitants of the castle go on searching for him (ll. 1144–47). While they search, she laments, and while she laments, Yvain looks at her and falls in love. When Lunete undertakes to produce him as a suitor for Laudine within three days, Laudine must meanwhile hold counsel with her men about defending her fountain against Arthur (ll. 1842–50). When Yvain is announced, she asks for him to be brought to her at once, "demantres qu'avuec moi n'est nus" (l. 1901), before other demands are made on her attention.

Yvain's companionship with the lion requires give and take: while Yvain eats, the lion waits his turn (ll. 3471–75). When they come to the fountain, Yvain almost gives way to grief and remorse and is on the point of killing himself in despair when Lunete, whose life has continued its own separate and perilous course, once again impinges on his actions. While he laments, she sees and hears him: "que que il einsi se demante" (l. 3563), someone else's problems need attention.

The peculiar anguish of Yvain's dilemma over the Harpin adventure is precisely because he is faced with two demands that are incompatible because they are simultaneous. The unjustly accused Lunete and the family persecuted by Harpin have no connection with one another. They just happen to be actors in two simultaneous dramas. The single common factor is that both parties have looked in vain for help from Gauvain and both have now no other hope than Yvain. In this densely populated

---

[9]Frappier, *Etude sur "Yvain,"* 220–21.

world, the hero's life has no vacuum waiting to be filled: he is pressed with more requests for help than it seems possible to cope with.

The problem here is the tightness of the time schedule. Yvain's time is not divided into the measured stages of an irresistible progress like Lancelot's. On the contrary, every moment that passes can change the direction of his action. Lunete's trial is to be the next day (ll. 3718–20); Harpin is due to arrive next day too, and before noon (ll. 3826–29). Yvain must decline to help if the giant does not arrive sufficiently early:

> "Qu'aillors mantir ne me covaingne;
> Que por rien je ne leisseroie,
> Que demain a midi ne soie
> Au plus grant afeire por voir,
> Que je onques poïsse avoir."          (ll. 3994–98)

The next day he waits till prime, then determines to leave. But the paralysis induced by the agony of this decision keeps him rooted to the spot until the giant arrives. Their combat takes so long that he is afraid of not arriving by noon to champion Lunete and indeed, he barely makes it in time (ll. 4406–07).

Yvain is still recovering from the wounds he receives in these perilously juxtaposed adventures when, quite unknown to him, a new crisis looms, which this time has no claim on either duty or friendship. His wounds are being treated in a house not far from the site of Lunete's ordeal. Meanwhile, in a different location, a new drama is in the making:

> Mes dedanz ce fu avenu,
> Que a la Mort ot plet tenu
> Li sire de la Noire Espine.          (ll. 4703–05)

The lord leaves behind him an inheritance quarrel which is of no personal concern to Yvain; but he will be drawn into it through the reputation he has acquired as the Knight of the Lion.

The appeals made to Yvain are random; the people he helps are increasingly distant from his own concerns. Yet the narrative does not disintegrate because the harmonious symmetry of the structure carries us on and imposes a coherent pattern on this biography that is not moving towards a conventional chivalrous climax. On the contrary, Yvain's public career ends on a note of something approaching anti–climax. This is one of the few points in which he is comparable to Lancelot. For both these heroes, it is their decision to follow a certain path that counts, rather than the thought of gaining or regaining public recognition. Chivalrous honour remains important to both, as chivalry remains their only mode of expression, but for each, the path they have chosen is never fully appreciated by their peers. Moreover, the public and personal sides of their lives remain separate. They do not win public acclamation like Erec with Enide. Chrétien abandons Lancelot in a tower; even in Godefroi's conclusion there is an explicit separation of his private life and his public role. Yvain's case is even more sharply divided: as soon as he can, he departs from Arthur's court and leaves behind all public life, with its potentially endless demands, in order to force a reconciliation with his wife. There can be no final, integrated triumph in a world crowded with independent, simultaneous crises.

## XII. The Disappearance of the Omniscient Narrator

The world of *Yvain* is more varied than that of *Erec*, more ambiguous than that of *Cligès* and more concrete than that of the *Charrette*. More than any other romance, *Yvain* approximates to the concept of a realistic, or rather, naturalistic, novel. Weakness, injustice, failure, greed, physical hardship, marital troubles and nervous breakdowns are more familiar and accessible to us as the matter of fiction than the didacticism of *Cligès* or the quasi-spirituality of the *Charrette*. In addition, one particular aspect of Chrétien's narrative technique in *Yvain* makes him appear even more modern than the naturalists, and that is the way he disappears as the omniscient narrator.

In the *Charrette* Chrétien told us plainly that his hero was a perfect lover and everything he shows us is compatible with this role. In *Yvain*, he withholds any such authoritative guidance. He transfers his presentation of the fountain to a series of internal narrators, whose descriptions do not quite tally. His presentation of the hero and heroine is made almost exclusively through the eyes of the characters concerned. In fact Chrétien goes much further than this and withdraws altogether behind a series of unreconciled contradictions.[1]

The first of these clashes occurs at the very beginning of the romance, in the first line of the narrative proper—in such a prominent position that it cannot have been placed there unconsciously. Chrétien has just taken up all his prologue telling us what a good king Arthur was, how his prowess teaches us to be brave and courteous, that at his court men really knew how to love, that the courtly dead are more agreeable to write about than the uncourtly living, and that he agrees with the Bretons that Arthur's renown will live forever. The tone is incontrovertibly didactic. It prepares us for another exemplary story in the style of *Lancelot*, though in this case it looks more like being the tale of the excellent subject of an excellent king. The allusion to the uncourtly living seems to have no function beyond acting as a foil to the glowing picture of a truly courtly world in the remote and glorious past. However, it is precisely this rejected uncourtliness that will become the cornerstone of the romance.

Nevertheless, as we can have no inkling yet of how far from ideal the content of the romance will be, it is a shock to read the transition from

---

[1]See the studies cited in note 1 of the previous chapter.

prologue to narrative. Chrétien tells us it is through King Arthur that we remember

> Li buen chevalier esleü,
> Qui an enor se traveillierent.
> Mes cel jor mout s'esmerveillierent
> Del roi, qui d'antre aus se leva,
> S'i ot de tes, cui mout greva. (ll. 40–44)

It is impossible to reconcile what Chrétien tells us with what he shows us. The shock does not lie in the criticism of Arthur: in *Erec* and in the *Charrette* we have seen him criticized by Gawain with increasing severity. Here, however, we have an Arthur quite differently placed. He is not pressured by any public circumstance, whether of his own making, as in *Erec*, or imposed by an outsider, as in the *Charrette*. Here, the imperfection is presented as a private whim, as unaccountable to his men as it is disconcerting to us, who have just heard his praises sung. Arthur was an admirable king, it seems, but on this occasion he was not. Of these two incompatible items of information, the former is given us directly on Chrétien's own authority. The unexplained caprice, the incomprehension of the other characters, the absence of any reconciling unity of vision, all these are typical of Chrétien's narrative technique in this romance.

The text is full of oppositions between what we expect and what actually happens. Calogrenant tells a tale "non de s'enor, mes de sa honte" (l. 60). The prologue to his tale is a whole string of oppositions. Within the space of ninety lines we find "mes" (but) used in the emphatic position at the head of the line no fewer than seven times (ll. 84; 102; 119; 128; 141; 147; 159) and "ainz" (rather) used in the same position three times (ll. 144; 160; 174). Between the prologue to the romance, and the telling of the tale which acts as prologue to the hero's career, Chrétien sets up an ineradicable sense of unresolved conflict. Not only do Calogrenant and the queen disagree, but their language continually expresses internal opposition. The harmonious evocation of courtesy is undermined, and future discourtesies prepared for. Worse, the characters who might be supposed to embody the courtly ideal are the very ones who are compromising it. Chrétien makes no attempt to reconcile the ideals he evoked in the prologue with the imperfections he shows in the narrative. After this, we can never again be sure of anything in *Yvain*, not even of what the author himself tells us.

To confirm our doubts, the opening sequence of contradictions is not an isolated case. An outrageous example occurs at the critical moment when the hero falls in love. Chrétien, after regretting that Love often degrades itself by lodging in unworthy places, adds:

> Mes ore est ele bien venue,
> Ci iert ele a enor tenue
> Et ci li fet buen demorer. (ll. 1391–93)

Sometimes, he goes on, Love favours blame rather than honour:

> Mes or n'a ele pas fet ceu,
> Ainz s'est logiee an un franc leu,
> Don nus ne li puet feire tort. (ll. 1403–05)

The whole point of the story is that the hero will wrong and dishonour Love. At this stage of the narrative, Chrétien is the only person who can possibly know this, yet he deliberately forbears to even hint as much.

Chrétien occupies this position throughout the romance: he has abdicated the role of omniscient author and assumes instead the less privileged position of spectator, looking at his characters and their crises as if he were nothing more than a sympathetic and intelligent member of his own public. Here Yvain still appears in a favourable light: on the level of pure chivalry, he has done what no-one expected, and out-done both Calogrenant and Esclados; on the level of courtesy he has out-done all the Arthurian court as Lunete makes clear, and she has no hesitation in espousing his cause (ll. 1314–16). No character in the story has any reason to suppose that Yvain will do anything other than honour Love when it comes to him.

Chrétien, however, quickly undermines the authority of his own comment by proceeding to show us this supposedly admirable lover presumptuously anticipating success with the woman who has the most right to hate him, and then stating that no man in Yvain's position ever loved "an si fole meniere" (l. 1513). If the author refuses to reconcile these discrepancies, he must wish us to feel their disconcerting effects. There is no reliable correlation between what the various characters appear to be and what they prove to be. We can take no-one's word for the truth of the matter, not even that of the author.[2]

Sometimes the discrepancy between appearance and reality is made explicit and we are invited to enjoy the comic effects of dramatic irony. It is paradoxical that *Yvain*, which contains more evil and suffering than any of Chrétien's previous romances, should be the first to contain explicit comedy. Lunete tells Yvain that anyone not terrified by it would find "solaz et deliz" in the spectacle of Esclados's men hunting vainly for an invisible quarry (ll. 1074–79), and Gawain laughs heartily at Lunete's story of how she persuaded her lady to marry Yvain and protected him from the hands of those who could not see him (ll. 2424–32). Yvain, who is no superhuman hero like Lancelot, can participate in a ludicrous adventure without losing anything of his essential nature. Yvain is always involved in the world and its imperfections; even in love he hides the reality of his feelings under a false appearance. We see him give Lunete one reason, while really having quite a different one, for wanting to watch the funeral procession of Esclados (ll. 1271–81).

---

[2]Grigsby notes "numerous confessions of authorial inadequacy in *Yvain*"; see "Narrative Voices," 270.

Lunete, in her turn, reminds him that it is often prudent to appear one way when one really feels another way (ll. 1325–26). Laudine puts up a spectacular appearance of grief (ll. 1150–65), but, as soon as the practicalities of her situation have been pointed out (ll. 1614–37), the appearance she puts up changes radically (ll. 1800–06). Evidence of the presence of Esclados's killer appears to his men, but they cannot perceive the reality of the admittedly extraordinary situation (ll. 1087–1143). Lunete amuses herself by pretending to Laudine on the one hand that she is bringing Yvain from Arthur's court (ll. 1820–44) and on the other hand pretending to Yvain that Laudine is still angry with him (ll. 1910–254). She and Chrétien's audience both know more than either the hero or the heroine.

In the grimmer world Yvain wakes up to after he is cured of his madness no character any more has full knowledge of what is going on. He recovers his memory of his past life, or at least of the part that led up to his madness, but he is bewildered by the state he finds himself in:

> Mes nuz se voit come un ivoire,
> S'a grant honte, et plus grant eüst,
> Se il s'avanture seüst;
> Mes n'an set plus que nuz se trueve.		(ll. 3020–23)

He has lost all awareness of his life with the hermit and feels only fear when he realizes the danger he was exposed to. He is entirely deceived by the courteous pretence of the damsel who cures him and who puts up an appearance of arriving on the spot by chance (ll. 3042–63). He never knows that she cured him and she never knows what sorrow caused his madness. Her mistress asks what became of the rest of the ointment, but this was in private (l. 3110) and so she never finds out what really happened to it and neither she nor Yvain ever know that the damsel lied about it. Neither of these ladies, nor indeed anyone at Norison, ever finds out why Yvain refuses to stay there. No single character is privy to everything that has been happening.

Chrétien places himself on the same level of imperfect knowledge. In his presentation of Gawain, Chrétien exploits to the full the possibilities of his own supposed ignorance by developing the disquieting effects produced by the discrepancies between what he tells us and what he shows us. A first indication of the possibilities Gawain offers in this respect came towards the end of *Charrette*, where we saw what a peculiarly ambiguous figure he cut as the knight who fails in comparison with the hero, but who nevertheless maintains the respect of the Arthurian court.

Gawain's function in *Yvain* is different. Yvain is not a superhuman hero who needs a more lowly foil: he is a much humbler figure who commits a major fault. All Gawain can do is offer the supreme example of pure prowess, of excellent fighting skills shorn of any particular concern for motivation. The only time when he directly confronts Yvain is in the final combat, and even here he remains potentially superior to the hero. Yvain is only able to achieve a draw because he is fighting on the right side and Gawain is not. Yet Chrétien makes much greater efforts than in the *Charrette* to avoid devaluing Gawain, and has him anticipate criticism by generously protesting that Yvain deserves to be called the victor (ll. 6342–49).

We may find fault with Gawain, but no character in the romance criticizes him and neither does the author. On the contrary, Chrétien praises him effusively in a passage where he calls him the sun of chivalry (ll. 2400–08). The next moment he shows this sun making a curious proposition to that unfortunate moon, Lunete. Gawain calls her his "amie" (l. 2420) and asks her not to change him for another, but then adds the disconcerting rider: "Se amander ne vos cuidiez" (l. 2437). Is this courteous modesty or careless cynicism? Chrétien gives us no help, makes no comment on what prompts Gawain to allow for inconstancy in Lunete, who does not have Laudine's *raisons d'état* for being fickle. The only certain point is that Gawain does not feel himself committed. After this one encounter, he seems to forget Lunete straight away.

Instead, he turns his attention to Yvain and makes a long speech to persuade him that he will deserve to lose Laudine's love if he neglects his chivalrous reputation (ll. 2484–538). No–one denies the principle he invokes, not even Laudine. It crosses no–one's mind that her fountain may be attacked in the absence of its defender. Gawain conveniently ignores the fact that Yvain has committed himself to marriage with Laudine and again betrays his ambivalent attitude to women when he admits that he would find it hard to follow his own advice

> "Se j'avoie si bele amie
> Con vos avez, sire conpainz."                    (ll. 2528–29)

The status of "wife" means nothing to him, but then the status of 'amie' means nothing either. Either he has already forgotten that he has just acquired an 'amie', or else he is being unflattering about her appearance. Worse, when the unfortunate Lunete is in imminent danger of her life as an indirect result of Gawain's influence on Yvain, he will not be available to render her the service he promised (l. 2423). She explains to Yvain that Gawain has gone in search of the queen and will never stop until he finds her (ll. 3712–15). Lunete, like all the characters in the romance, never dreams of criticizing Gawain, even when he has let her down. We are here in a position of superior knowledge to Lunete and cannot help wondering if it would affect her admiration for the sun of chivalry to know that he fails in his quest for the queen and reaches the kingdom of Gorre in a highly undignified fashion and too late. Almost certainly it would not affect her. Nowhere in Chrétien's works is there any overt criticism of Gawain, no matter what he does or fails to do. Like Arthur, his position as one of the mainstays of chivalry is unassailable, however little he may seem in some cases to deserve his reputation.

Yvain's attachment to Gawain is repeatedly stressed and is less comprehensible. Yvain is never disillusioned about his friend, though he might well have handed him some of the blame for his misfortune, since it was Gawain who pressured him into leaving Laudine in the first place, and did everything he could to keep him away (ll. 2538–43; 2672–78). Yvain's anguish at having to choose between defending Lunete and defending the family persecuted by Harpin is due to Gawain's unavailability, though both parties had sought his help. It would not be necessary to defend the heiress of Noire Espine if Gawain had not agreed unquestioningly to champion her unjust sister. Yet Yvain never mentions him except in the warmest terms. For him, the worst part of abandoning the family persecuted by Harpin is that they are related to "Mon seignor Gauvain que j'aim mout" (l. 4045) and they appealed to him "De par l'ome que il plus aimme" (l. 4072). He has no hesitation in calling him "mes sire Gauvains [. . .] li frans, li douz" (ll. 3698–99) to Lunete, for she is quite of the same opinion. The crisis of the last combat, as Chrétien tells us in elaborate detail (ll. 5998–6105), is that under the appearances of hate, the reality of the love between the two companions is not immediately apparent.

Chrétien never comments authoritatively on Gawain's actions or motivations. He places himself on the same level as his characters as regards predicting what Gawain is likely to do. If Yvain should fail to return as agreed and overstep the limit of the year, then he will only be reconciled with his lady with the greatest difficulty and, Chrétien adds:

> Je cuit qu'il le trespassera;
> Car departir nel leissera
> Mes sire Gauvains d'avuec lui.            (ll. 2667–69)

The prediction is as tentatively formulated as if Chrétien were an onlooker among a group of real people, offering an opinion on the probable future of the men he is observing.

It is only in his purely narrative interventions that Chrétien retains the decisive tone of his earlier romances. All these interventions are declarations of economy, expressions of his refusal to waste time and words on anything he considers inessential. Although at Yvain's wedding there is an abundance of people and pleasure,

> Plus que conter ne vos savroie,
> Quant lonc tans pansé i avroie.
> Miauz me vient teire, que po dire. –
> Mes ore est mes sire Yvains sire,
> Et li morz est toz oblïez.            (ll. 2161–65)

Chrétien is well able to describe courtly ceremonies, but he has not given us one since Erec's coronation. He hints in Cligès that his public did not appreciate long descriptions and Yvain's marriage hardly deserves one: it is far more important to get on with narrating what follows from it.

Nor will Chrétien spend time describing the public welcome given to Arthur when it is more important to inform us of how Gawain met Lunete:

> De la joie assez vos contasse,
> Se ma parole n'i gastasse;
> Mes solemant de l'acointance
> Vuel feire une brief remanbrance,
> Qui fu feite a privé consoil
> Antre la lune et le soloil. (ll. 2393–98)

Even this meeting is described briefly. Still less will he delay over the joy shared by the sick heiress of Noire Espine and her friends at obtaining the services of the Knight of the Lion. There would be too much to tell, says Chrétien: "Tot vos trespas jusqu'au monter" (l. 5840). She and we are to be transported without delay to Arthur's court.

Neither does sorrow always merit a long description. Chrétien will not delay over the tearful farewells Yvain takes of Laudine:

> Ne sai que vos doie conter,
> Comant mes sire Yvains s'an part. (ll. 2624–25)
>
> . . . .
>
> Trop i feroie grant demore. (l. 2633)

It is tactful to skip this short-lived sorrow: Chrétien will give us more detail about the real suffering Yvain endures when it is too late. Nor will he delay over the lamentations of the damsel who finds him:

> Ne sai qu'alasse demorant
> A conter le duel qu'ele an fist. (ll. 2918–19)

Instead, he makes her take her tears to her lady, who has the means of curing him.

Chrétien protests a great deal about his ignorance, but *Yvain* is the most obviously planned of all his romances. When Yvain seeks lodgings the night before he is to champion Lunete, he comes to a castle with strong walls, surrounded by a devastated area. Chrétien represses any untimely curiosity on our part:

> Assez an savroiz la reison
> Une autre foiz, quant leus sera. (ll. 3782–83)

In spite of what he would have us believe, everything has its pre-appointed place in the narrative.

Nevertheless, when we are being told about the actions of the hero, the tone of uncertainty is reassumed. Yvain repeats that he is sure of nothing. To the family he has rescued from Harpin

> . . . il respont qu'il ne les ose
> Asseürer de nule chose;

>  Qu'il ne set mie deviner,
>  S'il li doit bien ou mal finer.                    (ll. 4269–72)

Chrétien does everything he can to appear to share in this uncertainty. After Yvain defends Lunete, he refuses to commit himself to his hero's plight even to the extent of telling us how long it took for him to be healed (ll. 4696–701). At Arthur's court, Chrétien claims ignorance of the time that has elapsed since Gawain left (l. 5872). In the combat between Yvain and Gawain, Chrétien analyses their present feelings in detail, but he refuses to predict the outcome of the battle, continuing to place himself in the position of an onlooker who can anxiously reason thus:

>  Car, s'il font tant qu'il s'antrevaingnent,
>  Grant peor ai qu'il ne maintaingnent
>  Tant la bataille et la meslee,
>  Qu'ele iert de l'une part outree.                  (ll. 6091–94)

The possibilities of authorial ignorance are most fully developed in the episode of Pesme Avanture. Yvain and his accompanying damsel make their way into the fortress where their horses are stabled by those who hope to get them. Chrétien adds, quite gratuitously "Ne sai, s'il cuidoient savoir" (l. 5356). The author cannot vouch for the future in his own romance! Yvain then comes to the lord of the castle, whose daughter is reading to him "An un romanz, ne sai de cui" (l. 5366). The lord and his family hasten forward to welcome Yvain and, though the author alone can know the truth of the motivations he attributes to them, Chrétien protests: "Je ne sai, se il le deçoivent" (l. 5407) and goes on, entirely in the spirit of an anxious and uncertain onlooker:

>  Or doint Des que trop ne li cost
>  Ceste losange et cist servise!                     (ll. 5424–25)

as if he could not know the outcome of the very adventure he is composing.

Not content with ignorance, Chrétien creates a digression. The lord has a daughter who represents everything that is antipathetic to the hero, for she is closely connected with the evil custom of the castle and she is to be given to him against his will. Yet Chrétien is extravagant in his praise of her beauty: if the god of love saw her, he says, he would let no man love her but would become a man himself for her sake and wound himself with his own dart (ll. 5375–84). From this description, she must be more beautiful than Laudine, yet Yvain displays as little interest in her as in the undescribed lady of Norison. She certainly does not tempt his constancy as the Hospitable Damsel sought to tempt Lancelot's. Chrétien is playing the part of a spectator who, seeing each new character in turn, reacts in ignorance of the hero's point of view.

Chrétien even threatens a further digression on the nature of true love: he would talk all day and more on the subject, except that his audience would not let him; people do not know how to love any more—they do not even want to hear about it (ll. 5389-96). It is a return to the theme of his prologue and perhaps a rueful acknowledgement that his public did not appreciate the long analyses of *Cligès* and the *Charrette*. No doubt he is well aware of the relief of suspense he produces when he abandons this projected digression and returns to the action:

> Mes ore oëz an quel meniere,
> A quel sanblant et a quel chiere
> Mes sire Yvains fu herbergiez! (ll. 5397-99)

It looks like a reassuring resumption of straightforward narrative but nothing is as it seems, for it is here that he protests that he knows nothing about the host's motivations (l. 5407).

Chrétien is even reticent in his presentation of God, though God is more frequently alluded to and appealed to in *Yvain* than in any of Chrétien's previous romances. This proliferation of appeals for divine help is natural in a romance in which so much human folly produces so much danger for so many people. The first substantial reference to God seems designed to assure us that whatever follies human beings may commit, God is in his heaven and all is ultimately right with the world. Calogrenant pours too much water on the stone, but God protects him from the storm, which subsides when God wishes (ll. 451-54). Yvain, in his turn, pours water on the stone and God is still in charge (ll. 807-08). These assertions play their part in making the fountain credible, but they do not find an echo in the appeals made by the people facing peril. However much they need or deserve help, none of the prospective victims in *Yvain* is confident that God will send it to them. After the event, they may see the hero's arrival as providential (ll. 4908-09), but none of them, any more than Yvain, has any confidence about the future. Life, as the characters perceive it, more often appears random than providential.

Everyone is conscious of the workings of what they see as chance, of what happens 'par avanture.' The term 'avanture' as used in this romance has several meanings. The most straightforward sense denotes something that actually happened.[3] When Yvain tells Arthur what happened to him, and Lunete tells Yvain what happened to her, the term they use is 'avanture' (ll. 2295; 3717). The word also retains its chivalrous meaning, closely linked to 'mervoille': the combat between the lion and the serpent is a "mervoille" (l. 3353), but its outcome, involving the surprising gratitude of the lion, is an "avanture" (l. 3407). Calogrenant asks the churl if he knows anything "Ou d'avanture ou de mervoille" (l. 366) as if, for him, the terms are synonymous. The churl,

---

[3]For a more general study of the word "aventure," see Burgess, *Contribution à l'étude du vocabulaire précourtois*, 44-55.

who is ignorant of the concept of chivalrous adventure, can nevertheless put him on the path to the fountain and inform him that if he can return from it

> "Sanz grant enui et sanz pesance,
> Tu seras de meillor cheance
> Que chevaliers qui i fust onques."                    (ll. 405–07)

Yvain, when his turn comes, has better "cheance" at the fountain, and very good luck indeed when he pursues Esclados. He just happens to be leaning forward when the portcullises drop and Chrétien tells us:

> Toz eüst esté porfanduz,
> Se ceste avanture ne fust.                            (ll. 940–41)

Later, when he recovers from his madness, we find that two kinds of 'avanture' affect him: he would have been ashamed if he had known of his 'avanture', that is, what happened to him (l. 3022), and he cannot imagine by what chance, "par quel avanture" (l. 3026) clothes happen to be lying beside him.

The family persecuted by Harpin are filled with dread at what may happen to them:

> . . . d'une avanture s'esmaient,
> Qu'il atandent a l'andemain.                          (ll. 3826–27)

Gawain, the lord says, would come to help them "Se il seüst ceste avanture" (l. 3934), but the urgent news does not reach him. Instead, Yvain offers to put himself "an l'avanture et el peril" (l. 3945) lest a terrible 'mesavanture' should befall the lord's daughter. Her father can then tell his family that

> ". . . un prodome mout de bon' eire
> Nos a Des et buene avanture
> Ceanz doné. . . ."                                    (ll. 3972–74)

It is partly by a happy chance that a possible saviour has appeared. Yvain is aware of the element of chance involved even in fighting on the just side. As he says, before the final combat with Gawain:

> "Or me doint Des eür et grace,
> Que je par sa buene avanture
> Puisse desresnier sa droiture!"                       (ll. 5104–06)

It was only "par avanture" (l. 4880) that the damsel seeking his help for this just cause was able to find shelter on her way. Now Chrétien speculates on what would happen if "par avanture" (l. 6101) one of the friends were to wound the other seriously. The maidens at Pesme Avanture have given up any hope of deliverance (ll. 5295–97). The poor women who depend on Lunete are convinced that God has abandoned them when she is condemned to die and they exclaim: "Ha! Des, con nos as obliëes!" (l. 4361).

In fact right does always triumph, even though evil leaves its traces. Chrétien does not portray an indifferent God, only one whose mills grind more slowly and less visibly than in the more optimistic world of his first romance. We remember how Enide, overcome with grief and despair, is about to commit suicide when God intervenes and, full of pity for her, stays her hand (*Erec*, ll. 4670–73). Yvain, similarly overcome and similarly tempted, receives no such direct help. Nevertheless, the same 'avanture' that brings him back to the fountain and its unbearable associations (ll. 3490–95) has also brought him back to the point where he can begin to repair the consequences of his fault. He is prevented from killing himself by Lunete who, for her part, is wholly absorbed in thinking herself "la plus dolante riens qui vive" (l. 3574). They outdo one another in their lamentations for their separate, personal catastrophes until it transpires that this chance encounter gives Yvain a reason to spare his own life in order to save Lunete's.

It is not enough that he accepts this responsibility and offers to champion Lunete. He also has to be clear in his mind that this obligation outweighs his desire to help the relations of his dearest friend. After his long, hard fight with Harpin and his desperate ride to the scene of the trial, Yvain has to take on all three of Lunete's accusers. The odds against him are fearful, but Yvain is here more confident than at any moment since his madness:

> Mes buene fiance an lui a,
> Que Des et droiz li eideront,
> Qui a sa partie seront:
> An cez conpaignons mout se fie
> Et son lion ne rehet mie.          (ll. 4332–36)

Between God, justice and the lion who first occasioned his espousal of a rightful side, his hopes of success are not unreasonably borne out.

The unequivocal orthodoxy of this episode is perhaps designed to be a rational improvement on the story that inspired it. An unhappy woman, accused of treachery by a trio of evil and envious courtiers, lamented by a chorus of the common people and rescued from the stake by the hero, constitutes the main element of one of the most dramatic episodes of the Tristan story as it survives in the Beroul fragment. Once again, Chrétien spares his heroine all indignity. Guinevere was spared the degradation of lying like Iseut: Laudine is spared by having the whole drama transferred to her subordinate. Laudine, accused of nothing, keeps her dignity intact, but Lunete, accused unjustly, keeps our attention. She is an entirely sympathetic character: grateful, quick-witted and resourceful, she more than once takes the initiative and manipulates her mistress in everyone's best interests. She is almost

too well-rounded for a secondary figure, for her actions absorb our
interest and sympathy while Laudine remains aloof.

Lunete, innocent of any crime, invokes God's help unambiguously
(ll. 4409–11). Yvain, confident of the justice of his cause, does the same
(ll. 4443–48). The accusers insult his apparent folly, but they do not
protest the rightfulness of their cause, and still less do they mention
God. In this clear-cut case, there is none of the moral ambiguity we find
in Beroul, where the lovers, whose actions are culpable though their
natures are noble, appeal endlessly to God, and where the barons,
whose accusation is correct but whose motives are base, are never
allowed to pronounce God's name.

Gawain presents Chrétien with a delicate problem in this respect.
God had no place in the exclusively chivalrous life he advocated to
Yvain. The nearest he came was to exclaim:

> "Honiz soit de sainte Marie,
> Qui por anpirier se marie!"                  (ll. 2487–88)

In the fight with the Knight of the Lion, where each of them is the
champion of one of the sisters of Noire Espine, Gawain cannot appeal
for God's help in the unjust cause he defends against Yvain, and can
only mention God as he is about to acknowledge his wrong. He explains
to Arthur the providential outcome of the battle, which lasted, he says,

> "Tant que il, la soe merci,
> Si con De plot, mon non anquist,"            (ll. 6336–37)

otherwise, Yvain would have killed him

> "Par sa proesce et par le tort
> Celi qui m'avoit an chanp mis."              (ll. 6346–47)

There is no question of actual remorse. Gawain, unlike Yvain, is
incapable of change. Chrétien keeps his Arthurian background static,
the better to display the evolution of his hero. The author of the *Chevalier
à l'épée* noted that Chrétien never made Gawain the central figure of one
of his romances.[4] We can see why most clearly here. In contact with the
Knight of the Lion he is permitted a moment of moral insight, but he
remains an integrated part of Arthur's entourage, with no more permanent change effected in him by Yvain's superior motivation than was
effected in Kay by Yvain's superior prowess. When Yvain parts from
him now, it is decisively and without a backward glance, as he goes off
to make an unencumbered effort to achieve a reconciliation with
Laudine.

Arthur's court is not the ideal assembly the prologue led us to expect
and it is only with difficulty that justice is ultimately upheld there.

---

[4]See *Two Old French Gawain Romances*, ed. Johnston and Owen, 30. These romances have
even been attributed to Chrétien; see Owen, "Two More Romances by Chrétien de
Troyes?"

Laudine's domain is even less ideal: her men are incapable of defending the fountain and her advisers promote injustice against Lunete. Worse still is the Castle of Pesme Avanture, where Yvain is welcomed with elaborate piety. The lord's family hasten towards him, exclaiming:

> ". . . Or ça, biaus sire!
> De quanque Des puet feire et dire,
> Soiiez vos beneoiz clamez
> Et vos et quanque vos amez!"           (ll. 5403–06)

As the lord knows perfectly well that he will subject Yvain to a diabolical ordeal next morning, this must be the most blatant hypocrisy, of a kind avoided even by evil barons. Or is it? Does he really believe he is as helpless in maintaining his evil custom as he makes out? Chrétien will not tell us. He does not know, he says, if they are deceiving him. Invoking God is no longer an indication of innocence, or even of good faith.

Chrétien's protests of ignorance cannot help influencing us when we come to the end of the romance. The conclusion is extremely reasonable; almost too reasonable for modern sensibilities. First, Laudine is furious when she discovers that Lunete has tricked her into promising to be reconciled with a man "qui ne m'aimme ne prise" (l. 6762). Only that perjury is so base, she would rather go on enduring the storms of the Fountain than grant Yvain his peace but, as she has given her word, her resentment, which would have gone on smouldering forever, will be forgotten because she must make peace with him. Yvain sees that things are turning out well for him; he reminds her that one should have mercy on wrong–doers and that he has now paid for his folly; he promises her that he will not wrong her again.[5] Rather than perjure herself, she agrees to do all in her power to make peace between them and he thanks her heartily.

Laudine is too rational to be easily comprehensible. Her reaction represents the triumph of the will over the heart, of reason over sentiment. If she has really ceased to love him, how can she start to love him again, just because honour demands it? We are more familiar with the psychology envisaged by La Rochefoucauld: "Il est impossible d'aimer une seconde fois ce qu'on a véritablement cessé d'aimer" (Réflexions, nr. 286). Chrétien thinks differently. Love for him always retains an element of the voluntary and no–one in his romances ever loves or ceases to love in defiance of what they believe to be right. Laudine first hated Yvain as the man who had deprived her of the excellent Esclados, then loved him as the only man willing and able to

---

[5]Yvain's speech is more convincing to us than it can be to Laudine who, as Lyons points out, is unaware of Yvain's most recent and most significant adventures; see "Sentiment et rhétorique dans l'Yvain," 376. Diverres notes that Chrétien depicts Yvain throughout as Laudine's lover rather than her lord; see "Chivalry and fin'amor," 112. Payen also notes the particular dignity of the position given Laudine; see Motif du repentir, 389–90.

replace him, then hated him again as the man who proved himself
unworthy of her love. Now he has proved again his worth as the Knight
of the Lion and she has pledged her word to help him. Honour requires
that she change her 'corage' and forget her grievances. Laudine is never
idealized morally, but she has a scrupulous sense of honour. She
promises her good will: Yvain promises to wrong her no more. If there
are no concessions to sentimentality, there is a rational basis to their
future love and we have no reason to doubt their commitment.

    If we doubt, it is because Chrétien protests too much. He follows
Yvain's thanks with the assertion:

> Ore a mes sire Yvains sa pes,
> Si poez croire qu'onques mes
> Ne fu de rien nule si liez,
> Comant qu'il et esté iriez.                          (l. 6799–802)

We would not think of doubting it if we were not being told to believe
it by an author who has so often compromised his authority. Yvain's
past sorrows are effaced by his present joy and his life with Laudine
stretches out before him in a "pes sanz fin" (l. 6811). Chrétien gives us
no rational cause to disbelieve him; it is entirely a matter of presentation.
After a long and complex story involving joy, sorrow and many other
conflicting emotions, it is disconcerting to see all future complexity so
firmly ruled out. After all the conflicting claims made on the hero in the
past, his future prospects are unified to the point of blankness. After
gaining a wider experience than any of Chrétien's heroes, Yvain's past
is wiped out and his future swallowed up in unending peace. The lion
disappears from the narrative at line 5924: does the Knight of the Lion
also vanish? If Yvain had had the epic role of a Charlemagne or a
William of Orange, we would feel certain that, though some crises have
been resolved, the heroic struggle still goes on.[6] Yvain, the most socially
committed of all Chrétien's heroes, subsides into social oblivion.

    Even Yvain's joy is not easy to accept. We might be satisfied if
Chrétien had shown us more, as he showed us the joy of the reunited
Erec and Enide, and told us less, now that we no longer have any real
confidence in what he tells us. Chrétien knew his audience wanted more
information, but he cuts us short:

> Del Chevalier au Lion fine
> Crestiiens son romanz einsi;
> Qu'onques plus conter n'an oï,
> Ne ja plus n'an orroiz conter,
> S'an n'i viaut mançonge ajoster.                    (ll. 6814–18)

By omitting a convincingly detailed picture of Yvain's final joy while
consigning his hero to happy oblivion, Chrétien plants doubts and

---

[6]See *Roland*, ll. 3988–4001; *Le Couronnement de Louis*, ed. Langlois, ll. 2657–95; *Prise
d'Orange*, ed. Régnier, ll. 1886–88.

uncertainties in the minds of his audience corresponding to the doubtful and uncertain world he created for Yvain to live in.

*Yvain* is by far the most complex of Chrétien's first four romances. The plot hinges on a marvel, yet there is greater emphasis than anywhere else on the mundane. Characters and audience alike are continually obliged to focus on what is external and visible, but the importance of purely chivalrous motivation is nowhere more stressed, and this motivation comes from within. The hero sets out alone in the classic manner of romance, yet no knight's adventures are so inextricably linked with the characters he encounters. We are promised a tale of the chivalrous times of good King Arthur, but we are shown a court where chivalrous standards are not maintained and an entire fictional world in which evil always maintains its full weight in the balance against good. Yvain's adventures have nothing of the elusive mystery of Lancelot's, yet in the end they are even harder to account for, because their creator wilfully misleads us and obliges us to reach our own conclusions about Yvain and a world in which reality, for the first time, is not clearly perceptible.

# Conclusion

Chrétien's narrative technique in his first four romances varies greatly from each work to the next but it does not undergo a straightforwardly linear evolution. *Erec* and *Cligès* are narratives of exploration. In each, Chrétien asserts his individuality as a narrator primarily by negative means: he rejects current narrative material in order to explore the possibilities of imposing his own attitudes on his romances. *Lancelot* and *Yvain*, on the other hand, prove to be narratives of affirmation: in these romances Chrétien confidently and positively introduces what material he pleases.

*Erec* has its strongly positive side: in this romance, more than any other, Chrétien gives full play to the optimistic rationalism of his period. Erec is the confident hero of a confident craftsman, but because Chrétien is so intent on displaying rationally human values he deprives him of the help given to other heroes by the "marvellous." In *Cligès*, Chrétien rejects the Tristan model, and for a similar purpose. His lovers will learn the art of love in exemplary fashion. Their love will not be produced by magic potions or practised in defiance of the claims of honour and society. Their correctly disposed hearts and wills will triumph, though at the cost of delegating much of the action to subordinates. Honour is prized just as highly as in *Erec*, but it is given a different narrative expression. *Erec* is constructed of forward–looking, interlocking actions; *Cligès* is didactic and analytic.

In *Lancelot* and *Yvain*, Chrétien moves from rejecting the irrational to integrating it. Having established his mastery over such potentially unruly elements as the marvellous and arbitrary, he is now confident of dominating his material. He allows Lancelot no magical help, but he makes him the focus of the "marvellous" for the other characters of the romance who see him pursue his quest. After *Cligès*, the Tristan story is never again explicitly referred to, but Chrétien incorporates numerous elements from it into the *Charrette*, with the double purpose of improving on his model in terms of decency and probability and of showing us the superior will power of his hero and heroine.

*Yvain* was apparently written soon after *Lancelot*, for it is closely linked to it, partly by the three cross–references to the *Charrette* and partly by the way Chrétien systematically inverts procedures evidently still fresh in his mind. In *Lancelot* Chrétien concentrated all our attention on the mind of the hero. He internalized all the action as far as possible, to emphasize the exceptional motivation of the Knight of the Cart. In *Yvain*, we are presented with an imperfect hero making his way through an imperfect world. Lancelot's surroundings were shadowy and elusive: Yvain's are solidly material and presented in vivid, if partial, visual terms. Chrétien is now so confident of his ability to dominate the "marvellous" that he uses the legendary Fountain of Broceliande as the pivot of his plot and allows his less-than-perfect hero to benefit from magic props. He even gives him a moment of failure in which the implied comparison with Tristan is to his disadvantage.

Chrétien's prologues tell us about the evolution of his preoccupations. The *Erec* prologue speaks of Chrétien's concern with coherent narrative structure and of his self-confidence as a literary craftsman. Apart from the descriptive interludes, the easy and rapid flow of the narrative confirms this boasted ability to construct a 'bele conjointure'. The prologue to *Cligès* is even more strikingly the work of a self-conscious artist. Chrétien lists all his previous works, including his translations from Ovid and a story on the Tristan theme. Ovid and the Tristan legend remain his two most important literary sources. The immediate source of this second romance had only the merit of being ancient and therefore worthy of belief, but it prompts Chrétien to compose his famous celebration of the *translatio studii* and the *translatio imperii*. Full of confidence in his ability to handle his source material, he goes on to tell his story.

The exact interpretation of the prologue to the *Charrette* remains a matter of controversy, but even giving the contribution of Marie de Champagne its fullest possible weight in the choice and treatment of the topic, Chrétien contributed the narrative craftsmanship of which he is so proud. He hints in his prologue that he is more competent at handling language than his fellow-romancer Gautier d'Arras, and his confidence is justified. He is glad to write his romance at the countess's request. If her suggestions caused him any difficulties, he shows her and us that he is well able to cope with them.

The prologue to Yvain mentions no patron and no source. Chrétien gives the impression of indulging his personal tastes when he chooses to talk of the remote golden age of Arthurian excellence. It is the most deceptive of all the prologues, for the evocation of the past is designed to help us accept the "marvellous" fountain, and the contrast between the Arthur of the prologue and the Arthur of the tale is just the first in a series of oppositions and discrepancies throughout the narrative.

The *mise en scène* varies with each romance. In *Erec*, Arthur and his splendid court are presented with a brevity and lack of explanation that presuppose a fair amount of knowledge on the part of the audience. This conciseness matches the rapid, unjustified narrative style of the first Arthurian romance. In *Cligès*, Chrétien adopts a factual, informative manner reminiscent of chronicles such as Wace's. In the opening scene of the *Charrette*, Chrétien returns to the *Erec* type of courtly gathering, but with the disruptive elements much more forcibly presented: a mysterious and malevolent figure erupts on the scene and Arthur is

powerless to withstand him. The initiative passes to someone else, and
Guinevere's husband is eclipsed by her wholly devoted lover. The
opening of *Yvain* is the most complex and disturbing. The first word of
the narrative proper is "mes" (but) and all that follows contradicts all
that we have been led to expect.

Each of Chrétien's heroes is introduced in a different manner. Erec is
presented as the man who has everything: high birth, high reputation
and an excellent appearance. There is no hint of ambivalence in this
portrait which is in keeping with the earliest and most optimistic of
Chrétien's narratives. Erec will lapse, but briefly; his rehabilitation will
be more than adequate and his coronation at Nantes the most glorious
climax of any hero's career. Alexander and Cligès are presented as much
younger men, notable primarily for the excellence of their potential:
each in turn will illustrate an exemplary education in the arts of love and
war. Lancelot makes the most mysterious entrance: a nameless knight,
he rides up out of nowhere and displays the effects of a powerful inner
force by accepting the shame of riding in the cart. His low-key entrance
eases the transfer of our attention from Guinevere's inadequate
husband to her heroic and single-minded lover. Lancelot's anonymity
is part of his role. He acquires an identity from the episode of the cart,
but he never acquires a place in society. Yvain is different again.
Chrétien introduces him as one of a group of representative Arthurian
knights and, though he leaves Arthur's court almost at once, his
destiny will always be bound up with other members of society.

Given that all Chrétien's heroes are knights who can only express
themselves through chivalrous action, the way they move from one
action to the next is what most typically illustrates the evolution of
Chrétien's narrative technique. In *Erec*, nothing of the hero's pre-plot
life affects the narrative. Erec is already a fully-fledged Knight of the
Round Table; he is decisive and strong-willed in his pursuit of Yder and
winning of Enide. After his single lapse has been brought home to him,
he moves decisively forward to rehabilitate himself. His quest is
pursued with scarcely a backward glance. Erec does not reject the world
surrounding him, but the pace of his quest is so rapid that the narrator
has no time for it. Erec rides with all speed 'tant que' he reaches his next
objective. All intervening objects are swept aside.

Alexander's progress is more complex. He has an external, epic side to
him which finds expression in his support of Arthur against the traitor
Angres. He also has a wholly separate object of silent and private
meditation: inspired by Soredamors, he perfects himself gradually in
the art of love. He alternates between these two spheres of action until
he has reached full proficiency in both. His son goes further in
integrating the two aspects of knightly endeavour, for he proves himself
three times in battle before his lady's eyes. Chrétien's style in *Cligès* is,
however, didactic and expository rather than narrative. Alexander,

Soredamors and Fenice expose their thoughts and feelings in long monologues and Chrétien, far from hastening us forward as he had in *Erec*, invites us rather to look back and reflect as he concludes the monologues with a demonstrative "einsi se plaint. . ."

Lancelot's progress owes something to both the earlier romances. The first part of the *Charrette*, dealing with Lancelot's quest, shows the hero riding forward with the determination of an Erec; the second part, which deals with the realization of Lancelot's love affair, is treated more in the manner of *Cligès*: both hero and heroine deliberate in long interior monologues. But there are additional refinements. Lancelot does not ignore the world around him because he is anxiously pressing forward like Erec. He deliberately withdraws from it into an incommunicable meditation. His quest is pursued in narrative terms in the form of a zig-zag: Chrétien makes him alternate from demonstrating his love to demonstrating his no less exceptional prowess. He is so exceptional that he becomes a marvel in the eyes of the characters who behold him. His preoccupations are so withdrawn from the external world that Chrétien is obliged to measure his progress on his quest in terms of externally noted time and distance.

Yvain's progress is similar to Lancelot's only insofar as it is appropriate to the character Chrétien gives him. He is a less idealized, more representative figure than any of Chrétien's other heroes. With the single but important exception of his espousal of the lion's cause against the serpent, Yvain always acts as a member of a social group. He is a link in the social chain, a current in the stream of Arthurian life. His actions typically take place 'que que' other actions are taking place elsewhere. He does not forge ahead for a specific purpose like Erec, or towards a precise destination like Lancelot but, like his fellow characters in the romance, he makes his way forward piecemeal. Yvain does not pursue his own 'droit chemin', he is drawn into the paths of others.

There is evolution too in Chrétien's presentation of his heroines. He describes Enide's beauty on his own authority in a splendid rhetorical encomium and follows it up with her father's description of her 'sagesse'. Her beauty and worth make her the equal of Erec and account for the hero's love for her. His response to her furnishes the mainspring of the action. Chrétien does not describe his second heroine, Soredamors: he leaves the perception of her to Alexander, as part of his education in the art of love. He describes Fenice in a series of rhetorical negatives. This strong-minded heroine will be forced to defend her honour and integrity negatively, defining her position in terms of what she cannot bring herself to countenance. Chrétien does not describe Guinevere at all. A few of her golden hairs in a comb cast Lancelot into a profound and quasi-spiritual meditation, but the external object of his internalized love is left undescribed. Chrétien's description of Laudine is the most ingenious and economical of all: we watch Yvain watching her and observe the changing feelings of both parties. Like every other element of this romance, the heroine's beauty is not presented in isolation but as part of the perceptions and reactions of the characters.

Chrétien's treatment of the permanent secondary figures also undergoes a change. Arthur, Gawain and Kay are all transformed as Chrétien adapts their functions to each new romance. In *Erec*, King Arthur is a static figure and the more dynamic hero goes his own way, though he acknowledges Arthur's prestige and position. For the youthful Alexander, Arthur's court provides the essential criterion of prowess and Arthur appears younger in this second romance than anywhere else. Here he is a figure close to the epic hero depicted by Geoffrey and Wace. The change comes with *Lancelot*. Once Arthur is placed in the position of being the hero's rival, he is inevitably the loser. In the early part of the *Charrette*, Chrétien degrades him to the point of reminding us of the helpless husband of Fenice. In *Yvain*, though he is theoretically the mainstay of chivalry and sees justice done in the end, he does not recover the prestige lost in the *Charrette* and is exposed to criticism from all quarters.

The evolution of Gawain's status is just as striking. In *Erec* he is the privileged spokesman of peace and reason. In *Cligès* he sets the standard for the young hero to reach at the tournament near Oxford. As with Arthur, however, the *Charrette* marks a drop in his prestige. His character remains the same, but his function changes radically. He is no longer the criterion of prowess but the foil for a hero of superhuman motivation. He is still the courteous *raisonneur*, valued by all at his uncle's court, but when he is pitted against Lancelot, his prestige suffers. We are told of his qualities but we are shown his failure. In *Yvain*, Chrétien increases this discrepancy: he speaks of Gawain as the sun of chivalry, but shows him failing in the service of both love and justice.

Kay too evolves towards an increasing imperfection. In *Erec* he is simply tactless and obstinate. In the *Charrette* he is the faithful and valued servant of Arthur but endangers the queen through his selfish and overweening desire for glory. In *Yvain*, his irrepressibly evil tongue is a part of the permanent evils of life, which permeate even King Arthur's court.

There is a noticeably pessimistic direction in these changes. *Erec* is without doubt a wholly optimistic romance. If the hero falls from the highest standards of knightly excellence, he is able and willing to assume responsibility for his fault and his rehabilitation. All undeserved misfortune is wiped away without a trace. Even some of the villains are won over to the right side. The happy ending is circumstantial and convincing.

*Cligès* represents the triumph of the right kind of will but, though all the four main characters succeed in perfecting themselves in the art of love, none of them has the power of an Erec to put their will directly into operation. Alexander and Soredamors need the queen as intermediary; Cligès and Fenice need the support of Thessala and Jehan. In this romance it is no longer enough to know how to act. One must be prepared to endure suffering as well.

The *Charrette* seems to promise a return to the triumphantly chivalrous world of *Erec*. Lancelot's service to Arthur's subjects is beyond anything that has been achieved before by any hero and his love for Guinevere is carried to a greater extreme than anything we have seen before. Yet this very excellence in both love and chivalry degrades by contrast the hitherto unassailable criterion of Arthur and his court. Such exceptional love and prowess can function only in the context of a remote and shadowy territory which Arthur never enters and where his nephew proves a failure.

*Yvain* is the most pessimistic of Chrétien's romances. The brilliant presentation of the "marvellous" Fountain, the picturesque glimpses of courtly décor, the liveliness and humour of certain scenes and the harmonious structure of the narrative make *Yvain* a very attractive romance, yet the essence of the story is much darker than anything we find in its predecessors. All the characters struggle against the material obstacles of the world. The hero is no longer sustained by an inner vision as Lancelot was. Yvain is a fully integrated member of an imperfect world. He has one moment of solitary moral choice when he decides to come to the rescue of the noble lion. After that, he struggles continually in a world in which culpable folly, whether of inadequacy or excess, inflicts endless misfortunes on the weak, and in which even his best efforts do not eradicate the sources and effects of an omnipresent evil.

The relative pessimism of *Yvain* must not be exaggerated. Chrétien remains an optimist in his continued belief in free will. All his heroes and heroines remain responsible for their actions. In all four of these romances Chrétien rejects the fatalism of the Tristan story. Yvain is the only hero who is shown, momentarily, to be less admirable than Tristan, but he rapidly recovers control of his mind and his motivations. In all of these romances Chrétien also rejects the fatalism of the Pyramus story. He never accepts the irrational and the absurd: neither love nor death is ever brought about by a tragic accident or a blind and indifferent fate. As with the Tristan story, there is a perceptible evolution in his treatment of the Pyramus theme. In the optimistic world of Erec, the innocent heroine's hand is stayed by the direct intervention of a merciful God. In *Cligès*, the hero's readiness to follow the heroine's supposed death is only a device to show the quality of a love that might otherwise seem too easily won. In the *Charrette*, the mistaken belief in the loved one's death enables Lancelot, and to a much greater degree Guinevere, to realize fully the quality of their love and decide how to act. In *Yvain*, the justly self–reproachful hero is saved from suicide by the indirect intervention of providence, when he hears of Lunete's even more pitiful plight.

Chrétien's position in his narratives undergoes considerable change. All that remains constant throughout these four romances is his repeated protest that he will pass over unnecessary detail. In *Erec* he is a self–effacing narrator. The presentation is dramatic, and his interventions are few. He briefly accounts for a custom and protests a little awkwardly about a marvel, but his characteristic interventions are his two refusals to go back over earlier parts of his narrative. All our interest and attention is constantly directed forward. In *Cligès*, Chrétien intervenes in order to reject the external descriptions which were such a feature of *Erec*. Drama is replaced by monologue, which Chrétien invites us to dwell on. *Cligès* is didactic, and Chrétien allows himself a long intervention to justify the reserve of his hero, whereas in *Erec* he had justified no part of his narrative. In *Lancelot* he returns to some degree to the dramatic manner of *Erec*, but he also comments on the exceptional quality of the hero's motivations.

In *Yvain* he abandons the position he held in the earlier romances as omniscient narrator. Yvain as a character is easier to come to terms with than Lancelot, even though the narrator of the *Charrette* was much more straightforward than the narrator of *Yvain*. Chrétien makes us participate in the action of the *Charrette* by showing us the events of the quest as they appear to Lancelot, a man withdrawn from external concerns. Chrétien makes us participate in the events of the *Chevalier au Lion* by allowing us only the partial, sometimes deceptive view of the world that the characters have. At times we have a privileged position and can enjoy the play of dramatic irony. More often we, like the hero, are deprived of guidance or even misled. We can no longer be sure that appearance coincides with reality, but appearance is all we have to go on.

The most striking quality of these four romances is their variety. Who would believe that the author of *Erec* was also the author of *Cligès* if he had not told us so himself? The contrast between *Lancelot* and *Yvain* is more subtle but just as real. Plenty of other vernacular narratives survive from the twelfth century, and among them there are individual works which at moments equal or even surpass comparable passages from Chrétien, but there is no other writer who comes anywhere near him in creative scope and technical innovation. Chrétien is not alone among his contemporaries in his concern for craftsmanship, but he is more eloquent on the subject than any other romancer and more successful in realizing his aims. He remains one of the most challenging of medieval writers and the variety of interpretations of his romances has not yet succeeded in exhausting all the resources of his art.

# Bibliography

A comprehensive list of studies on Chrétien up to 1975 is to be found in Douglas Kelly, *Chrétien de Troyes: An Analytic Bibliography* (London, 1976). A supplementary volume is to be published in 1988.

An annual bibliography of all Arthurian literature is published in the *Bulletin Bibliographique de la Société Internationale Arthurienne*.

References listed below are confined to the texts and critical works mentioned in this study.

## ABBREVIATIONS

*BBSIA*   Bulletin Bibliographique de la Société Internationale Arthurienne
*CFMA*   Classiques Français du Moyen Age
*FMLS*   Forum for Modern Language Studies
*PMLA*   Publications of the Modern Language Association
*SATF*   Société des Anciens Textes Français
*TLF*   Textes Littéraires Français

## WORKS BY OR ATTRIBUTED TO CHRÉTIEN DE TROYES

Full details of pre-1974 editions of works attributed to Chrétien are given on pages 19–23 of Kelly's bibliography. Listed below are the editions used in this study.

*Erec*   *Kristian von Troyes: Erec und Enide.* Edited by Wendelin Foerster. Romanische Bibliothek, 13. Halle, 1934.

*Cligès*   *Kristian von Troyes: Cligès.* Edited by Wendelin Foerster, edition abridged by Alfons Hilka. Romanische Bibliothek, 1. Halle, 1921.

*Lancelot*   *Der Karrenritter (Lancelot) und das Wilhelmsleben (Guillaume d'Angleterre) von Christian von Troyes.* Edited by Wendelin Foerster. Halle, 1899.

*Yvain*   *Chrestien de Troyes: Yvain (Le Chevalier au Lion).* The Critical Text of Wendelin Foerster with Introduction, Notes and Glossary by T. B. W. Reid. Manchester, 1942; rev. rpt 1974.

*Perceval*   *Chrétien de Troyes: Le Roman de Perceval ou le Conte du Graal.* Edited by William Roach. TLF, 71. 2d ed. Geneva and Paris, 1959.

Brakelmann, Jules, ed. *Les plus anciens chansonniers français (XIIe siècle).* Paris, 1870–1891. (Includes three lyrics of Chrétien, and discussion: 42–49.)

*Les Chansons courtoises de Chrétien de Troyes.* Edited by Marie–Claire Zai. Publications Universitaires Européennes, Series 13. French Language and Literature, 27. Bern and Frankfurt, 1974.

*Chrétien de Troyes: Guillaume d'Angleterre, roman du XIIe siècle.* Edited by Maurice Wilmotte. CFMA, 55. Paris, 1927.

*Philomena: conte raconté d'après Ovide par Chrétien de Troyes.* Edited by C. de Boer. Paris, 1909.

*Two Old French Gawain Romances: "Le Chevalier à l'épée" and "La Mule sans frein."* Edited by R. C. Johnston and D. D. R. Owen. Edinburgh and London, 1972.

### TEXTS AND REFERENCE WORKS

Abelard. *Historia Calamitatum*. Edited by J. Monfrin. 2nd ed. Paris, 1962.

*Andreas Capellanus on Love*. Edited and translated by P. G. Walsh. London, 1982.

*The Apocryphal New Testament*. Edited and translated by M. R. James. Oxford, 1921.

*Bernard de Ventadour, troubadour du XIIe siècle: Chansons d'amour*. Edited by Moshé Lazar. Bibliothèque française et romane. Série B: Editions critiques de textes, 4. Paris, 1966.

Beroul  *The Romance of Tristran by Beroul: A Poem of the Twelfth Century*. Edited by Alfred Ewert. 2 vols. Vol. 1: Oxford, 1939; rpt 1970. Vol. 2: Oxford, 1970.

Boethius. *Philosophiae Consolatio*. Edited by Ludwig Bieler. Corpus Christianorum Series Latina, 94. Turnholt, 1957.

Brut  *Le Roman de Brut de Wace*. Edited by Ivor Arnold. 2 vols. SATF. Paris, 1938; 1940.

Cicero. *De Senectute, De Amicitia, De Divinatione*. Edited and translated by William Armistead Falconer. Loeb Classical Library. London and Cambrige, Mass., rpt 1946.

*Saint Augustine: The City of God Against the Pagans*. Ed. B. Dombart, rev. A Kolb. Trans. G. E. McCracken, E. M.Sanford and William M. Green. 7 vols. Loeb Classical Library. London and Cambridge, Mass., 1957–72.

*Le Couronnement de Louis: Chanson de geste du XIIe siècle*. Edited by Ernest Langlois. CFMA, 22. Paris, rpt 1969.

*Die Disciplina Clericalis des Petrus Alfonsi*. Edited by Alfons Hilka and Werner Söderhjelm. Heidelberg, 1911.

Eneas  *Eneas: Roman du XIIe siècle*. Edited by J.-J. Salverda de Grave. CFMA, 44 and 62. Paris, 1925; 1929.

[Floire et Blancheflor]: *Le Conte de Floire et Blancheflor*. Edited by Jean-Luc Leclanche. CFMA, 105. Paris, 1980.

*La Folie Tristan de Berne*. Edited by Ernest Hoepffner. 2d ed. Paris, 1949.

*La Folie Tristan d'Oxford*. Edited by Ernest Hoepffner. 2d ed. Paris, 1943; rpt 1963.

*Gautier d'Arras: Eracle*. Edited by Guy Raynaud de Lage. CFMA, 102. Paris, 1976.

Geoffrey of Monmouth. *Historia Regum Britanniae*. Edited in Edmond Faral, *La Légende arthurienne: Etudes et documents* (part I, vol. 3, no. 2, 63–303). Paris, 1929.

Giraldus Cambrensis. *Topographia Hibernica et Expugnatio Hibernica*. Edited by James F. Dimock as vol. 5 of *Opera*. London, 1857.

———— . *Expugnatio Hibernica: The Conquest of Ireland by Giraldus Cambrensis*. Edited and translated by A. B. Scott and F. X. Martin. Dublin, 1978.

*Jean Bodels Saxenlied*. Edited by F. Menzel and E. Stengel. Ausgaben und Abhandlungen aus dem Gebiete der romanischen Philologie, 99 and 100. Marburg, 1906; 1909.

John of Salisbury. *Policratici Libri VIII*. Edited by Clemens C. I. Webb. 2 vols. Oxford, 1909.

*Les Lais de Marie de France*. Edited by Jean Rychner. CFMA, 93. Paris, 1966.

*Narcisse: Conte ovidien français du XIIe siècle*. Edited by Martine Thiry–Stassin and Madeleine Tyssens. Bibliothèque de la Faculté de Philosophie et Lettres de l'Université de Liège, 211. Paris, 1976.

Ovid. *L'Art d'Aimer*. Edited and translated by Henri Bornecque. Collection des Universités de France publiée sous le patronage de l'Association Guillaume Budé. Paris, 1924, rev. rpt 1967.

Ovid. *Metamorphoses*. Edited by William Andersen. Leipsig, 1977.

*Piramus et Tisbé: Poème du XIIe siècle*. Edited by C. de Boer. CFMA, 26. Paris, 1921.

*La Prise d'Orange: Chanson de geste de la fin du XIIe siècle*. Edited by Claude Régnier. Bibliothèque française et romane. Série B: Editions critiques de textes, 5. 4th ed. Paris, 1972.

*Proverbes français antérieurs au XVe siècle*. Edited by Joseph Morawski. CFMA, 47. Paris, 1925.

Raynaud, Gaston. *Bibliographie des chansonniers français des XIIIe et XIVe siècles.* Paris, 1884.

*Renaut de Beaujeu: Le Bel Inconnu.* Edited by G. Perrie Williams. CFMA, 38. Paris, rpt 1967.

Roland    *La Chanson de Roland.* Edited by F. Whitehead. 2d ed. Oxford, 1946.

Rou    *Le Roman de Rou de Wace.* Edited by A. J. Holden. 3 vols. SATF. Paris, 1970–73.

*The Saga of Tristram and Isönd.* Translated by Paul Schach. Lincoln, Nebr., 1973.

Thèbes    *Le Roman de Thèbes.* Edited by Guy Raynaud de Lage. CFMA, 94 and 96. Paris, 1966; 1968.

Thomas. *Le Roman de Tristan par Thomas: poème du XIIe siècle.* Edited by Joseph Bédier. 2 vols. SATF. Paris, 1902; 1905.

Tristrant    *Eilhart von Oberg: Tristrant.* Edited and translated by Danielle Buschinger. Göppingen, 1976.

Tristrant    *Eilhart von Oberge's Tristrant.* Translated by J. W. Thomas. Lincoln, Nebr., 1978.

Troie    *Le Roman de Troie par Benoît de Sainte-Maure.* Edited by Léopold Constans. 6 vols. SATF. Paris, 1904–12.

*La Vie de Saint Alexis.* Edited by C. Storey. Oxford, 1968.

*Walter Map: De Nugis Curialium.* Edited by M. R. James. Oxford, 1914.

## STUDIES

Auerbach, Erich. *Mimesis: The Representation of Reality in Western Literature.* Translated by Willard R. Trask. Princeton, 1953; rpt 1973.

Beer, Gillian. *The Romance.* The Critical Idiom, 10. London, 1970.

Benson, Robert L. and Giles Constable, eds. *Renaissance and Renewal in the Twelfth Century.* Oxford, 1982.

Benton, John F. "The Court of Champagne as a Literary Center." *Speculum* 36 (1961): 551-91.

Bertolucci, Valeria. "Di nuovo su 'Cligès' e 'Tristan'." *Studi Francesi* 6 (1962): 401-13.

Bezzola, Reto R. *Le Sens de l'aventure et de l'amour (Chrétien de Troyes).* Paris, 1947.

Bezzola, Reto R. *Les Origines et la formation de la littérature courtoise en occident (500-1200).* 3 parts, 5 vols. Paris, 1958-63.

Bloch, Marc. *La Société féodale.* Paris, 1939; rpt 1968.

Bogdanow, Fanni. "The Love Theme in the *Chevalier de la Charrette.*" *Modern Language Review* 67 (1972): 50-61.

Booth, Wayne C. *The Rhetoric of Fiction.* Chicago and London, 1961; rpt 1973.

Brodeur, Arthur G. "The Grateful Lion: a Study in the Development of Mediaeval Narrative." *PMLA* 39 (1924): 485-524.

Brooke, Christopher. *The Twelfth-Century Renaissance.* London, 1969.

Burgess, Glyn S. *Contribution à l'étude du vocabulaire pré-courtois.* Publications romanes et françaises, 110. Geneva, 1970.

———. "Sen(s) 'Meaning' in Twelfth-Century Literature." *Romania* 99 (1978): 389-95.

———. *Chrétien de Troyes: "Erec et Enide."* London, 1984.

Busby, Keith. *Gauvain in Old French Literature.* Amsterdam, 1980.

Carasso-Bulow, Lucienne. *The Merveilleux in Chrétien de Troyes' Romances.* Geneva, 1976.

Chydenius, J. *Love and the Medieval Tradition.* Helsinki, 1977.

Colby, Alice. *The Portrait in Twelfth-Century French Literature: An Example of the Stylistic Originality of Chrétien de Troyes.* Geneva, 1965.

Cook, Robert G. "The Ointment in Chrétien's *Yvain.*" *Medieval Studies* 31 (1969): 5-14.

Curtius, Ernst Robert. *European Literature and the Latin Middle Ages.* Translated by Willard R. Trask. London, 1953.

Diverres, A. H. "Some thoughts on the *sens* of *Le Chevalier de la Charrette.*" *FMLS* 6 (1970): 24-26.

———. "Chivalry and *fin'amor* in *Le Chevalier au Lion.*" In *Studies in Medieval Literature and Languages in Memory of Frederick Whitehead,* 91-116. Manchester, 1973.

———— . "Yvain's Quest for Chivalric Perfection." In *An Arthurian Tapestry: Essays in Memory of Lewis Thorpe*, 214–28. Glasgow, 1981.

Duby, Georges. *Medieval Marriage: Two Models from Twelfth-Century France*. Translated by Elborg Forster. Baltimore, 1978.

Faral, Edmond. *Recherches sur les sources latines des contes et romans courtois du Moyen Age*. Paris, 1913.

———— . *Les Arts poétiques du XIIe et du XIIIe siècle*. Paris, 1924.

Ferrante, Joan M. "The Conflict of Lyric Conventions and Romance Form." In *Pursuit of Perfection: Courtly Love in Medieval Literature*, edited by J. M. Ferrante and G. D. Economou, 135–73. New York and London, 1975.

Foulon, Charles. "Le *Rou* de Wace, l'*Yvain* de Chrétien de Troyes et Eon de l'Etoile." *BBSIA* 17 (1965): 93–102.

Fourrier, Anthime. *Le Courant réaliste dans le roman courtois en France au Moyen-Age*. Paris, 1960.

Frappier, Jean. *Le Roman breton*. Les Cours de Sorbonne. 4 vols. Paris, 1950–64.

———— . "La Brisure du couplet dans *Erec et Enide*." *Romania* 86 (1965): 1–21.

———— . *Chrétien de Troyes*. Connaissance des Lettres, 50. Paris, rev. ed. 1968.

———— . *Etude sur "Yvain" ou "Le Chevalier au Lion" de Chrétien de Troyes*. Paris, 1969.

———— . "Le Prologue du *Chevalier de la Charrette* et son interprétation." *Romania* 93 (1972): 337–47.

———— . "Remarques sur le texte du *Chevalier de la Charrette*." In *Mélanges d'histoire littéraire, de linguistique et de philologie romanes offerts à Charles Rostaing*, 1:317–31. Liège, 1974.

Frye, Northrop. *Anatomy of Criticism: Four Essays*. Princeton, 1957; rpt 1971.

Gallais, Pierre. "Recherches sur la mentalité des romanciers français du moyen âge: les formules et le vocabulaire des prologues. I." *Cahiers de civilisation médiévale* 7 (1964): 479–93.

———— . "De la naissance du roman: à propos d'un article récent." *Cahiers de civilisation médiévale* 14 (1971): 69–75.

———— . "Littérature et médiatisation: réflexions sur la genèse du genre romanesque." *Etudes littéraires* 4 (1971): 39–73.

———— . *Perceval et l'initiation*. Paris, 1972.

———— . *"Tristan et Iseut" et son modèle persan*. Paris, 1974.

Geschiere, Lein. "Deux vers d'*Yvain*." In *Mélanges de linguistique romane et de philologie médiévale offerts à Maurice Delbouille*, 2:231–49. Gembloux, 1964.

Gilson, Etienne. *La Philosophie au Moyen Age*. Paris, 1944; rev. ed. 1962.

Griffin, Nathaniel E. "The Definition of Romance." *PMLA* 38 (1923): 50–70.

Grigsby, John L: "Narrative Voices in Chrétien de Troyes: a Prolegomenon to Dissection." *Romance Philology* 31 (1978–79): 261–76.

Guyer, Foster, E. "The Influence of Ovid on Crestien de Troyes." *Romanic Review* 12 (1921): 97–134, 216–47.

Haidu, Peter. *Aesthetic Distance in Chrétien de Troyes: Irony and Comedy in "Cligès" and "Perceval."* Geneva, 1968.

———— . *Lion-queue-coupée: l'écart symbolique chez Chrétien de Troyes*. Geneva, 1972.

Hall, Robert A. "The Silk Factory in Chrestien de Troyes' *Yvain*." *Modern Language Notes* 56 (1941): 418–22.

Harris, Julian. "The Rôle of the Lion in Chrétien de Troyes' *Yvain*." *PMLA* 64 (1949): 1143–63.

Haskins, Charles Homer. *The Renaissance of the Twelfth Century*. Cambridge, Mass., 1927.

Hilka, Alfons. "Der Tristanroman des Thomas und die *Disciplina Clericalis*." *Zeitschrift für französische Sprache und Literatur* 45 (1919): 38–46.

Hunt, Tony. "The Rhetorical Background to the Arthurian Prologue: Tradition and the Old French Vernacular Prologues." *FMLS* 6 (1970): 1–23.

———— . "Tradition and Originality in the Prologues of Chrestien de Troyes." *FMLS* 8 (1972): 320–44.

———— . "The Dialectic of *Yvain*." *Modern Language Review* 72 (1977): 285–99.

———— . "Redating Chrestien de Troyes." *BBSIA* 30 (1978): 209–37.

——— . "Chrestien de Troyes: The Textual Problem." *French Studies* 33 (1979): 257-69.

——— . *Chrétien de Troyes: "Yvain"*. London, 1986.

Jackson, W. T. H. "The Nature of Romance." *Yale French Studies* 51 (1974): 12-25.

Jauss, Hans-Robert. "Littérature médiévale et théorie des genres." *Poétique* 1 (1970): 79-101.

Jones, Rosemarie. *The Theme of Love in the "Romans d'Antiquité."* London, 1972.

Jonin, Pierre. *Les Personnages féminins dans les romans français de Tristan au XIIe siècle: étude des influences contemporaines.* Aix-en-Provence, 1958.

——— . "Aspects de la vie sociale au XIIe siècle dans *Yvain*." *L'Information littéraire* 16 (1964): 47-54.

Kelly, Douglas. "Two Problems in Chrétien's *Charrette*: the Boundary of Gorre and the use of *'novele'*." *Neophilologus* 48 (1964): 115-21.

——— . *"Sens" and "Conjointure" in the "Chevalier de la Charrette."* The Hague and Paris, 1966.

——— . "The source and meaning of *conjointure* in Chrétien's *Erec*." *Viator* 1 (1970): 179-200.

——— . *"Matière* and *genera dicendi* in Medieval Romance." *Yale French Studies* 51 (1974): 147-59.

Kennedy, Angus J. "The Portrayal of the Hermit-Saint in French Arthurian Romance: The Remoulding of a Stock Character." In *An Arthurian Tapestry: Essays in Memory of Lewis Thorpe*, 69-82. Glasgow, 1981.

Ker, W. P. *Epic and Romance: Essays on Medieval Literature.* London, 1908.

Köhler, Erich. "Le Rôle de la 'coutume' dans les romans de Chrétien de Troyes." *Romania* 81 (1960): 386-97.

Lacy, Norris J. *The Craft of Chrétien de Troyes: An Essay on Narrative Art.* Leiden, 1980.

Laurie, Helen C. R. *"Eneas* and the *Lancelot* of Chrétien de Troyes." *Medium Aevum* 37 (1968): 142-56.

——— . "The 'Letters' of Abelard and Heloise: A Source for Chrétien de Troyes?" *Studi Medievali* 27 (1986): 123-46.

Lazar, Moshé. *Amour courtois et 'fin'amors' dans la littérature du XIIe siècle.* Paris, 1964.

Lewis, C. S. *The Allegory of Love: A Study in Medieval Tradition.* Oxford, 1936, rpt 1972.

——— . *The Discarded Image.* Cambridge, 1964, rpt 1974.

Lonigan, P. R. "The *Cligès* and the Tristan legend." *Studi Francesi* 18 (1974): 201-12.

——— . *Chrétien's "Yvain": A Study of Meaning through Style.* New York, 1978.

Loomis, Roger Sherman. *Arthurian Tradition and Chrétien de Troyes.* New York, 1949.

——— , ed. *Arthurian Literature in the Middle Ages: A Collaborative History.* Oxford, 1959.

Lot-Borodine, Myrrha. "Tristan et Lancelot." In *Medieval Studies in Memory of Gertrude Schoepperle Loomis*, 21-24. Paris and New York, 1927.

Luttrell, Claude. *The Creation of the First Arthurian Romance: A Quest.* London, 1974.

——— . "The Arthurian Traditionalist's Approach to the Composer of Romance: R. S. Loomis on Chrétien de Troyes." *Oeuvres et Critiques* 5, no. 2 (1980-81): 23-30.

Lyons, Faith. "La Fausse mort dans le *Cligès* de Chrétien de Troyes." In *Mélanges de linguistique et de littérature romanes offerts à Mario Roques*, 1:167-77. Baden and Paris, 1950.

——— . " 'Entencion' in Chrétien's *Lancelot*." *Studies in Philology* 51 (1954): 425-30.

——— . "Sentiment et rhétorique dans l'*Yvain*." *Romania* 83 (1962): 370-77.

——— . "Interprétations critiques au XXe siècle du Prologue de *Cligès*: la *Translatio studii* selon les historiens, les philosophes et les philologues." *Oeuvres et Critiques* 5, no. 2 (1980-81): 39-44.

Maddox, Donald. "Trois sur deux: Théories de bipartition et de tripartition des oeuvres de Chrétien de Troyes." *Oeuvres et Critiques* 5, no. 2 (1980-81): 91-102.

Mâle, Emile. *L'Art religieux du XIIe siècle en France: étude sur les origines de l'iconographie du moyen âge.* 3d ed. Paris, 1928.

Ménage, René. *"Erec et Enide*: quelques pièces du dossier." In *Mélanges de langue et de littérature françaises du Moyen Age et de la Renaissance offerts à Charles Foulon*, 2:203-21. Rennes, 1980.

Micha, Alexandre. *"Eneas et Cligès."* In *Mélanges de philologie romane et de littérature médiévale offerts à Ernest Hoepffner*, 237-43. Paris, 1949.

_____ . "Tristan et Cligès." *Neophilologus* 36 (1952): 1–10.

Mullally, Evelyn. "The Order of Composition of *Lancelot* and *Yvain*." *BBSIA* 36 (1984): 217–29.

Newstead, Helaine. "Narrative Technique in Chrétien's *Yvain*." *Romance Philology* 30 (1976–77): 431–41.

Nitze, William A. "A Note on Two Virgilian Commonplaces in Twelfth–Century Literature." In *Mélanges de linguistique et de littérature offerts à Alfred Jeanroy*, 439–46. Paris, 1928.

Noble, Peter. "Alis and the Problem of Time in *Cligés*." *Medium Aevum* 39 (1970): 28–31.

_____ . "The Character of Guinevere in the Arthurian Romances of Chrétien de Troyes." *Modern Language Review* 67 (1972): 524–35.

Ollier, Marie–Louise. "The Author in the Text: The Prologues of Chrétien de Troyes." *Yale French Studies* 51 (1974): 26–41.

Owen, D. D. R. *The Vision of Hell: Infernal Journeys in Medieval French Literature.* Edinburgh and London, 1970.

_____ . "Profanity and its Purpose in Chrétien's *Cligès* and *Lancelot*." *FMLS* 6 (1970): 37–48.

_____ . "Two More Romances by Chrétien de Troyes?" *Romania* 92 (1971): 246–60.

_____ . "Chrétien and the *Roland*." In *An Arthurian Tapestry: Essays in Memory of Lewis Thorpe*, 139–50. Glasgow, 1981.

Paré, G., A. Brunet and P. Tremblay. *La Renaissance du XIIe siècle: les écoles et l'enseignement.* Paris and Ottawa, 1933.

Paris, Gaston. "Cligès." *Journal des Savants* (1902): 57–69, 289–309, 345–57, 438–58, 641–56. Reprinted in *Gaston Paris: Mélanges de littérature française du Moyen Age*, edited by Mario Roques, 229–327. Paris, 1912.

Payen, Jean–Charles. *Le Motif du repentir dans la littérature française médiévale (des origines à 1230).* Publications romanes et françaises, 98. Geneva, 1968.

_____ . "Lancelot contre Tristan: la conjuration d'un mythe subversif (réflexions sur l'idéologie romanesque au Moyen Age)." In *Mélanges de langue et de littérature médiévales offerts à Pierre Le Gentil*, 617–32. Paris, 1973.

_____ . "Une approche classiciste du roman médiéval: Jean Frappier, lecteur de Chrétien de Troyes." *Oeuvres et Critiques* 5, no. 2 (1980–81): 45–52.

Pelan, Margaret. *L'Influence du "Brut" de Wace sur les romanciers français de son temps.* Paris, 1931.

Pickford, C. E. "The Good Name of Chrétien de Troyes." In *An Arthurian Tapestry: Essays in Memory of Lewis Thorpe*, 389–401. Glasgow, 1981.

Polak, Lucie. *Chrétien de Troyes: "Cligés."* London, 1982.

Press, A. R. "Le Comportement d'Erec envers Enide dans le roman de Chrétien de Troyes." *Romania* 90 (1969): 529–38.

Propp, Vladimir. *Morphologie du conte.* Translated by Tzvetan Todorov. Paris, 1970.

Reid, T. B. W. "Chrétien de Troyes and the Scribe Guiot." *Medium Aevum* 45 (1976): 1–19.

Ribard, Jacques. *Chrétien de Troyes. Le Chevalier de la Charrette: essai d'interprétation symbolique.* Paris, 1972.

Rychner, Jean. "Le Prologue du *Chevalier de la charrette*." *Vox Romanica* 26 (1967): 1–23.

_____ . "Le Sujet et la signification du *Chevalier de la charrette*." *Vox Romanica* 27 (1967): 50–76.

_____ . "Le Prologue du *Chevalier de la charrette* et l'interprétation du roman." In *Mélanges offerts à Rita Lejeune*, 2:1121–35. Gembloux, 1969.

_____ . "Encore le Prologue du *Chevalier de la charrette*." *Vox Romanica* 31 (1972): 263–71.

Schoepperle, Gertrude. *Tristan and Isolt: A Study of the Sources of the Romance.* 2 vols. Frankfurt and London, 1913.

Seay, Albert. *Music in the Medieval World.* Englewood Cliffs, N.J., 1965.

Shirt, David. "*Cligés*: Realism in Romance." *FMLS* 13 (1977): 368–80.

_____ . "Chrétien's *Charrette* and its Critics, 1964–74." *Modern Language Review* 73 (1978): 38–50.

_____ . "*Cligès*–A Twelfth–Century Matrimonial Case-book?" *FMLS* 18 (1982): 75–89.

Smalley, Beryl. *Historians in the Middle Ages.* London, 1974.

Southern, R. W. *The Making of the Middle Ages*. London, 1953; rpt 1973.

⸻ . *Medieval Humanism and Other Studies*. Oxford, 1970.

Stevens, John. *Medieval Romance*. London, 1973.

Sturm-Maddox, Sara. "*Hortus non conclusus*: critics and the *Joie de la Cort*." *Oeuvres et Critiques* 5, no. 2 (1980–81): 61–71.

Topsfield, L. T. *Chrétien de Troyes: A Study of the Arthurian Romances*. Cambridge, 1981.

Uitti, Karl. "Narrative and Commentary: Chrétien's Devious Narrator in *Yvain*." *Romance Philology* 33 (1978–79): 160–7.

Van Hamel, A. G. "*Cligès et Tristan*." *Romania* 33 (1904): 465–89.

Vinaver, Eugène. "Les deux pas de Lancelot." In *Mélanges pour Jean Fourquet*, 355–61. Paris and Munich, 1969.

⸻ . *A la recherche d'une poétique médiévale*. Paris, 1970.

⸻ . *The Rise of Romance*. Oxford, 1971.

Wetherbee, Winthrop. *Platonism and Poetry in the Twelfth Century: The Literary Influence of the School of Chartres*. Princeton, 1972.

Whitteridge, Gweneth. "The Date of the *Tristan* of Beroul," *Medium Aevum* 28 (1959): 167–71.

Wilmotte, Maurice. *L'Evolution du roman français aux environs de 1150*. Paris, 1903.

Zaddy, Zara P. *Chrétien Studies*. Glasgow, 1973.

⸻ . "*Le Chevalier de la Charrette* and the *De Amore* of Andreas Capellanus." In *Studies in Medieval Literature and Languages in Memory of Frederick Whitehead*, 363–99. Manchester, 1973.

# Index

239

PUBLICATIONS

OF

# The American Philosophical Society

The publications of the American Philosophical Society consist of PROCEEDINGS, TRANSACTIONS, MEMOIRS, and YEAR BOOK.

THE PROCEEDINGS contains papers which have been read before the Society in addition to other papers which have been accepted for publication by the Committee on Publications. In accordance with the present policy one volume is issued each year, consisting of four quarterly numbers, and the price is $24.00 net per volume. Individual copies may be purchased at $10.00 per copy.

THE TRANSACTIONS, the oldest scholarly journal in America, was started in 1769. In accordance with the present policy each annual volume is a collection of monographs, each issued as a part. The current annual subscription price is $70.00 net per volume. Individual copies of the TRANSACTIONS are offered for sale.

Each volume of the MEMOIRS is published as a book. The titles cover the various fields of learning; most of the recent volumes have been historical. The price of each volume is determined by its size and character, but subscribers are offered a 20 per cent discount.

The YEAR BOOK is of considerable interest to scholars because of the reports on grants for research and to libraries for this reason and because of the section dealing with the acquisitions of the Library. In addition it contains the Charter and Laws, and lists of members, and reports of committees and meetings. The YEAR BOOK is published about April 1 for the preceding calendar year. The current price is $12.00. A separate volume of GRANTEES' REPORTS is published annually. The listed price is $10.00.

An author desiring to submit a manuscript for publication should send it to the Editor, American Philosophical Society, 104 South Fifth Street, Philadelphia, Pa. 19106.

www.ingramcontent.com/pod-product-compliance
Lightning Source LLC
Chambersburg PA
CBHW080923100426
42812CB00007B/2351